25th International Conference on Computational Linguistics

(COLING 2014)

System Demonstrations

Dublin, Ireland
23 - 29 August 2014

Editors:

Lamia Tounsi Rafal Rak

ISBN: 978-1-63439-196-2

Printed from e-media with permission by:

Curran Associates, Inc.
57 Morehouse Lane
Red Hook, NY 12571

Some format issues inherent in the e-media version may also appear in this print version.

Printed by Curran Associates, Inc. (2014)

For permission requests, please contact the Association for Computational Linguistics at the address below.

Association for Computational Linguistics
209 N. Eighth Street
Stroudsburg, Pennsylvania 18360

Phone: 1-570-476-8006
Fax: 1-570-476-0860

acl@aclweb.org

Additional copies of this publication are available from:

Curran Associates, Inc.
57 Morehouse Lane
Red Hook, NY 12571 USA
Phone: 845-758-0400
Fax: 845-758-2634
Email: curran@proceedings.com
Web: www.proceedings.com

COLING 2014

The 25th International Conference on Computational Linguistics

Proceedings of the Conference System Demonstrations

Editors
Dr. Lamia Tounsi, CNGL, Dublin City University
Dr. Rafal Rak, NaCTeM, University of Manchester

August 23-29, 2014
Dublin, Ireland

Preface

This volume contains papers from the system demonstration session of the 25th International Conference on Computational Linguistics (COLING 2014) held in Dublin, Ireland. The conference is organized by the Centre for Global Intelligent Content (CNGL) and held at the Helix Conference Centre at Dublin City University (DCU) from 25 to 29 August 2014, under the auspices of the International Committee on Computational Linguistics (ICCL).

The demonstration session complements the conference's presentation and poster sessions and is focused on working software systems that are the tangible outcomes of research on computational linguistics.

As a result of a rigorous review process, we accepted 28 papers out of 45 submissions. The program committee consisted of 35 members and two chairs from both academia and industry. Each member evaluated two or three papers, which amounted to two reviews per paper. The acceptance criteria we followed during the selection process included the quality of work as well as the utility and demonstrability potential of the presented systems. Consequently, most of the accepted systems are user-interactive and feature rich graphical user interfaces.

First and foremost we would like to thank the program committee for their hard work and dedication to help make this event a success. Our special thanks also go to the people who made COLING 2014 and this volume possible. We thank Programme Chairs, Prof. Junichi Tsujii (Microsoft Research) and Prof. Jan Hajic (Charles University), General Chairs, Prof. Josef van Genabith (Universität des Saarlandes/DFKI) and Professor Andy Way (CNGL, DCU) , the chairs of the local organizing committee, Dr. Cara Green (CNGL, DCU) and Dr. John Judge (CNGL/NCLT, DCU), and Publications Chairs, Dr. Joachim Wagner (CNGL, DCU), Dr. Liadh Kelly (CNGL, DCU) and Dr. Lorraine Goeuriot (CNGL, DCU), for their tireless work.

Lamia Tounsi and Rafal Rak

COLING 2014 Demonstration Programme Co-chairs

25 July 2014

Organizers:

Demonstration Chairs

Lamia Tounsi, CNGL, Dublin City University, Ireland
Rafal Rak, NaCTeM, University of Manchester, UK

Program Committee:

Michiel Bacchiani, Google Inc.
Kay Berkling, Cooperative State University, Karlsruhe
Ann Bies, Linguistic Data Consortium
William Black, University of Manchester
Francis Bond, Nanyang Technological University
Chris Brew, Nuance Communications
Aoife Cahill, Educational Testing Service
Vittorio Castelli, IBM
Md. Faisal Mahbub Chowdhury, IBM
Léa Deleris, IBM
Martin Emms, Trinity College Dublin
Guillaume Gravier, IRISA and INRIA Rennes
Keith Hall, Google Research
Derrick Higgins, Educational Testing Service
Keikichi Hirose, University of Tokyo
Frank Hopfgartner, Technische Universität Berlin
Daxin Jiang, Microsoft STC-A
John Kelleher, Trinity College Dublin
Adam Kilgarriff, Lexical Computing Ltd
BalaKrishna Kolluru, Toshiba
Seamus Lawless, Trinity College Dublin
Saturnino Luz, Trinity College Dublin
Nitin Madnani, Educational Testing Service
Hilary McDonald, Trinity College Dublin
Helen Meng, Chinese University of Hong Kong
Peter Mika, Yahoo Labs
Tony O'Dowd, KantanMT
Florian Pinel, IBM
Johann Roturier, Symantec
Andrew Rowley, University of Manchester
Frédérique Segond, Viseo Research
Swapna Somasundaran, Educational Testing Services
Tomoki Toda, Nara Institute of Science and Technology
Xinglong Wang, Brandwatch
Jason Williams, Microsoft Research

Table of Contents

Conference Program

25/08/2014

(10:15 - 12:25) Demo session 1

An Error Analysis Tool for Natural Language Processing and Applied Machine Learning
Apoorv Agarwal, Ankit Agarwal and Deepak Mittal

Claims on demand – an initial demonstration of a system for automatic detection and polarity identification of context dependent claims in massive corpora
Noam Slonim, Ehud Aharoni, Carlos Alzate, Roy Bar-Haim, Yonatan Bilu, Lena Dankin, Iris Eiron, Daniel Hershcovich, Shay Hummel, Mitesh Khapra, Tamar Lavee, Ran Levy, Paul Matchen, Anatoly Polnarov, Vikas Raykar, Ruty Rinott, Amrita Saha, Naama Zwerdling, David Konopnicki and Dan Gutfreund

Copa 2014 FrameNet Brasil: a frame-based trilingual electronic dictionary for the Football World Cup
Tiago Torrent, Maria Margarida Salomão, Fernanda Campos, Regina Braga, Ely Matos, Maucha Gamonal, Julia Gonçalves, Bruno Souza, Daniela Gomes and Simone Peron

Creating Custom Taggers by Integrating Web Page Annotation and Machine Learning
Srikrishna Raamadhurai, Oskar Kohonen and Teemu Ruokolainen

How to deal with students' writing problems? Process-oriented writing support with the digital Writing Aid Dutch
Lieve De Wachter, Serge Verlinde, Margot D'Hertefelt and Geert Peeters

Processing Discourse in Dislog on the TextCoop Platform
patrick saint-dizier

UIMA Ruta Workbench: Rule-based Text Annotation
Peter Kluegl, Martin Toepfer, Philip-Daniel Beck, Georg Fette and Frank Puppe

(15:15 - 17:25) Demo session 2

Discourse Relations in the Prague Dependency Treebank 3.0
Jiří Mírovský, Pavlína Jínová and Lucie Poláková

Lightweight Client-Side Chinese/Japanese Morphological Analyzer Based on Online Learning
Masato Hagiwara and Satoshi Sekine

MultiDPS – A multilingual Discourse Processing System
Daniel Anechitei

25/08/2014 (continued)

Sanskrit Linguistics Web Services
Gérard Huet and Amba Kulkarni

TICCLops: Text-Induced Corpus Clean-up as online processing system
Martin Reynaert

Trameur: A Framework for Annotated Text Corpora Exploration
Serge Fleury and Maria Zimina

TweetGenie: Development, Evaluation, and Lessons Learned
Dong Nguyen, Dolf Trieschnigg and Theo Meder

26/08/2014

(10:15 - 12:25) Demo session 3

A Sentence Judgment System for Grammatical Error Detection
Lung-Hao Lee, Liang-Chih Yu, Kuei-Ching Lee, Yuen-Hsien Tseng, Li-Ping Chang and Hsin-Hsi Chen

CLAM: Quickly deploy NLP command-line tools on the web
Maarten van Gompel and Martin Reynaert

CRAB 2.0: A text mining tool for supporting literature review in chemical cancer risk assessment
Yufan Guo, Diarmuid Ó Séaghdha, Ilona Silins, Lin Sun, Johan Högberg, Ulla Stenius and Anna Korhonen

Nerdle: Topic-Specific Question Answering Using Wikia Seeds
Umar Maqsud, Sebastian Arnold, Michael Hülfenhaus and Alan Akbik

NTU-MC Toolkit: Annotating a Linguistically Diverse Corpus
Liling Tan and Francis Bond

RDF Triple Stores and a Custom SPARQL Front-End for Indexing and Searching (Very) Large Semantic Networks
Milen Kouylekov and Stephan Oepen

What or Who is Multilingual Watson?
Keith Cortis, Urvesh Bhowan, Ronan Mac an tSaoir, D.J. McCloskey, Mikhail Sogrin and Ross Cadogan

26/08/2014 (continued)

(15:15 - 17:25) Demo Session 4

A Marketplace for Web Scale Analytics and Text Annotation Services
Johannes Kirschnick, Torsten Kilias, Holmer Hemsen, Alexander Löser, Peter Adolphs, Heiko Ehrig and Holger Düwiger

DKPro Agreement: An Open-Source Java Library for Measuring Inter-Rater Agreement
Christian M. Meyer, Margot Mieskes, Christian Stab and Iryna Gurevych

Distributional Semantics in R with the wordspace Package
Stefan Evert

Method51 for Mining Insight from Social Media Datasets
Simon Wibberley, David Weir and Jeremy Reffin

MT-EQuAl: a Toolkit for Human Assessment of Machine Translation Output
Christian Girardi, Luisa Bentivogli, Mohammad Amin Farajian and Marcello Federico

OpenSoNaR: user-driven development of the SoNaR corpus interfaces
Martin Reynaert, Matje van de Camp and Menno van Zaanen

THE MATECAT TOOL
Marcello Federico, Nicola Bertoldi, Mauro Cettolo, Matteo Negri, Marco Turchi, Marco Trombetti, Alessandro Cattelan, Antonio Farina, Domenico Lupinetti, Andrea Martines, Alberto Massidda, Holger Schwenk, Loïc Barrault, Frederic Blain, Philipp Koehn, Christian Buck and Ulrich Germann

An Error Analysis Tool for Natural Language Processing and Applied Machine Learning

Apoorv Agarwal
Department of Computer Science
Columbia University
New York, NY, USA
apoorv@cs.columbia.edu

Ankit Agarwal
NextGen Invent Corp.
Shrewsbury, MA, USA
ankit.agarwal@ngicorporation.com

Deepak Mittal
NextGen Invent Corp.
Shrewsbury, MA, USA
deepak.mittal@ngicorporation.com

Abstract

In this paper we present a simple to use web based error analysis tool to help computational linguists, researchers building language applications, and non-technical personnel managing development of language tools to analyze the predictions made by their machine learning models. The only expectation is that the users of the tool convert their data into an intuitive XML format. Once the XML is ready, several error analysis functionalities that promote principled feature engineering are a click away.

1 Introduction

A typical machine learning (ML) pipeline involves conversion of *examples* into a structured representations, followed by training a model on these examples, followed by testing the model. Most Natural Language Processing (NLP) tasks involve (broadly) two types of structured representations: feature vectors (in which examples are represented as vectors in $\mathbb{R}^n$) and abstract representations such as strings and trees. Classification models assign each test example an integer, corresponding to the predicted class. Regression models assign each test example a real number. Throughout this process, frequently asked questions include: is there a bug in the code that converts text into a feature vector or structured representation, which models (trained using different learning algorithms) make the right prediction on what kind of examples? Which models trained on which set of features/structures make the right prediction on what kind of examples? Is a pair of models statistically significantly different? Answers to these questions give us a deeper understanding of the learning process, which in turn results in principled feature engineering and model selection.

We spend a lot of time writing quick and dirty scripts to make connections between different aspects of the learning process (features, structures, predictions, models). These scripts are often task dependent and need to be re-written for each task. More time is spent in compiling a report so our findings may be shared with other collaborators. Frustrated with this day-to-day and repetitive script writing, we decided to design and implement an easy-to-use error analysis tool that helps in answering the aforementioned questions in a few clicks. The following are the two main contributions of this work:

1. Design: the tool provides a common framework for performing error analysis of a wide range of NLP tasks. In designing and implementing this tool, we had to abstract away from specific task definitions, feature representations, and structure representations in order to bring different aspects of a task into a unified interface.

2. Web based: the tool is web-based, meaning that users can access a URL and upload files to access the functionalities of the tool. Each user can optionally generate an identifier, which can be shared with other users, enabling other users to access the same error analysis session.

2 The Tool

In the following sub-sections, we give details of the basic functionalities of the tool, followed by details of a few advanced functionalities. We explicate the functionalities using the ACE relation extraction task as a running example.

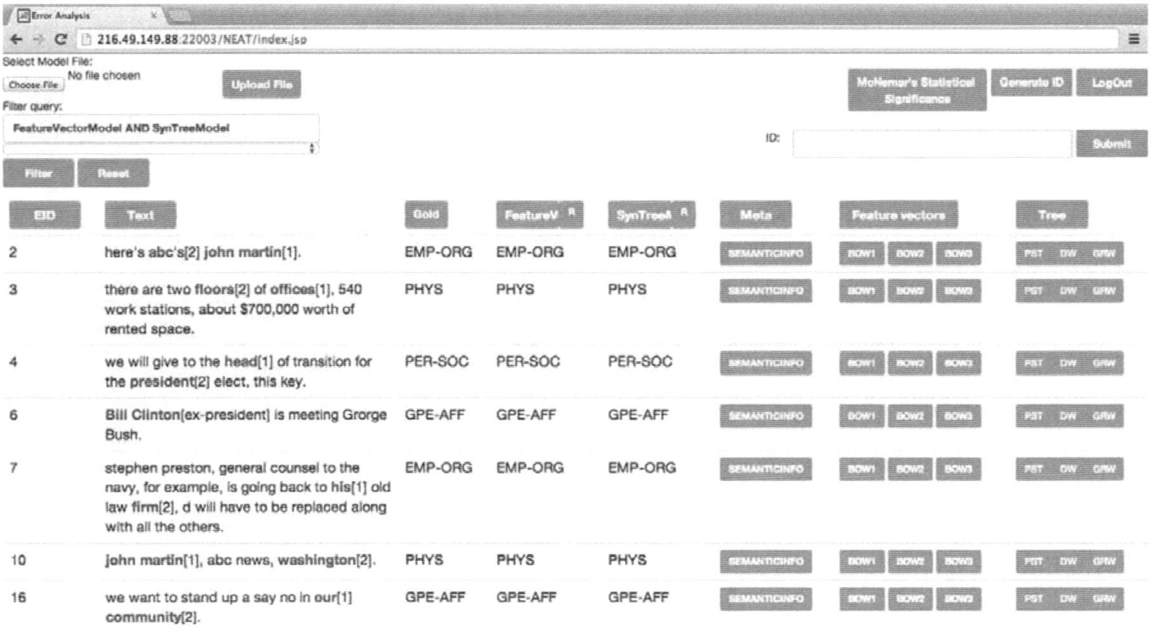

Figure 1: A screenshot of the tool loaded with ACE relation extraction task data.

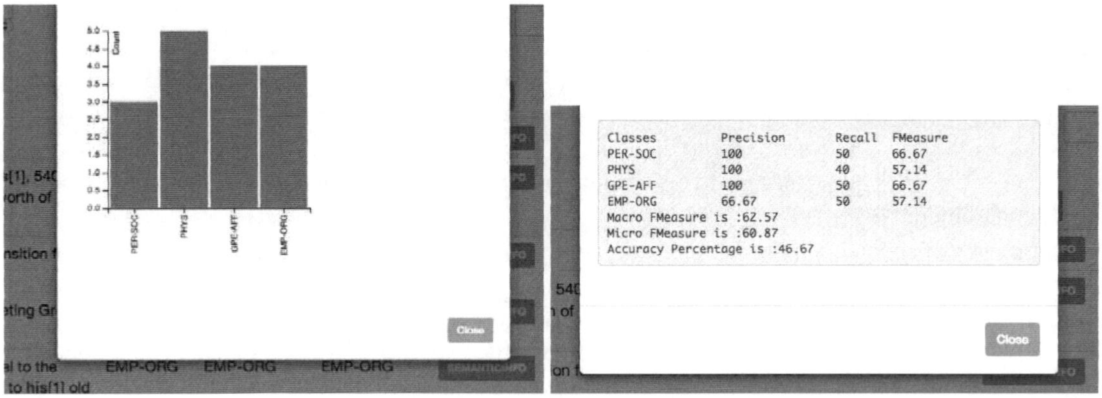

Figure 2: Screenshots of pop-ups on sample ACE data. The first pop-up shows the gold class distribution. The second pop-up shows evaluation metrics for one of the models.

2.1 ACE Relation Extraction

ACE (Automatic Content Extraction) relation extraction is a popular and well-established NLP task (Doddington et al., 2004). Given a sentence, and two entity mentions (usually referred to as *target* entities), the goal is to detect a relation between the two entities (relation detection), and if a relation exists, to identify the type of the relation (relation classification). There is a pre-defined list of relations for the ACE relation extraction task: ART, DISC, EMP-ORG, GPE-AFF, PER-SOC, PHYS, OTHER. Researchers have developed a wide range of features for the task (Kambhatla, 2004; Zhao and Grishman, 2005; Zhang et al., 2006). There is also a large body of work that has explored the space of tree structure representations (Zelenko et al., 2003; Culotta and Sorensen, 2004; Zhou et al., 2007; Nguyen et al., 2009; Agarwal and Rambow, 2010; Agarwal et al., 2014). Relation extraction is a complex task, with features ranging from simple bag-of-words to more complex semantic features, and with tree structures ranging from simple parse trees to more complicated tree structures.

2.2 Basic Functionalities

Figure 1 presents a screenshot of the tool loaded with the ACE relation extraction data. The column labeled **EID** is the example identifier assigned to each example, the column labeled **Text** has the example in text format, the column labeled **Gold** has the gold class of each example (may be a real number for regression type tasks), the columns labeled **FEATUREVECTORMODEL** and **SYNTREEMODEL** have predictions of respective models. The column labeled **FEATUREVECTORS** has the different types of feature vector representations, and the column labeled **TREES** has the different types of tree structure representations for each example. Note that the number of columns and their names are not hard-coded. The number of columns, their names and their order is automatically inferred from the XML input specified by the user (section 2.4).

The column labeled **Text** in Figure 1 shows the sentence with the target entities highlighted. The relations may be directed from one target entity to the other. The numbers next to the highlighted entities specify the direction of the relation (from entity marked as [1] to entity marked as [2]). Highlighting certain parts of input text with a tag (in this case target identifiers) is a general feature of the tool. There are other popular NLP tasks in which this functionality may come in handy. For example, for parts-of-speech tagging and named entity recognition tasks, features are extracted with respect to part of a text, which may be highlighted to understand the input example.

The column labeled **Gold** in Figure 1 shows the gold label for each example. Clicking on the column label pops up a window with a histogram that shows the distribution of the gold class (Figure 2).

The column labeled **FEATUREVECTORMODEL** shows the predictions made by a model that was trained only on feature vectors. The column labeled **SYNTREEMODEL** shows the predictions made by a model that was trained only on syntactic tree structures. There is an icon next to the column name, marked as **R**. Clicking on this icon pops up a window with a result table that summarizes the performance of that model (Figure 2). Built-in metrics include precision, recall, and F1-measure (with respect to each class), alongside the macro- and micro-F1 measures and percentage accuracy. This list of metrics may be easily extended in the code.

The way in which a user specifies the predictions per model is simple – the user is required to create a two column file (EID, prediction) and load the file into the tool using the "Browse" and "Upload File" buttons (upper left corner of Figure 1). The tool uses the **EID** to assign each prediction a row and therefore the predictions may be specified in any order.

In section 2.3 we discuss an advanced functionality of the tool that allows the user to *filter* the loaded set of examples based on boolean queries on the correctness of predictions of various models.

The column labeled **Meta** contains meta-data associated with each example. In our research, we are currently experimenting with features and tree structures derived from the output of a semantic frame parser called Semafor (Chen et al., 2010). Semafor labels the input text with frame information – frame evoking elements, frame elements, their spans and types. The output of a Semafor parse is quite complex. Visualizing the annotations produced by Semafor, along with other features and dependency trees, is helping us design novel features and tree structures for the task of relation extraction. The user of the tool has full control over the type of meta-data, and the number of types of meta-data that (s)he might want to upload in the error analysis interface.

The column labeled **FEATUREVECTORS** lists the different types of features that one may design for a task. Clicking one of the feature vector types pops up a window that shows the value of features for a particular example. For instance, clicking "BOW1" for the first example will show a pop-up that contains the following: "some:0.2 administration:0.6". These are words (and their tf-idf scores) that appear in the text between the start of the sentence and the occurrence of the first target.

The column labeled **Trees** shows the different types of tree structures that a user may design for a task. Clicking on a particular type of tree (button) will bring up a picture of the tree. Note – we do not require the user to provide the pdf with the tree diagram. The tool converts a tree specified in a standard text format, such as this "(ROOT (A B))", into a dot file, which is automatically converted into a pdf file.

2.3 Other Functionalities

Notice the text box labeled "Filter Data" in Figure 1. Users of the tool may specify complex queries to filter out the examples that do not satisfy the filter. For example, a query such as "**FeatureVectorModel** AND NOT **SynTreeModel**" will filter out examples that do not satisfy the following condition: examples that **FeatureVectorModel** predicted correctly but **SynTreeModel** predicted incorrectly. Similarly a query such as "**FeatureVectorModel** OR **SynTreeModel**" will filter out examples that both the models predicted incorrectly. We have implemented two binary operations (AND and OR) and a unary operation (NOT). These operations may be combined with model names to form complex queries. The tool automatically saves the past 10 filter conditions, which may be accessed through a drop down menu under the filter text box.

Notice the button labeled "McNemar's Statistical Significance" in Figure 1 (upper right corner). Clicking this button pops up a window that shows, in tabular format, the McNemar's statistical significance p-value for all pairs of models loaded in the interface.

Notice the "Generate ID" button on the top right corner of Figure 1. If a user of the tool wants to share his/her session (and analysis) with other collaborators, the user can generate a unique identifier by clicking this button. This identifier may be shared with other collaborators who may visit the tool website, enter the identifier in the text box labeled "ID" and gain access to the same session. Of course, a user might want to save the generated identifier for him/her-self for returning to an older session. The web service handles concurrent requests.

2.4 Input XML Representation

```
<example EID="..." GOLD="...">
   <Text> ... </Text>
   <Meta-[NAME]> ... </Meta-[NAME]>
   <Tree-[NAME]> ... </Tree-[NAME]>
   <Feat-[NAME]> ... </Feat-[NAME]>
</example>
```

Figure 3: XML format to be specified by the user.

Figure 3 shows the input XML schema expected from the user. Each example may be specified within the XML tag "example". Example identifier and its gold class may be specified as attributes of the element "example". Each example may have associated text, and a number of "Meta", "Feat", and "Tree" prefixed tags. We use this prefix to determine how to render the content of each element. For example, the content of the tag prefixed by "Meta" and "Feat" is shown as is on the interface, whereas the content of the tag prefixed by "Tree" is converted to a pdf with a picture of the tree.

3 Related Work

Stymne (2011) present an error analysis tool for machine translation. El Kholy and Habash (2011) present an error analysis tool, Ameana, for NLP tasks that use morphologically rich languages. Both these tools are specific in terms of the NLP tasks they tackle. While such tools are important (because tasks such as machine translation are quite complex and require customized solutions), the goal of the tool we present in this paper is different. The goal of our tool is to replace the day-to-day, quick and dirty script writing process (required to make connections between different aspects of an NLP task) by a web based user friendly solution. The design of this tool is novel, and to the best of our knowledge there is no such publicly available web based error analysis tool.

4 License and Contact Information

The error analysis tool is available[1] for free for research purposes under the GNU General Public License as published by the Free Software Foundation.

Acknowledgements

We would like to thank Jiehan Zheng and Aakash Bishnoi for contributing to the user interface code. We would also like to thank Caronae Howell for her insightful comments.

References

Apoorv Agarwal and Owen Rambow. 2010. Automatic detection and classification of social events. In *Proceedings of the 2010 Conference on Empirical Methods in Natural Language Processing*, pages 1024–1034, Cambridge, MA, October. Association for Computational Linguistics.

Apoorv Agarwal, Sriramkumar Balasubramanian, Anup Kotalwar, Jiehan Zheng, and Owen Rambow. 2014. Frame semantic tree kernels for social network extraction from text. *14th Conference of the European Chapter of the Association for Computational Linguistics.*

Desai Chen, Nathan Schneider, Dipanjan Das, and Noah A. Smith. 2010. Semafor: Frame argument resolution with log-linear models. In *Proceedings of the 5th International Workshop on Semantic Evaluation*, pages 264–267, Uppsala, Sweden, July. Association for Computational Linguistics.

Aron Culotta and Jeffrey Sorensen. 2004. Dependency tree kernels for relation extraction. In *Proceedings of the 42nd Meeting of the Association for Computational Linguistics (ACL'04), Main Volume*, pages 423–429, Barcelona, Spain, July.

G. Doddington, A. Mitchell, M. Przybocki, L. Ramshaw, S. Strassel, and R. Weischedel. 2004. The automatic content extraction (ace) program–tasks, data, and evaluation. *LREC*, pages 837–840.

A. El Kholy and N. Habash. 2011. Automatic error analysis for morphologically rich languages. In *MT Summit XIII*, September.

Nanda Kambhatla. 2004. Combining lexical, syntactic, and semantic features with maximum entropy models for extracting relations. In *Proceedings of the ACL 2004 on Interactive poster and demonstration sessions*, page 22. Association for Computational Linguistics.

Truc-Vien T. Nguyen, Alessandro Moschitti, and Giuseppe Riccardi. 2009. Convolution kernels on constituent, dependency and sequential structures for relation extraction. *Conference on Empirical Methods in Natural Language Processing.*

Sara Stymne. 2011. Blast: A tool for error analysis of machine translation output. In *Proceedings of the ACL-HLT 2011 System Demonstrations*, pages 56–61, Portland, Oregon, June. Association for Computational Linguistics.

Dmitry Zelenko, Chinatsu Aone, and Anthony Richardella. 2003. Kernel methods for relation extraction. *The Journal of Machine Learning Research*, 3:1083–1106.

Min Zhang, Jie Zhang, Jian Su, and Guodong Zhou. 2006. A composite kernel to extract relations between entities with both flat and structured features. In *Proceedings of COLING-ACL.*

Shubin Zhao and Ralph Grishman. 2005. Extracting relations with integrated information using kernel methods. In *Proceedings of the 43rd Meeting of the ACL.*

GuoDong Zhou, Min Zhang, DongHong Ji, and QiaoMing Zhu. 2007. Tree kernel-based relation extraction with context-sensitive structured parse tree information. In *Proceedings of EMNLP-CoNLL.*

[1] www.ngicorporation.com/NEAT

Claims on demand – an initial demonstration of a system for automatic detection and polarity identification of context dependent claims in massive corpora

Ehud Aharoni IBM Haifa Research Lab, Haifa, Israel

Carlos Alzate IBM Dublin Research Lab, Ireland

Roy Bar-Haim IBM Haifa Research Lab, Haifa, Israel

Yonatan Bilu IBM Haifa Research Lab, Haifa, Israel

Lena Dankin IBM Haifa Research Lab, Haifa, Israel

Iris Eiron IBM Haifa Research Lab, Haifa, Israel

Daniel Hershcovich IBM Haifa Research Lab, Haifa, Israel

Shay Hummel IBM Haifa Research Lab, Haifa, Israel

Mitesh Khapra IBM Bangalore Research Lab, India

Tamar Lavee[1] IBM Haifa Research Lab, Haifa, Israel

Ran Levy IBM Haifa Research Lab, Haifa, Israel

Paul Matchen IBM YKT Research Lab, US

Anatoly Polnarov Hebrew University, Jerusalem, Israel

Vikas Raykar IBM Bangalore Research Lab, India

Ruty Rinott IBM Haifa Research Lab, Haifa, Israel

Amrita Saha IBM Bangalore Research Lab, India

Naama Zwerdling IBM Haifa Research Lab, Haifa, Israel

David Konopnicki IBM Haifa Research Lab, Haifa, Israel

Dan Gutfreund IBM Haifa Research Lab, Haifa, Israel

Noam Slonim[2] IBM Haifa Research Lab, Haifa, Israel

Abstract

While discussing a concrete controversial topic, most humans will find it challenging to swiftly raise a diverse set of convincing and relevant claims that should set the basis of their arguments. Here, we demonstrate the initial capabilities of a system that, given a controversial topic, can automatically pinpoint relevant claims in Wikipedia, determine their polarity with respect to the given topic, and articulate them per the user's request.

1 Introduction

The ability to argue in a persuasive manner is an important aspect of human interaction that naturally arises in various domains such as politics, marketing, law, and health-care. Furthermore, good decision making relies on the quality of the arguments being presented and the process by which they are resolved. Thus, it is not surprising that argumentation has long been a topic of interest in academic research, and different models have been proposed to capture the notion of an argument (Freeley and Steinberg, 2008).

A fundamental component which is common to all these models is the concept of *claim* (or *conclusion*). Specifically, at the heart of every argument lies a single claim, which is the assertion the argument aims to prove. Given a concrete topic, or context, most humans will find it challenging to swiftly raise a diverse set of convincing and relevant claims that should set the basis of their arguments.

[1] Present affiliation: Yahoo!

[2] Corresponding author, at noams@il.ibm.com

In this work we demonstrate the initial capabilities of a system that, given a controversial topic, can automatically pinpoint relevant claims in Wikipedia, determine their polarity with respect to the given topic, and articulate them per the user's request.

2 Basic concepts and associated challenges

We define and rely on the following two concepts:
Topic: Short, usually controversial statement that defines the subject of interest.
Context Dependent Claim (CDC): General, and concise statement, that directly supports or contests the given Topic.

Given these definitions, as well as a few more detailed criteria to reduce the variability in the manually labeled data, human labelers were asked to detect CDCs for a diverse set of Topics, in relevant Wikipedia articles. The collected data were used to train and assess the performance of the statistical models that underlie our system. These data are freely available for academic research (Aharoni et al 2014).

The distinction between a CDC and other related texts can be quite subtle, as illustrated in Table 1. For example, automatically distinguishing a CDC like S1 from a statement that simply defines a relevant concept like S4, from a claim which is not relevant enough to the given Topic like S5, from a statement like S6 that merely repeats the given Topic in different words, or from a statement that represents a relevant claim which is not general enough like S7, is clearly challenging. Further, CDCs can be of different flavors, ranging from factual assertions like S1 to statements that are more of a matter of opinion (Pang and Lee 2008) like S2, adding to the complexity of the task. Moreover, our data suggest that even if one focuses on Wikipedia articles that are highly relevant to the given Topic, only ≈2% of their sentences include CDCs.

Furthermore, since CDCs are by definition concise statements, they typically do not span entire Wikipedia sentences but rather sub-sentences. This is illustrated in Table 2. There are many optional boundaries to consider when trying to identify the exact boundaries of a CDC within a typical Wikipedia sentence. This task further complicates the CDC detection problem. Thus, we are faced with a large number of candidate CDCs, of which only a tiny fraction represents positive examples that might be quite reminiscent of some of the negative examples. Finally, automatically determining the correct Pro/Con polarity of a candidate CDC with respect to the Topic poses additional unique challenges. Nonetheless, by breaking the problem into a set of modular tangible problems and by employing various techniques - specifically designed to the problems at hand - we obtain promising results, demonstrated by the capabilities of our system.

Topic	The sale of violent video games to minors should be banned
(Pro) CDC	*S1: Violent video games can increase children's aggression*
(Pro) CDC	*S2: Video game publishers unethically train children in the use of weapons* Note, that a valid CDC is not necessarily factual.
(Con) CDC	*S3: Violent games affect children positively*
Invalid CDC 1	*S4: Video game addiction is excessive or compulsive use of computer and video games that interferes with daily life.* This statement defines a concept relevant to the Topic, not a relevant claim.
Invalid CDC 2	*S5: Violent TV shows just mirror the violence that goes on in the real world.* This statement is not relevant enough to the Topic.
Invalid CDC 3	*S6: Violent video games should not be sold to children.* This statement simply repeats the Topic, and thus is not considered a valid CDC.
Invalid CDC 4	*S7: "Doom" has been blamed for nationally covered school shooting.* This statement is not general enough to represent a CDC, as it focuses on a specific single video game.

Table 1. Examples of CDCs and invalid CDCs.

Because violence in video games is interactive and not passive, critics such as Dave Grossman and Jack Thompson argue that ***violence in games hardens children to unethical acts****, calling first-person shooter games ``murder simulators", although no conclusive evidence has supported this belief.*

Table 2. A CDC is often only a small part of a single Wikipedia sentence - e.g., the part marked in bold in this example.

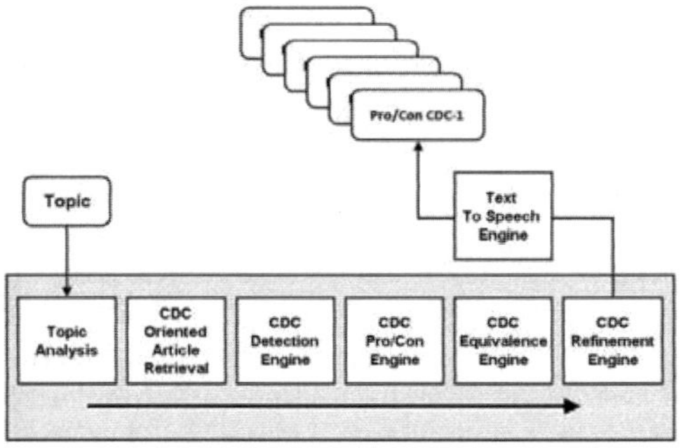

Figure 1. High level architecture of the demonstrated system.

3 High Level Architecture

The demonstrated system relies on a cascade of engines, depicted in Figure 1. In general, these engines rely on various IR, NLP and ML technologies, as well as different resources and lexicons like WordNet (Miller, 1995). Some engines are more mature than others, and, correspondingly, already employ a complex inner architecture, that will be discussed in more detail elsewhere. Given a Topic, the **Topic Analysis engine** starts with initial semantic analysis of the Topic, aiming to identify the main concepts mentioned in this Topic and the sentiment towards each concept. Next, the **CDC Oriented Article Retrieval** engine employs IR and opinion mining techniques in order to retrieve Wikipedia articles that with high probability contain CDCs. Next, the **CDC Detection engine** relies on a combination of NLP and ML techniques to zoom-in within the retrieved articles and detect candidate CDCs. A detailed description of this engine can be found in (Levy et al 2014). Next, the **CDC Pro/Con engine** aims to automatically determine the polarity of the candidate CDC with respect to the given Topic by analyzing and contrasting the sentiment towards key concepts mentioned in the Topic and within the candidate CDC. Next, the **CDC Equivalence engine** uses techniques reminiscent of automatic paraphrase detection to identify whether two candidate CDCs are semantically equivalent, so to avoid redundancy in the generated output. Finally, the **CDC Refinement engine** aims to improve the precision of the generated output, based on the results collected thus far; e.g., using a simple rule-based approach, we remove candidate CDCs for which the predicted Pro/Con polarity has low confidence. The remaining predictions are sent to the **Text To Speech engine** that articulates the top CDC predictions at the user's request.

4 Summary

Given a Topic, the demonstrated system is currently focused on detecting and articulating relevant CDCs. Combining this system with technologies that could automatically detect evidence to support these CDCs, may give rise to a new generation of automatic argumentation systems. In principle, such systems may swiftly detect relevant CDCs in massive corpora, and support these CDCs with evidence detected within other articles, or even within entirely different corpora, ending up with automatically generated arguments that were never explicitly proposed before in this form by humans. The system described herein represents an important step in pursuing this vision.

Acknowledgments

We would like to thank our colleagues in the IBM debating technologies team who participate in generating more advanced versions of the system presented in this work, and further continue to contribute to essential aspects of this project. These include Priyanka Agrawal, Indrajit Bhattacharya, Feng Cao, Lea Deleris, Francesco Dinuzzo, Liat Ein-Dor, Ron Hoory, Hui Jia Zhu, Qiong Kai Xu, Abhishek Kumar, Ofer Lavi, Naftali Liberman, Yosi Mass, Yuan Ni, Asaf Rendel, Haggai Roitman, Bogdan Sacaleanu, Dafna Sheinwald, Eyal Shnarch, Mathieu Sinn, Orith Toledo-Ronen, Doron Veltzer and Yoav Katz.

References

Austin J. Freeley and David L. Steinberg. 2008. *Argumentation and Debate*. Wadsworth, Belmont, California.

Ehud Aharoni, Anatoly Polnarov, Tamar Lavee, Daniel Hershcovich, Ran Levy, Ruty Rinott, Dan Gutfreund, and Noam Slonim. 2014. "A Benchmark Dataset for Automatic Detection of Claims and Evidence in the Context of Controversial Topics", in *Proceedings of the First Workshop on Argumentation and Computation, ACL 2014, to appear.*

Bo Pang and Lillian Lee. 2008. "Opinion mining and sentiment analysis" in *Foundations and Trends in Information Retrieval*, Vol. 2, pp. 1-135.

George A Miller. 1995. " WordNet: A Lexical Database for English" in *Communications of the ACM*, Vol. 38, pp. 29-41.

Ran Levy, Yonatan Bilu, Daniel Hershcovich, Ehud Aharoni and Noam Slonim. 2014. "Context Dependent Claim Detection." In *Proceedings of the* 25th *International Conference on Computational Linguistics, COLING 2014, to appear.*

Copa 2014 FrameNet Brasil: a frame-based trilingual electronic dictionary for the Football World Cup

Tiago T. Torrent, Maria Margarida M. Salomão, Fernanda C. A. Campos, Regina M. M. Braga, Ely E. S. Matos, Maucha A. Gamonal, Julia A. Gonçalves, Bruno C. P. Souza, Daniela S. Gomes and Simone R. Peron

Federal University of Juiz de Fora – FrameNet Brasil
tiago.torrent@ufjf.edu.br; mm.salomao@uol.com.br
{fernanda.campos|regina.braga|ely.matos}@ufjf.edu.br;
mauchaandrade@gmail.com; julia.goncalves@ifsudeste.edu.br;
brunopereiradesouza@yahoo.com.br;danielasimoesgomes@gmail.com;
speronjf@yahoo.com.br

Abstract

This paper presents the Copa 2014 FrameNet Brasil software (C-14/FN-Br): a frame-based trilingual electronic dictionary covering the domains of Football, Tourism and the World Cup. The dictionary relies on the infrastructure of FrameNet and is meant to be used by tourists, journalists and the staff involved in receiving foreign visitors. Vocabulary from the three domains is made available in English, Spanish and Brazilian Portuguese. Every lexical unit in the dictionary is described against an interlingual background frame.

1 Introduction

The idea of building a frame-based electronic dictionary is not new. Fillmore and Atkins (1992) paper on the semantics of Risk and its neighbors already propose the general guidelines for a lexical resource in which frames would play the key role of organizing lexical units (LUs) – the pairing of a lemma and a frame – and the relations among them. Five years after the Risk paper, Berkeley FrameNet was launched not only to materialize those general guidelines, but also to go beyond them (Fillmore et al. 2003a; 2003b). Currently, Berkeley FrameNet has described 1,164 frames and 12,713 LUs, which, in turn, are attested in 195,590 annotated sentences[1]. Additionally, there are framenets being developed for several languages other than English, such as Chinese (You and Liu, 2005), German (Boas, 2002), Japanese (Ohara et al., 2004), Spanish (Subirats and Petruck, 2003), Swedish (Borin et al., 2010), and Brazilian Portuguese (Salomão, 2009), among others.

However, although FrameNet and its sister projects have made considerable impact in Computational Linguistics, the frame-based approach for creating lexical resources envisioned by Fillmore and his collaborators has not been fully exploited in creating commercial electronic dictionaries, i.e. pieces of software focusing not on an expert user, but in the non-linguist. The Copa 2014 FrameNet Brasil Project (C-14/FN-Br) aims to fill in this blank.

Covering the domains of Football – whose frames were defined by the Semantec group at UNISINOS (Chishman et al., 2013) –, Tourism and the World Cup itself – both modeled by the FrameNet Brasil group at the Federal University of Juiz de Fora –, the dictionary is meant to be used by tourists, journalists and the staff involved both in the organization of the event and in receiving foreign visitors. Vocabulary from the three domains is made available in English, Spanish and Brazilian Portuguese. Every LU in the dictionary is described against a background frame, which is the same for the three languages. Hence, relying on the infrastructure of framenet, C-14/FN-Br serves as a proof of concept that frames – at least the crosscultural ones – can be used as an interlingua.

2 The Database

The C-14/FN-Br database is fully multilingual, in the sense that, besides comprising LUs from the

[1]Data retrieved from http://framenet.icsi.berkeley.edu on December 17th 2013.

three languages, the frames and Frame Elements (FEs) – the participants and props in a frame – modeled are represented in the three languages as well. This procedure aims to provide the software with a trilingual interface, meaning that the user may choose in which language s/he wants to interact with the software.

To populate the database, C-14/FN-Br uses the same software developed for Berkeley FrameNet, the FrameNet Desktop, with some minor changes, the most important of which being the Translation Relation, the Language Index, the Grammatical Function and Phrase Type Correspondence Tables, and the LU Link.

2.1 Translation Relation

The original FrameNet database works with eight different frame-to-frame relations: Inheritance, Using, Subframe, Perspective on, Precedes, Causative of, Incohative of and See also (Fillmore et al. 2003b; Ruppenhofer et al. 2010). Those relations structure the network of frames, defining which frame is a type – Inheritance – or a part – Subframe – of another, or even if it comes before another frame – Precedes.

For the development of C-14/FN-Br, an additional relation was created: Translation. Since it is a symmetric relation between representations of the same conceptual structure, the Translation relation requires all FE in one representation to be mapped to FEs in the other.

With this relation, the software is able to link the set of LUs evoking a frame in a given language to the set of LUs evoking the same frame in another language. Also, the Translation relation provides the dictionary user with the possibility of accessing the frame description in all the three interface languages, which may or may not be the same as the language of the word being looked up.

2.2 Language Index

A framenet-like database is composed of both a set of frames, FEs and the relations among them, and a set of annotations. In the annotation sets, sentences are labeled not only in regards to the FEs occurring in them, but also in regards to the Grammatical Functions (GFs) and Phrase Types (PTs), i.e. the linguistic material, in which they are instantiated.

Each language requires its own set of GFs and PTs, which were defined by the correspondent framenet projects (see Ruppenhofer et al., 2010; Spanish FrameNet, 2013; Torrent and Ellsworth, 2013). In C-14/FN-Br, GF and PT labels for English, Spanish and Brazilian Portuguese are included in the database and made available for the lexicographer when annotating a sentence. A Language Index (*en*, for English; *es*, for Spanish, and *br*, for Brazilian Portuguese) was created and ascribed to the layers containing those labels and also to the frames. During the process of importing aanotation corpora into the Desktop, the Language Index in the annotation set is unified with that of the layers, thus providing the relevant GF and PT labels for each sentence.

2.3 Grammatical Function and Phrase Type Correspondence Tables

Another change made to the database was the creation of a relational table in which GF and PT labels in the three languages are associated to each other. The purpose of this table is to provide the software with a base for comparing valence patterns of the lexical units in the dictionary. Through such a comparison, C-14/FN-Br is able to suggest the best translation equivalents for a given word in the other two languages covered by the dictionary (see Torrent et al., forthcoming).

2.4 LU Link

The last change incorporated to the C-14/FN-Br database is the LU Link. Through this relation, LUs evoking the same frame in different languages can be linked to each other as translation equivalents. The process of assigning those equivalences is based on the analysis of the lexicographer. The LU Link tool is specially important for defining equivalence relations between nouns evoking entities, such as city and stadiums names, since their valence patterns are not informative enough for the automatic suggestion of translation equivalents.

3 The Application

C-14/FN-Br was developed as a web app and can be accessed at http://dicionariodacopa.com.br. On the client side, the web interface is built using HTML5 and Javascript. Data is stored in a MySQL database and is delivered to clients through a PHP5 web service. Data transfer uses AJAX techniques.

Every piece of information in the multilingual framenet-like database of C-14/FN-Br is, to some extent, used for presenting information to the final user. Thus, besides being able to search for LUs and their equivalents in the other languages, users can also see the frame and the FEs evoked by the lexical item, as well as selected annotated sentences, images and videos, which illustrate the meaning evoked by the word.

Since the dictionary is aimed at a non-specialist audience, adaptations in the Frame Semantics terminology were made. Frames are called scenes (or *esceneas* and *cenas*, in Spanish and Portuguese) and Frame Elements are called participants (or *participantes*). Frame-to-frame relations also had their names changed into more transparent concepts. For instance, instead of presenting the names Inheritance and Subframe, the software shows these relations as nominal predicates, respectivelly, “is a type of” and “is a part of”.

3.1 Query Modes

Users may access the information in the dictionary in four different ways: by searching a word, by typing a sentence, by browsing the list of frames grouped by cognitive domains, and by exploring the frame grapher.

The first mode is similar to the one found in the majority of electronic dictionaries (Pastor and Alcina, 2010): users are presented a list of words in alphabetical order and a search box. Icons with the Brazilian, British and Spanish flags provide the possibility of choosing the language to which the words being looked up belong.

When a given lemma is paired with more than one frame in the dictionary, that is, it is polysemous, C-14/FN-Br shows a disambiguation screen to the user, in which s/he can choose in which scene s/he wants to explore the meaning of the word. Alternatively, if the user types in a sentence containing the LU s/he wants to look up, the dictionary may infer the most appropriate scene, using the frame disambiguation tool.

3.2 Frame Disambiguation

The frame disambiguation tool chooses, among the frames evoked by the various LUs of a lexeme, the best fit for a given context. First, a text-matching script identifies lemmas in the sentence the user types in. Second, all frames evoked by the LUs grouped under those lemmas are retrieved and each possible combination of frames forms a cluster. Since it is very unlikely that two or more LUs evoke the same frame in one sentence, and since frames in FrameNet are related to each other via frame-to-frame relations, cluster formation is extended so as to include related frames. The similarity/proximity between frames is assessed within each cluster, based on the weights ascribed to each frame-to-frame relation. The cluster in which relations between frames are stronger receive higher grades, enabling C-14/FN-br to present to the user the most probable meaning of a polysemous word given the sentential context provided in the query. Currently, the frame disambiguation tool works only for verbal lexical units.

3.3 Frame Grapher

The two other query modes focus on frames, not on LUs. Users can either browse a list of the frames defined for each domain, accessing their definitions and FEs, or explore the frame grapher, a dynamic graph in which frames are linked to each other via frame-to-frame relations. The purpose of the grapher is to show to the user, in an interactive tool, how the domains of the World Cup, Football and Tourism are organized. Through this tool it is possible not only to access the vocabulary evoking a specific stage of the World Cup, such as the Playoffs, for example, but also to see that it is a part of the World Cup that precedes the Final Match and comes after the Group Stage.

3.4 Multimedia Features and External Links

As an additional resource for understanding the frame evoked by each lexical unit, the dictionary provides the users with pictures and annotated pieces of video illustrating some of the frames. Currently, video annotation is made using a free web tool from Mozilla Corporation: PopcornMaker (https://popcorn.webmaker.org).

Also, users may follow a link to the websites from which the example sentences for each LU were collected, thus being able to read travel blogs, news and other pieces of text related to the domains coverd by the dictionary.

4 Preliminary Analytics

The C-14/FN-Br web app was launched on June 4th 2014, one week prior to the World Cup. During the first month, from 6/4/2014 to 7/4/2014, the app was accessed 1,883 times by 1,367 different users, with a total of 12,322 pages visited, i.e. an average of 6.54 pages per session. Bounce rate during the first month was of 22.68%, and the average session duration was 3 minutes and 52 seconds.

The web app was accessed from 59 different coutries. Table 1 lists the top ten countries in number of sessions. For each country, the percentage of new sessions, the bounce rate, the average number of pages visited and the average session duration is also presented.

Country	Sessions	New users	Bounce rate	Pages per session	Session duration
Brazil	1,352(71.80%)	924(68.39%)	22.26%	6.99	00:04:21
United States	75(3.98%)	57(4.22%)	29.33%	4.49	00:02:23
Spain	71(3,77%)	65(4.81%)	14.08%	6.11	00:02:39
Colombia	31(1.65%)	16(1.18%)	41.94%	3.32	00:02:13
Peru	31(1.65%)	27(2.00%)	12.90%	6.45	00:03:47
United Kingdom	30(1.59%)	18(1.33%)	36.67%	6.17	00:02:49
Venezuela	27(1.43%)	24(1.78%)	29.63%	4.89	00:03:05
Germany	24(1.27%)	22(1.63%)	16.67%	4.62	00:01:23
France	19(1.01%)	18(1.33%)	10.53%	5.89	00:02:04
Canada	18(0.96%)	10(0.74%)	11.11%	6.56	00:02:09
Other	205(10.88%)	170(12.58%)	---	---	---
Total/Average	**1,883(100%)**	**1,351(100%)**	**22.68%**	**6.54**	**00:03:52**

Table 1. Sessions per country.

Although 71.80% of the sessions originated from Brazil, only 65.00% (1,224) of them were opened from devices in which the default language was Brazilian Portuguese. Devices in which English is the default language represent 18.00% of the total (339 sessions), while those whose default language is Spanish stand for 10.20% (192 sessions). Those data might point to the fact that the app has been used by foreigners visitng Brazil during the World Cup, however, the information on the default language retrieved from the analytics software is not competely reliable, since it is set by the user while configuring the device for the first time.

Nevertheless, stronger data supporting the claim that the app has been used by foreigners while visiting Brazil come from the analysis of the number of clicks received by each link in the first page of the app, in which users choose the interface language in their first visit – this page is not shown after the second time the same device accesses C-14/FN-Br. In the 1,367 sessions opened in this page, Brazilian Portuguese was chosen as the interface language 794 times, English was chosen 202 times and Spanish 160 times. 211 sessions were closed before any clicks were recorded.

Regarding the query modes offered in the main menu, Table 2 presents the users' behavior in regards to the interface language chosen. Totals presented in the last row of the table include visits by both first-time and returning users and do not include sessions in which no query mode was selected and users simply accessed information about the project or quit the app. Data in Table 2 show that the word search was the most used query mode in all three languages, representing at least half of the users'choices. Neverthless, the other query modes oferred by C-14/FN-Br were tested by a substantial number of users.

Query Modes	Brazilian Portuguese	English	Spanish
Search a word	543 (54.08%)	206 (60.41%)	142 (66.98%)
Type in a sentence	141 (14.04%)	52 (15,25%)	26 (12.26%)
See the meaning	174 (17.33%)	42 (12.31%)	27 (12.73%)
Explore the network	146 (14.54%)	41 (12.02%)	17 (8.01%)
Total	**1,004 (100%)**	**341 (100%)**	**212 (100%)**

Table 2. Query modes chosen by users according to each of the possible interface languages.

5 Conclusion

This paper presented C-14/FN-Br, a frame-based trilingual electronic dictionary covering the domains of football, tourism and the Word Cup. Our aim with this research was both to extend the use of FrameNet to the construction of lexical resources for non-linguists and to explore the use of frames as interlingual representations.

Acknowledgments

The authors thank the National Council for Scientific and Technological Development – CNPq – (grant #474270/2011-4), the Minas Gerais State Research Foundation – FAPEMIG – (grant #CHE-APQ-00567-12), and the Federal University of Juiz de Fora (grant #PAGP-24975/12-14) for funding this project. The authors are grateful to the Semantec Group at UNISINOS, for providing the Football frames, and to Berkeley FrameNet and Spanish FrameNet, for the helpful insights on the English and Spanish frames and lexical units.

References

Carlos Subirats and Miriam R. L. Petruck. 2003. Surprise: Spanish FrameNet! *Proceedings of the 17th International Conference of Linguists*. Prague, Czech Republic.

Charles J. Fillmore and Beryl T. Atkins. 1992. Toward a Frame-Based Lexicon: the semantics of RISK and its neighbors. In Adrienne Lehrer and Eva F. Kittay (eds.). *Frames, Fields and Contrasts*. Routledge, New York. 75-102.

Charles J. Fillmore, Christopher R. Johnson and Miriam R. L. Petruck. 2003a. Background to FrameNet. *International Journal of Lexicography*, 16(3): 235-250.

Charles J. Fillmore, Miriam R. L. Petruck, Joseph Ruppenhofer and Abby Wright. 2003b. FrameNet in action: the case of attaching. *International Journal of Lexicography*, 16(3):297-332.

Hans C. Boas. 2002. Bilingual FrameNet Dictionaries for Machine Translation. *Proceedings of The Third International Conference on Language Resources and Evaluation*. Las Palmas, Spain.

Joseph Ruppenhofer, Michael Ellsworth, Miriam R. L. Petruck, Christopher R. Johnson and Jan Scheffczyk. 2010. *FrameNet II: Extended Theory and Practice*. ICSI, Berkeley, USA.

Kyoko H. Ohara, Seiko Fujii, Toshio Ohori, Ryoko Suzuki, Hiroaki Saito and Shun Ishizaki. 2004. The Japanese FrameNet Project: An Introduction. *Proceedings of the LREC 2004 SatelliteWorkshop: Building Lexical Resources from Semantically Annotated Corpora*. Lisboa, Portugal.

Lars Borin, Danna Dannélls, Markus Forsberg, Maria Toporowska Gronostaj and Dimitrios Kokkinakis. 2010. Swedish FrameNet++. *Proceedings of the Swedish Language Technology Conference*. Linköping, Sweden.

Liping You and Kaiying Liu. 2005. Building Chinese FrameNet Database. *Proceedings of the 2005 IEEE International Conference on Natural Language Processing and Knowledge Engineering*. ICCS Shangai Normal University, Shangai, China.

Maria Margarida M. Salomão. 2009. FrameNet Brasil: um trabalho em progresso. *Calidoscópio*, 7(2): 171-182.

Rove L. O. Chishman, Diego S. Souza and João G. Padilha. 2013. Kicktionary_Br: um relato sobre a anotação semântica de um corpus voltado ao domínio do futebol. *Veredas,* 17(1): 101-116.

Spanish FrameNet. 2013. Spanish FrameNet web site. http://sfn.uab.es:8080/SFN/.

Thomas Schmidt. 2007. The Kicktionary: A Multilingual Resource of the Language of Football. In Georg Rehm, Andreas Witt and Lothar Lemnitzer (eds.). *Data Structures for Linguistic Resources and Applications*. Gunter Narr, Tübingen, Germany. 189-196.

Tiago T. Torrent and Michael Ellsworth. 2013. Behind the Labels: criteria for defining analytical categories in FrameNet Brasil. *Veredas,* 17(1): 44-65.

Verónica Pastor and Amparo Alcina. 2010. Search Techniques in Electronic Dictionaries: a classification for translators. *International Journal of Lexicography*, 23(3): 333-357.

Creating Custom Taggers by Integrating Web Page Annotation and Machine Learning

Srikrishna Raamadhurai* **Oskar Kohonen*** **Teemu Ruokolainen****
*Aalto University, Department of Information and Computer Science, Finland
**Aalto University, Department of Signal Processing and Acoustics, Finland
firstname.lastname@aalto.fi

Abstract

We present an on-going work on a software package that integrates discriminative machine learning with the open source WebAnnotator system of Tannier (2012). The WebAnnotator system allows users to annotate web pages within their browser with custom tag sets. Meanwhile, we integrate the WebAnnotator system with a machine learning package which enables automatic tagging of new web pages. We hope the software evolves into a useful information extraction tool for motivated hobbyists who have domain expertise on their task of interest but lack machine learning or programming knowledge. This paper presents the system architecture, including the WebAnnotator-based front-end and the machine learning component. The system is available under an open source license.

1 Introduction

A typical development cycle of a natural language processing (NLP) tool involves several different experts whose time is often limited as well as expensive. In particular, rule-based systems need experts to construct the rules, while data-driven systems require domain experts to produce annotated training data and machine learning experts to train the systems. Because of the required investment, tasks which lack commercial or academic interest are often left completely without applicable tools. Nevertheless, we believe that there exist many relatively simple tasks where necessary annotation for a machine learning system could be produced by motivated hobbyists who possess domain expertise but lack machine learning or programming knowledge. For example, consider identifying fields in classified ads such as product name, dimensions and price, or segmenting individual posts in a web forum. To this end, we present a software package that integrates discriminative machine learning with the open source WebAnnotator system (Tannier, 2012).

The combination of an annotation tool and machine learning is, of course, not a new idea, as it goes back at least to the Alembic system (Day et al., 1997), which was developed to accelerate the process of tailoring NLP tools to new domains, languages, and tasks, by attempting to reduce the work load of human annotators by employing pre-taggers learned from previously annotated data. Despite these ideas being around for a long time, they do not seem to have been integrated into a web-browser previously. Since a large amount of information is consumed using the web-browser, it is desirable to be able to train and apply automatic analysis tools directly within that context.

The paper is organized as follows. In Section 2, we review how the system is used, its general architecture and details related to how the machine learning is implemented. Section 4 provides discussion and conclusions on the work.

2 System

In this section we present in some detail the system that integrates discriminative machine learning with the open source WebAnnotator (Tannier, 2012). We review the usage of the system, its software architecture, the central aspects related to how machine learning is applied: the employed Conditional

Random Fields-method, indexing and pre-processing web-pages, how training sets are constructed, and the applied feature extraction. Finally, we review how the trained system is applied to new web-pages.

The latest version of the software can be found at `https://github.com/okohonen/semantify`.

2.1 Overview of Usage

The system is installed as an add-on to the Firefox browser. Subsequently, it can be activated for any web page. The user can train several different models by indicating which model a particular annotation belongs to. The user can also define the tag set used for annotation. To annotate, the user highlights parts of the page with the mouse and selects the desired tag from the shown menu. Assigned annotations are denoted by colors. This process is presented in Figure 1 (a). When the user is done, she stores the annotated page as shown in Figure 1 (b). The system then stores the annotated page in its page index. Meanwhile, in the background, the system automatically produces a training set that contains all the pages annotated so far and learns a tagger. The user can ask the system to tag a new page as shown in Figure 1 (c), in which case the system pre-processes and tags the current page using the latest trained model. The system then adds the annotations matching the output of the machine learning model to the viewed web page. The automatically assigned tags are visually distinct from the manually annotated ones (lighter color scheme). The automatic taggings can then be corrected manually and added to the training set. An example of an automatically annotated page is shown in figure 1 (d).

2.2 Overview of Architecture

The system architecture consists of two main components, namely, 1) an add-on to the Firefox-browser that allows annotation of web pages directly in the browser window, and 2) a machine learning component for annotating new pages. The browser add-on extends the WebAnnotator system (Tannier, 2012) by integrating it with the machine learning component and with functionality to show and edit the tags produced by the trained taggers. The machine learning component indexes the annotated web pages, pre-processes them to produce training sets of sentences, and trains models that can then be applied to new data. The Firefox add-on is implemented in Javascript and XUL while the machine learning component is implemented in Python. To bridge the language gap they communicate using XMLHTTPRequest. The machine learning component implements the well-known conditional random field (CRF) method, a discriminative modeling framework for sequence labeling (Lafferty et al., 2001).

2.3 Conditional Random Fields

Our system implements the linear-chain CRF model (Lafferty et al., 2001) which can inherently accommodate the arbitrary, overlapping features described below in Section 2.7. The CRF model is estimated based on the available training set of exemplar input-output sequence pairs. Test instances are decoded using the standard Viterbi search (Lafferty et al., 2001).

CRF parameter estimation is most commonly associated with the maximum likelihood approach employed by Lafferty et al.(2001). However, in our system, we rely on the averaged perceptron algorithm following Collins (2002a). (Note that the CRFs correspond to discriminatively trained hidden Markov models, and Collins (2002a) employs the latter terminology.) We apply the averaged perceptron learning approach for its simplicity and competitive performance (Zhang and Clark, 2011).

2.4 Web Page Index

The web page index in the machine learning component stores the annotated pages using the internal format of WebAnnotator, which is simply the original HTML-page augmented with <span>-tags to encode and visualize the annotations. Apart from annotated pages, it is also possible to index unannotated pages if one has a particular set of pages that are to be tagged by the model.

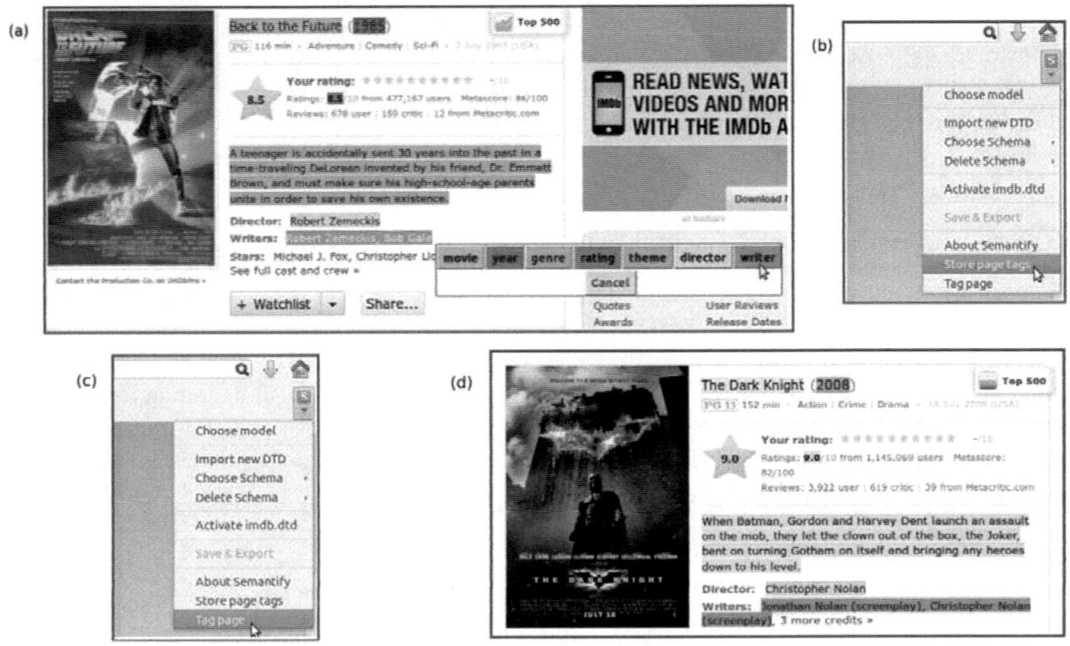

Figure 1: Sample screenshots of the tool depicting typical scenarios.

2.5 Pre-processing

We parse the HTML using the Beautiful Soup-library[1], extracting the visible text parts. Subsequently, we tokenize the text by splitting at white space and at non-alphanumeric characters. The token sequence is grouped into sentences based on punctuation and HTML-tags. We consider that if an HTML-tag defines a new block then it also starts a new sentence (e.g. <div> starts a block, while <span> does not). For each token position we apply feature functions that are described in detail in Section 2.7.

The user's annotations are stored as `span`-tags that are identified by their `class` attributes. The `span`-tags are parsed so that the label information is extracted, but they are ignored when calculating the feature functions which should be identical regardless of how the page is annotated. If the user has not assigned any label we assume a default `Outside` class.

2.6 Building the Training Sets

The CRF parameter estimation requires training and development sets which must be drawn from annotated web pages in the page index. A special characteristic of the data set is that the label distribution is typically very skewed towards many `Outside` taggings and few non-`Outside` taggings. To ensure that the development set gets sufficiently many non-`Outside` taggings, we use use a modulus-based scheme that assigns 10% of the sentences to the development set while making sure that there are enough sentences containing taggings from each class. The training set and development set are formed by concatenating the preprocessed files for each individual page.

2.7 Feature Extraction

In addition to standard first-order state transition features, the CRF model includes feature functions which operate on the token sequence of the sentence and the HTML-tree of the page. We use *orthographic features* and *HTML-features* which consider the token string and HTML-tree, respectively. For orthographic features, we use the word in lower case, and generalized character-based following Collins (2002b). We extract features based on the following properties of the current node in the HTML-tree: parent nodes and the class-attribute. For the parent nodes we calculate both individual features for im-

[1] http://www.crummy.com/software/BeautifulSoup/

mediate parents as well as very specific features that concatenates all parents up to the `body`-tag. For the class-attribute we provide it both as it is and apply the same generalization functions as in the orthographic feature set. One could also extract features from other attributes than `class`. However, we suspect that they are less informative for the tagging task compared to the `class`-attribute which is often used to indicate structural properties of the page content. We also window the features to consider the previous and next positions in the input.

2.8 Annotating New Pages Automatically

When the user asks the system to tag a new page, the current page is sent to the machine learning component for preprocessing. The latest trained CRF is applied to the preprocessed page and each token is assigned a tag. We produce <span>-tags similar to the internal format used by WebAnnotator, but with distinct attributes so the browser extension can distinguish manual and automatic annotation. To produce the modified HTML-page, we need to know the position in the HTML-string for each token in the preproessed file. In order to achieve this, we create an index of the HTML-string during preprocessing that maps every token to its original position in the string.

3 Discussion

For a software tool of the presented kind, the key performance measures are: accuracy on the task at hand, as a function of the number of annotations; and training time. As both measures are specific to task and implementation, addressing them both experimentally would require a large number of experiments which is not feasible in the allowed space. However, for illustration purposes, we will present a simple example application.

In general, for the proposed system to yield high accuracy, it needs to learn the desired categories from a few annotated examples. This requires input features that predict the desired target category well. The key benefit of the discriminative training employed is the ability to use a large set of rich and overlapping features. This allows the construction of feature sets that yield good performance on several different tasks, reducing the need for task-specific feature engineering which requires domain and programming expertise. Future work includes identifying additional features that yield good performance in a number of different tasks.

For training time, it would be ideal if the system could be trained in real time, that is, once the user has submitted an annotated web page to the system, the training would be completed when the user wants to apply the model to a new web page. This would require training times on the order of a few seconds. Training time depends mostly on the employed classifier, training algorithm, and the number of sequences and tokens in the training set. We had assumed that training time would not be an issue, even for a naive implementation, because a typical user would only gather small data sets. However, it turned out that while the annotation may be small in the number of annotated web pages, typical web pages were larger in terms of token counts than we had anticipated and more advanced training techniques may be needed to reach real-time performance.

To illustrate the properties related to tagging web pages using the current implementation, we present a simple example application of the system to the task of extracting fields from the Internet Movie Database (IMDB).[2] We annotated 50 web pages from IMDB, each describing a different movie. The following fields were annotated: *director*, *genre*, *title*, *rating*, *theme*, *writer*, and *release year*. It should be noted that this task is from the easier end of the spectrum, as the fields can be extracted with a high accuracy using the markup structure alone. For experimental purposes, we performed cross-validation with training, development, and test sets constructed from 36, 4, and 10 web pages respectively. The system yielded the following token F-scores by category, director: 73%, genre: 99%, title: 86%, rating: 100%, theme: 100%, writer: 80%, and release year: 100%. This level of performance is promising, as several fields were extracted with perfect, or near perfect accuracy. The training times for the 36-page training sets varied between 1.5 and 3.5 minutes on a standard desktop computer (Intel i5-2500 with 16Gb RAM). The variance in training time is explained by the employed stopping criterion which

[2]http://www.imdb.com

terminates training based on the performance on the development set, resulting in varying numbers of passes over the training data. In the above example task, the training set sizes were on average: 22K sequences, 133K tokens, and 30K features.

The empirical training times are longer than what could be considered real-time performance. The goal of the current implementation has been accuracy rather than execution time, and for the latter, there is certainly room for improvement. However, for real-time performance, the improvement needed is large enough that a different training procedure may be necessary. A promising approach, that suits the setting well, is using online training, such that one would only train on the latest submitted web-page. Furthermore, it is usually the case, that the non-`Outside` annotation is concentrated on a fairly small subpart of the web page. This structure could be utilized to reduce computational cost. These approaches will be evaluated in future work.

4 Conclusions

We presented on-going work on a software package that integrates discriminative machine learning with the open source WebAnnotator system of Tannier (2012). The system allows users to annotate web pages directly within their web browser and train a machine learning tagger applicable for annotating new web pages. We hope the software evolves into a useful information extraction tool for motivated hobbyists who have domain expertise on their task of interest but lack machine learning or programming knowledge.

In future work, we plan to investigate the following aspects of the system. The utility of the system should be evaluated in real-life tasks and for the target user group. The machine learning component could then be improved further based on user experience. Perhaps most importantly, the extracted features can be improved using both generic and task-specific features. Also, while the system currently applies only supervised learning, it would be a natural setting to apply semi-supervised learning.

Acknowledgements

The work was funded by an Exploratory Research Project grant from Aalto Science Institute, the Academy of Finland research project on Multimodal Language Technology, Langnet (Finnish doctoral programme in language studies), and the Academy of Finland under the Finnish Centre of Excellence Program 2012–2017 (grant no. 251170).

References

Michael Collins. 2002a. Discriminative training methods for hidden Markov models: Theory and experiments with perceptron algorithms. In *Proceedings of the ACL-02 conference on Empirical methods in natural language processing*, volume 10, pages 1–8.

Michael Collins. 2002b. Ranking algorithms for named-entity extraction: Boosting and the voted perceptron. In *Proceedings of the 40th Annual Meeting on Association for Computational Linguistics*, pages 489–496. Association for Computational Linguistics.

David Day, John Aberdeen, Lynette Hirschman, Robyn Kozierok, Patricia Robinson, and Marc Vilain. 1997. Mixed-initiative development of language processing systems. In *Proceedings of the Fifth Conference on Applied Natural Language Processing*, ANLC '97, pages 348–355, Stroudsburg, PA, USA. Association for Computational Linguistics.

John Lafferty, Andrew McCallum, and Fernando C.N. Pereira. 2001. Conditional random fields: Probabilistic models for segmenting and labeling sequence data. In *Proceedings of the Eighteenth International Conference on Machine Learning*, pages 282–289.

Xavier Tannier. 2012. WebAnnotator, an Annotation Tool for Web Pages. In *Proceedings of the 8th International Conference on Language Resources and Evaluation (LREC 2012)*, Istanbul, Turkey, May.

Yue Zhang and Stephen Clark. 2011. Syntactic processing using the generalized perceptron and beam search. *Computational Linguistics*, 37(1):105–151.

How to deal with students' writing problems? Process-oriented writing support with the digital Writing Aid Dutch

Lieve De Wachter
KU Leuven /
Dekenstraat 6
3000 Leuven
Belgium
lie-
ve.dewachter@
ilt.kuleuven.
be

Serge Verlinde
KU Leuven /
Dekenstraat 6
3000 Leuven
Belgium
serge.verlinde@
ilt.kuleuven.
be

Margot D'Hertefelt
KU Leuven /
Dekenstraat 6
3000 Leuven
Belgium
mar-
got.dhertefelt
@ilt.kuleuven.
be

Geert Peeters
[KU Leuven /
Dekenstraat 6
3000 Leuven
Belgium
geert.peete
rs@ilt.kule
uven.
be

Abstract

Students at universities and colleges in Belgium as well as abroad often experience difficulties with writing (academic) texts in their native language. Several needs analyses have pointed out that the most frequent writing problems in Dutch are text structure and cohesion, academic style and, to a lesser extent, spelling. Despite many interventions such as extra writing classes or workshops, the transfer between theory and practice often remains problematic. From students' and teachers' perspective there is a strong need for effective and process-oriented support. This presentation focuses on the digital Writing Aid Dutch, which makes students aware of typical areas of concern in their texts and provides them with individualized feedback. Writing Aid Dutch is not based on NLP techniques but makes extensive use of databases and analyzes texts using complex queries and string matching techniques. Two effect analyses and user experience studies have revealed that texts improve significantly on use of passives and vague words and on structure and cohesion. Writing Aid Dutch stimulates students' self-learning process and students perceive it as a very relevant tool. Throughout the design process of the writing aid user-friendliness has been inquired about as well.

1 Introduction

Students at Flemish universities and colleges often have difficulties with writing, irrespective of the educational field they are in (Berckmoes and Rombouts, 2009; Berckmoes et al., 2010; De Wachter and Heeren, 2011; Peters and Van Houtven, 2010). A needs analysis in which different sources and methods were triangulated and that was carried out among first year students of KU Leuven (Belgium) revealed that the most frequent writing problems of students are situated on the level of (1) text structure and cohesion, (2) style and, to a lesser extent, (3) spelling (De Wachter & Heeren, 2011). The results of this needs analysis are strikingly similar to those of previously conducted studies in Flanders. Despite several interventions, such as writing classes or extra workshops, the transfer between theory and the actual writing assignment remains difficult for many students. This is not only frustrating for students but also for teachers, who often have to correct the same mistakes again and again.

In this paper, the online Writing Aid Dutch is presented, which responds to the strong need for effective writing support for native speakers of Dutch. Its aim is to offer all students of KU Leuven Association (a total number of more than 102.000 students) process-oriented and individualized writing support and to shift the correction workload of teachers and assistants from repeating and superficial mistakes to more important aspects of the text, so that more useful feedback can be given. Writing Aid Dutch guides students through their writing process by making them aware of the most frequent writing problems in their texts situated on the level of text structure, style and spelling. It does not correct and 'judge' students' writing mistakes, but marks potential problem fields and provides students with balanced and concise feedback, tips, examples and links to informative websites. That way, students' self-learning processes, autonomy and responsibility are encouraged.

For Dutch, very few writing tools have been developed, most of them being commercialized ('WoDy'/Sensotec©), not elaborated enough (Language Tool Dutch/Naber, 2014) or not attuned to the target audience ('Klinkende Taal'/Gridline©). The development of Writing Aid Dutch fits in with an international trend of responding to students' writing problems by means of electronic writing assistance systems. More specifically, it corresponds to the attention shift from product assessment to process-oriented support (Dale and Kilgarriff, 2011; Fontana et al, 2006; Gikandi et al., 2011). Also writing assistance systems such as Amadeus (Fontana et al., 2006) or Helping Our Own (Dale and Kilgarriff, 2011) are specifically being developed to assist students throughout their writing process.

2 Writing Aid Dutch

2.1 Interface

The interface of Writing Aid Dutch is simple and user-friendly: after students have copy-pasted or keyed in their text in the input field, they can click on three coloured buttons that each represent one of three problem areas: (1) text structure and cohesion, (2) style and (3) spelling. Each button is subdivided into separate buttons that represent specific textual elements corresponding to the general level. In the first level, the student can check use of reference words, use of structure words, most frequent words of the text, recurring sentence patterns, sentence length and paragraph length. More general statistics concerning text structure and cohesion, viz. the total number of words, sentences and paragraphs of the text are given as well. Lastly, the readability index (or complexity index) of the text is calculated. In the style level, passives, nominalizations, personal language use, long-winded constructions, informal and subjective words, formal and archaic words, vague words and word combinations can be checked. The last level on which students can check their text is spelling, where typing mistakes, wrongly spelled words and abbreviations are marked by a spell-checker. When students click on one of these separate buttons, the specific element becomes marked in the text.

2.2 Underlying system and techniques

Writing Aid Dutch does not make us of NLP techniques but uses databases and mostly string and pattern matching to analyze texts in a detailed and accurate way. For some metrics, however, other techniques are used. For sentence and paragraph length in the level of text structure and cohesion, for example, a minimal and maximal boundary is set. The readability index that is calculated in the same level is partly based on the Flesch-Douma index, the readability formula based on Flesch (1948) but adapted to Dutch. Despite a number of objections, such as the idea that long sentences are not always more complex than shorter ones (Jansen and Lentz, 2008), this formula has proven to be a reliable predictor of a text's readability and complexity. However, to make the formula even more accurate we have added word frequency, seeing that words that are highly frequent are more understandable than infrequent words.

The implementation of the spell-checker has been (and still is) a labour-intensive work. It is based on a word list containing over eight hundred thousand headwords supplied with linguistic information such as word class, article, plural form, past form, participle etc. The spell-checker functions in various steps and conditions and a word will become marked only when it has not been recognized after these selection criteria are met. One of these criteria, for example, takes into account context in order to check whether the word is part of a word group that has not been recognized as a fixed expression. Concretely, the context is limited to a span of four words left and right. The spell-checker is designed in a way that it is partly self-supportive. Unrecognized words automatically appear in a separate database, so that they can be checked and if necessary added manually to the word list.

3 Comparison to other existing systems

The concern of students' poor writing skills is not confined to Belgium alone but is shared internationally and has already resulted in many digital aids and tools offering writing support for students (Dugan and Polanski, 2006; Graham and Perin, 2007; Gray et al., 2005; Taylor and Paine, 1993). Desktop applications such as SWAN (Scientific Writing AssistaNt, Kinnunen et al., 2012) or web applications such as the Language Tool Style and Grammar Checker (Naber, 2014) or Spell Check Plus (Nadashi and Sinclair, 2014) offer writing assistance to students who write at an L2 level or in their native language. Unlike these systems, Writing Aid Dutch is not NLP based. Such writing systems do not always guarantee a better text analysis as the accuracy of the suggested feedback or corrections often remains unsatisfactory. Moreover, these systems are rather time-consuming as students have to pass several ‘stages’ before receiving any feedback on their text. Students are often also provided with an overwhelming amount of information, which makes that they lose sight of the relevant feedback and of lose responsibility towards their text. Lastly, many writing aids do not focus on the writing process itself but rather on the product and do not encourage students’ writing skills development, suggesting corrections immediately (Napolitano and Stent, 2009).

4 Impact: effect analyses and user experience studies

The effectiveness of the writing aid has been investigated, on the one hand, in a one-group design study among higher education students of KU Leuven and two partner institutions (n = 34). Despite the fact that such a design has limited minimal internal validity and almost no external validity (Sytsma, 2002), we have chosen for this design because of the restricted research scope of the project. Through triangulation of different research methods, however, the validity issue has to a certain extent been resolved. The 34 students participating in the experiment were asked to rewrite their own writing product with Writing Aid Dutch. This has resulted in 68 texts: 34 texts written without the writing aid (version 1) and 34 texts written with it (version 2). Before and after students rewrote their text with Writing Aid Dutch, they filled in a questionnaire that inquired about their writing difficulties and whether they gained insight into their text after using the writing aid. After the experiment, a focus interview was held in which these issues were discussed further.

The effectiveness of Writing Aid Dutch has, on the other hand, also been investigated among 79 final-year students of secondary education. In this investigation, different methods have also been triangulated as well: texts written with and without Writing Aid Dutch have been analysed and students and teachers have been questioned in questionnaires and focus interviews respectively (Wyers, 2014). As such, the empirical data in both effect studies have been completed with judgmental data (Leakey, 2011). Our first research question was whether use of Writing Aid Dutch leads to qualitatively better texts in the short term. Second, we wanted to evaluate students’ perception of their learning process.

Because of the small total number of students participating in both experiments and the limited one-group design, only indications rather than generalisable results can be given. Higher education students improve significantly for use of passives and vague words when Writing Aid Dutch is used. Secondary school students improve especially on the level of structure and cohesion, more specifically for sentence and paragraph length and recurring patterns and words. In both investigations, students highly appreciated Writing Aid Dutch and considered it very relevant for their field of education. They also indicated that Writing Aid Dutch gave them insight into their own text and stimulated them to reflect on their own writing process.

During the development of the writing aid, user experiences from 50 students of different KU Leuven Association institutions were gathered as well in an online questionnaire. These experiences enabled us to review and adapt the writing aid throughout its development. The results were also very positive: all students would recommend the writing aid to their fellow students. From the three levels, they found text structure and cohesion the most useful, followed by style and then spelling.

5 Conclusion

Writing Aid Dutch responds to a strong need for effective, process-oriented writing support in Dutch. More specifically it offers help in the domains that students have problems with most. The writing aid aims at offering students insight into their text and at stimulating their self-learning process, autonomy and responsibility. From a computational point of view, it has been demonstrated that a system based on string and pattern matching techniques and a lot of data can be correct, fast and detailed. Moreover, Writing Aid Dutch is a durable and partly self-supportive web application that can be adapted at any time. For now, only students of KU Leuven Association have access to the writing aid. However, collaborations with publishers or the Dutch Language Union are not excluded and will make the tool possibly available for a larger audience.

References

Berckmoes, D., Rombouts, H., 2009. Rapport verkennend onderzoek naar knelpunten taalvaardigheid in het hoger onderwijs. [Report preliminary investigation of higher education students' difficulties of literacy skills]. Antwerp: Linguapolis/University of Antwerp. Available at: <http://webh01.ua.ac.be/linguapolis/mom/Intern_rapport_verkennend_onderzoek_naar_knelpunten_taalvaardigheid_in_het_hoger_onderwijs-Monitoraat_op_maat.pdf> [Accessed 27 June 2012].

Berckmoes, D., Rombouts, H., Hertogs, K., 2010. Taalstimulering academisch Nederlands voor studenten aan de Universiteit Antwerpen. Monitoraat op maat. Rapport derde jaar, september 2008 – augustus 2009 [Language stimulation academic Dutch for students at the University of Antwerp. Report third year]. Linguapolis/University of Antwerp.

Dale, R., Kilgarriff, A. 2011. Helping Our Own: The HOO 2011 Pilot Shared Task. *Proceedings of the 13th European Workshop on Natural Language Generation*, pp. 242–249.

De Wachter, L., Heeren, J., 2011. Taalvaardig aan de start. Een behoefteanalyse rond taalproblemen en remediëring van eerstejaarsstudenten aan de KULeuven [Entry-level academic language skills. A needs analysis of language problems and remedy of first year university students at the University of Leuven]. Leuven Language Institute/University of Leuven. Retrieved from https://ilt.kuleuven.be/cursus/docs/Behoefteanalyse_TaalVaST.pdf

Dugan, R.F. Jr., Polanski, V.G., 2006. Writing for computer science: a taxonomy of writing tasks and general advice. *Journal of Computing Sciences in Colleges*, 21(6), pp. 191-203.

Flesch. R., 1948. A new readability yardstick. *Journal of Applied Psychology*, 32, pp. 221-233.

Fontana, N.M., Caldeira, S.M.A., De Oliveira, L.C.F., Oliveira Jr., O.N. 2006. Computer assisted writing. Applications to English as a foreign language. *CALL*, 6(2), pp. 145-161.

Gikandi, J.W., Morrow, D., Davis, N.E. 2011. Online formative assessment in higher education: a review of the literature. *Computers & Education*, 57, pp. 2333-2351.

Graham, S., Perin, D., 2007. *Writing next: Effective strategies to improve writing of adolescents in middle and high schools – A report to Carnegie Corporation of New York.* Washington, DC: Alliance for Excellent Education. Available at: http://www.all4ed.org/files/WritingNext.pdf [Accessed 12 September 2012].

Gray, E.F., Emerson, L., MacKay, B., 2005. Meeting the demands of the workplace: science students and written skills. *Journal of science education and technology*, 14(4), pp. 425-435.

Jansen, C., Lentz, L., 2008. Hoe begrijpelijk is mijn tekst? De opkomst, neergang en terugkeer van leesbaarheidsformules [How understandable is my text? The rise, downfall and comeback of readability formulas]. Available at: http://www.kennislink.nl/publicaties/hoe-begrijpelijk-is-mijn-tekst [Accessed 1 January 2014].

Kinnunen, T., Leisma, H., Machunik, M., Kakkonen, T., Lebrun, J.L., 2012. SWAN – Scientific Writing AssistaNt. A tool for helping scholars to write reader-friendly manuscripts. *Proceedings of the 13th conference of the European chapter of the association for computational linguistics*, pp. 20-24.

Leakey, J., 2011. *Evaluating computer-assisted language learning. An integrated approach to effectiveness research in CALL.* Bern: Peter Lang.

Naber, D. 2014. Language Tool Style and Grammar Checker. Available at: www.languagetool.org [Accessed 1 January 2014].

Nadashi, T., Sinclair, S., 2001-2014. Spell Check Plus. Nadaclair Language Technologies. Available at: < http://spellcheckplus.com> [Accessed 1 January 2014].

Napolitano, D.M., Stent, A., 2009. TechWriter: an evolving system for writing assistance for advanced learners of English. *CALICO Journal,* 26(3), pp. 611-625.

Peters, E., Van Houtven, T., 2010. De weg naar materiaalontwikkeling is geplaveid met behoeftes [The way to material design is paved with needs]. In: E. Peters, T. Van Houtven, eds. 2010. *Taalbeleid in het hoger onderwijs. De hype voorbij?*. Leuven: Acco. pp. 71-85.

Sytsma, S., 2002. The basics of experimental design. Available at: http://courses.washington.edu/bio480/Basics_of_Experimental_Design.pdf [Accessed 20 November 2012].

Taylor, H.G., Paine, K.M., 1993. An inter-disciplinary approach to the development of writing skills in computer science students. *Proceedings of the SIGCSE Technical Symposium on Computer Science Education*, pp. 274-278.

Wyers, J. 2014. Schrijfvaardigheid ondersteunen. Een effectstudie naar de inzetbaarheid van een elektronische schrijfhulp in het secundair onderwijs [Supporting writing skills. An effect study of the implementation of an electronic writing aid in secondary education]. Dissertation, unpublished.

Processing Discourse in Dislog on the TextCoop Platform

Patrick Saint-Dizier
IRIT-CNRS, 118 route de Narbonne
31062 Toulouse Cedex France
stdizier@irit.fr

Abstract

This demo presents the TextCoop platform and the Dislog language, based on logic programming, which have primarily been designed for discourse processing. The linguistic architecture and the basics of discourse analysis in TextCoop are introduced. Application demos include: argument mining in opinon texts, dialog analysis, and procedural and requirement texts analysis. Via prototypes in the industry, this framework has now reached the TRL5 level.

1 Introduction

The TextCoop platform and the Dislog language (for Discourse in Logic) have been primarily designed for discourse processing. TextCoop was initially a research prototype which reached some maturity via its use in research, in teaching and in applications developed in cooperation with the industry. We estimate that the **TRL5 level** has now been reached. The kernel of TextCoop is now freely available under a **Creative Commons BY** licence. It is so far used by about 25 research groups or companies mainly in Europe. The foundations, the methodological elements, and the performances of TextCoop are published in (Saint-Dizier 2014). TextCoop is a platform that supports:
(1) **Dislog**, which is a language based on logic programming designed to describe in a declarative way discourse structures and the way they can be bound to form larger structures, via selective binding rules. An authoring tool has been developed to help rule specification,
(2) **an engine** associated with a set of processing strategies. This engine offers several mechanisms to deal with ambiguity and **concurrency** when different discourse structures can be recognized on a given text fragment,
(3)**a set of active constraints** that check for the well-formedness of discourse structures (e.g. precedence, dominance, co-occurence or not) which can be parameterized by the grammar writer,
(4) **input-output facilities**: the input-output streams are in XML or html formats. TextCoop can be quite directly connected to text databases or to editorial suites (e.g. Scenari), it can also, via some coding, process MS Word or Excel files,
(5) a set of **lexical resources** which are frequently used in discourse analysis (e.g. connectors),
(6) a set of about 180 **generic rules** that describe 12 frequently encountered discourse structures such as reformulation, illustration, cause, contrast, concession, etc.

2 Discourse Processing Challenges

In discourse analysis, Rhetorical Structure Theory, RST (Man et al. 1988), has been very influential in the emergence of computational models of discourse structure. RST can be used to represent the structure of e.g. explanations, reformulations, elaborations, illustrations, causes, etc. Following RST principles, almost 80 relatively general purpose relations have been introduced with various aims (http://www.sfu.ca/rst/).

In a number of 'real' texts, we observed that relations between nuclei and satellites are more complex than postulated by the RST:

- they may be one-to-many or even many-to-many.
- a satellite can be a nucleus for another relation,
- a nucleus and its related satellites may be non-adjacent,
- a nucleus may be linked to several satellites of different types,
- some types of satellites may be embedded into their nucleus.

This entails quite complex processing strategies and well-formedness controls that have been developed in the TextCoop platform.

Identifying discourse relations is a real challenge since linguistic cues are relatively limited. Relations are investigated together with their linguistic markers in e.g. (Delin et al. 1994), (Marcu 1997), (Miltasaki et al. 2004). They are then applied in e.g. for language generation (Rossner et al. 1992) and (Saito et al. 2006), with an extensive study on how markers can be quite systematically acquired. (Stede 2012) develops a typology of markers.

There are at the moment a few well-known and widely used language processing environments. They are essentially used for sentence processing. The reasons are essentially that the sentence level and its substructures are the crucial levels of analysis for a large number of investigations based on information extraction, opinion analysis, or machine translation. However, investigations and projects on e.g. summarization, language generation or question-answering do require an intensive discourse analysis level.

Mainly dedicated to sentence processing with some limited discourse analysis capabilities, let us note the GATE platform (http://gate.ac.uk/) which is widely used, and the Linguastream (http://www.linguastream.org) system which is based on a component architecture, making the system really flexible. RST was first used in natural language generation as a powerful means to structure arguments in a coherent way. The GETARUNS system (http://project.cgm.unive.it/getaruns.html), based on the LFG grammar approach, has some capabilities to process discourse structures and argumentation. (Marcu 1997, 2000) developed a large and robust discourse analyzer for the purpose of automatic summarization. Finally the Hilda system is a discourse parser based on a support vector machine classification (Hernault et al. 2010).

3 Main Features of Dislog and TextCoop

Dislog rule system extends the possibilities offered by regular expressions. Rules are composed of terminal, preterminal and non-terminal symbols (used to encode grammars specific to a phenomenon: e.g. temporal expressions). Symbols are associated with feature structures. The language allows optionality and iterativity markers over non-terminal and preterminal symbols. Dislog also allows 'gap' symbols, which are symbols that stand for finite sequences of words of no interest for the rule which must be skipped. Dislog offers the possibility to specify in a gap a list of elements which must not be skipped: when such an element is found before the termination of the gap, then the gap fails. Finally, rules are associated with a pattern that allows the construction of a representation based on XML tags or on dependencies.

As an illustration consider the simple rules for the 'advice' structure as expressed in technical texts:

Advice → verb(V,pref,infinitive), gap(G), punctuation(P)./

[it,is], adv(prob), gap(G1), exp(advice1), gap(G2), eos./ exp(advice2), gap(G), eos.

Resources: verb(pref): choose, prefer, ...

exp(advice1): a good idea, better, recommended, preferable

exp(advice2): a tip, an advice, best option, alternative, etc. ... adv(prob): probably, possibly, ...

For the first element of the rule (verb + gap + punctuation) the pattern that elaborates the resulting XML structure could be written as follows: <advice> V, G, P </advice>

where V, G and P are respectively the strings of words corresponding to the verb, the gap and the punctuation, as specified in the rule. In that case, the result is:

<advice> It is better to mention the capacity of high bandwidth probes </advice>, because these can be used for advanced tests.

Besides these relatively standard features, Dislog and TextCoop have the following original features which are of much interest for discourse processing and application development:

- Dislog allows the use of **knowledge (e.g. ontologies) and reasoning procedures** via a specific field in the rules. Reasoning can be used e.g. to resolve analysis ambiguities or to elaborate a semantic representation. Predefined reasoning predicates are included, additional ones can be encoded by the grammar writer.
- Dislog has two types of rules, which basically have the same format: rules to recognize discourse structures as illustrated above and **selective binding rules** whose goal is to bind discourse structures, adjacent or not, to form larger units (e.g. an illustration with what is illustrated, an argument conclusion with its support(s), a goal-title and its instructions and warnings in a procedure, or an evaluative expression and its related arguments in opinion analysis). Bounding nodes are defined that limit the distance between discourse units which can be bound.
- TextCoop offers **concurrency and synchronization mechanisms**, which can be parameterized, in order to manage conflicts or priorities among discourse relations,
- TextCoop offers a **variety of processing strategies** which may be selected by the rule author. For example, right-to-left processing is recommended when the main linguistic cues are to the right in the rule. TextCoop has a by-default left-to-right strategy.
- TextCoop also offers **active constraints that express discourse structure well-formedness constraints** (dominance, non-dominance, precedence, strict adjacence, etc.) which are checked at each step of the parsing process. These can be parameterized depending on the discourse structures.

4 The Demos

4.1 The Basics of TextCoop

We first propose to present the overall linguistic architecture of the system and the structure of discourse analysis rules. Typical rule examples will be considered so that the audience gets a clear idea of their form and how to create or update rules and corresponding lexical data. Elements of our rule authoring system will be outlined. To illustrate rules, text samples will be processed and the results explained.

The audience can also propose text fragments that the system will process according to a predefined set of discourse analysis rules, or a given set of new or updated rules produced during the demo (this can be done quite fast). Finally relevant cases where reasoning is useful to resolve ambiguities will be presented. We will focus in particular on cases where ontologies help to disambiguate the assignment of discourse structures, e.g. between elaboration and illustration.

4.2 Argument mining in opinion texts

In (Garcia et al. 2012), we show how arguments can be extracted from opinion texts, in conjunction with evaluative expressions, so that it is possible to know **why** consumers are happy or unhappy with a certain product. In this work we shown that a number of arguments are composed of a more or less explicit evaluative expression (the conclusion in argumentation theory) followed by a support, expressed by means of discourse structures. For example, in *well located hotel, close to the museums and restaurants* the positive evaluation related to the location is further supported by an illustration (or an elaboration), which indicates why it is well located. Similarly, restrictions (attacks) can be expressed by contrast or concessive relations.

We show (1) how discourse structures relevant to the expression of argument supports or attacks are expressed in Dislog and how they are recognized in texts, (2) how they are bound to their related evaluative expressions, which may not be adjacent, by means of selective binding rules.

The result is (1) opinion texts with discourse structure annotations in XML, (2) a set of marks assigned to each evaluated attribute indicating the consumer satisfaction level, and (3) a list of supports or attacks for each of these attributes. This project is now an industrial prototype. A synthesis of these supports and attacks remains an open problem.

4.3 Procedural and requirement text analysis and improvement

This is a large project (Lelie) whose aim is to help technical writers to improve the way they produce procedural texts, specifications or requirements (Barcellini et al. 2012), (Kang et al. 2013). We address here the detection of inappropriate discourse structures. The discourse structure of technical documents is analyzed (including titles and instructions). Then error diagnosis are produced (1) according to the fact that some text fragments do not follow authoring guidelines as specified by the company or (2) that sentences have very complex discourse structures which may entail ambiguities or intensive understanding efforts from operators.

In this demo, we outline (1) the recognition of discourse structures typical of technical texts (advice, warnings, instructions, titles, prerequisites, evaluations, etc. mainly explanation structures) and how they are temporally or causally connected. Then, we show (2) how error diagnosis rules can be written in Dislog and (3) how technical texts are then tagged with appropriate error diagnosis and correction recommendations. Parts of this project are an industrial prototype 'Lelie for requirements'.

4.4 Analysis of dialogue structures

The project (Farmer) on which this demo is based involves a cooperation between Dundee, Potsdam, Toulouse and Warsaw universities. Its goal is to extract arguments for or against a certain controversial issue in a dialogue. RST as well as IAT (Budzynska et al 2013) are considered as a theoretical framework.

In this demo, we show how Dislog can be used to identify (1) elementary dialogue units, (2) the illocutionary acts and forces associated with each unit and (3) the nature of the transitions between units, based on discourse and dialogue patterns. These three points are realized using Dislog rules in different manners. They will be shown and demonstrated on the BBC Moral Maze corpus.

References

Barcellini, F., Grosse, C., Albert, C., Saint-Dizier, P., Risk Analysis and Prevention: LELIE, a Tool dedicated to Procedure and Requirement Authoring, LREC, Istanbul, May 2012.

Budzynska, K., Janier, M., Reed, C., Saint-Dizier, P., Theoretical Foundations for Illocutionary Structure Parsing, CMNA, Springer, 2013.

Delin, J., Hartley, A., Paris, C., Scott, D., Vander Linden, K., 1994. Expressing Procedural Relationships in Multilingual Instructions, Proceedings of the Seventh International Workshop on Natural Language Generation, pp. 61-70,Maine, USA.

Garcia Villalba, M., Saint-Dizier, P. 2012. *A framework for extracting arguments in opinion texts*, international journal of cognitive intelligence and natural intelligence (IJCINI), IGI Global, 6(4).

Hernault, H., Prendinger, H., du Verle, D., Ishizuka, M. 2010. *HILDA: A Discourse Parser Using Support Vector Machine Classification*, Discourse and Dialogue Vol 1(3).

Kang, J., Saint-Dizier, P. 2013. Requirement Mining in Safety Documents, CMNA, Roma.

Mann, W., Thompson, S. 1988. *Rhetorical Structure Theory: Towards a Functional Theory of Text Organisation*, TEXT 8(3) pages 243-281.

Marcu, D. 1997. The Rhetorical Parsing of Natural Language Texts, ACL97.

Marcu, D, 2000. *The Theory and Practice of Discourse Parsing and Summarization*, MIT Press.

Miltasaki, E., Prasad, R., Joshi, A., Webber, B. 2004. Annotating Discourse Connectives and Their Arguments, proceedings of new frontiers in NLP.

Rosner, D., Stede, M. 1992. Customizing RST for the Automatic Production of Technical Manuals, in R. Dale, E. Hovy, D. Rosner and O. Stock eds., *Aspects of Automated Natural Language Generation*, LNAI, Springler-Verlag.

Saint-Dizier, P. 2014. *Challenges of discourse processing: the case of technical documents*, Cambridge Scholars.

Saito, M., Yamamoto, K., Sekine, S. 2006. Using Phrasal Patterns to Identify Discourse Relations, ACL06.

Stede, M. 2012. *Discourse Processing*, Morgan and Claypool Publishers.

UIMA Ruta Workbench: Rule-based Text Annotation

Peter Kluegl[12] **Martin Toepfer**[2] **Philip-Daniel Beck**[2] **Georg Fette**[2] **Frank Puppe**[2]

[1]Comprehensive Heart Failure Center
University of Würzburg, Straubmühlweg 2a
Würzburg, Germany
pkluegl@uni-wuerzburg.de

[2]Department of Computer Science VI
University of Würzburg, Am Hubland
Würzburg, Germany
first.last@uni-wuerzburg.de

Abstract

UIMA Ruta is a rule-based system designed for information extraction tasks, but it is also applicable for many natural language processing use cases. This demonstration gives an overview of the UIMA Ruta Workbench, which provides a development environment and tooling for the rule language. It was developed to ease every step in engineering rule-based applications. In addition to the full-featured rule editor, the user is supported by explanation of the rule execution, introspection in results, automatic validation and rule induction. Furthermore, the demonstration covers the usage and combination of arbitrary components for natural language processing.

1 Introduction

Components for natural language processing and information extraction nowadays often rely on statistical methods and their models are trained using machine learning techniques. However, components based on manually written rules still play an important role in real world applications and especially in industry (Chiticariu et al., 2013). The reasons for this are manifold: The necessity for traceable results, the absence or aggravated creation of labeled data, or unclear specifications favor rule-based approaches. When the specification changes, for example, the complete training data potentially needs to be annotated again. In rule-based components, adaptions in a small selection of rules typically suffice. Rule-based approaches are also used in combination with or when developing statistical components. While models are often trained to solve one specific task in an application, the remaining parts need to be implemented as well. Furthermore, rules can be applied for high-level feature extraction and for semi-automatic creation of labeled data sets. It is often faster to define one rule for a specific pattern than to annotate repeating mentions of a specific type.

Unstructured Information Management Architecture (UIMA) (Ferrucci and Lally, 2004) is a framework for analyzing unstructured data and is extensively applied for building natural language processing applications. Two popular systems built upon UIMA are the DeepQA system Watson (Ferrucci et al., 2010) and the clinical Text Analysis and Knowledge Extraction System (cTAKES) (Savova et al., 2010). UIMA allows the definition of scalable pipelines of interoperable components called analysis engines, which incrementally add and modify meta information of documents mostly in form of annotations. The semantics and features of annotations are given by their types, which are specified in type systems.

This demonstration gives an overview on the UIMA Ruta Workbench (Kluegl et al., 2014), a development environment for the UIMA Ruta language. The rule language provides a compact representation of patterns while still supporting high expressivity necessary for solving arbitrary tasks. The UIMA Ruta Workbench includes additional tools that accelerate the efficient creation of components and complete pipelines. The user is supported in all aspects of the development process like specification of rules and type systems, debugging, introspection of the results, and quality assessment. UIMA Ruta is developed by an active community[1] and is released like UIMA under the industry-friendly Apache License 2.0.

[1]http://uima.apache.org/ruta.html

The rest of the paper is structured as follows: Section 2 compares UIMA Ruta to a selection of related systems. The rule language and the tooling support are introduced in Section 3. Section 4 provides an overview of the content of the demonstration and Section 5 concludes with a summary.

2 Related Systems

Rule-based systems for information extraction and natural language processing in general have a long history and thus we can only give a short comparison to a selection of related systems especially based on UIMA. The probably most noted rule-based system is JAPE (Cunningham et al., 2000). It is open source and integrated into the GATE (Cunningham et al., 2011) framework. JAPE propagates a clear separation of condition and action parts, and an aggregated execution of rules of one phase in a finite state transducer whereas UIMA Ruta allows freer positioning of actions for a more compact representation and applies the rules sequentially. Nevertheless, UIMA Ruta is able to compete well concerning performance and provides a high expressiveness. AFST (Boguraev and Neff, 2010) is also based on finite state transduction over annotations and additionally allows vertical patterns, which are also supported in UIMA Ruta. SystemT (Chiticariu et al., 2010) defines rules in declarative statements similar to SQL and applies them using an optimized operator graph. Our system takes first steps in this direction with the concept of variable matching directions, but still provides a compact language for more flexible operations. Other rule-based systems for UIMA are the IBM LanguageWare Resource Workbench[2], Zanzibar[3] and UIMA Regexp[4].

Most of the freely available rule-based systems provide only minimal development support. Good development environments and tooling are usually found in at least partially commercial systems. The development environment of SystemT (Chiticariu et al., 2011), for example, provides an editor with syntax highlighting and hyperlink navigation, an annotation provenance viewer, a contextual clue discoverer, regular expression learner, and a rule refiner. One intention of UIMA Ruta consists in providing strong tooling support that facilitates every step in the development process. The UIMA Ruta Workbench includes most features of related systems, but still introduces a few new and useful tools.

3 UIMA Ruta

UIMA Ruta (Rule-based Text Annotation) consists of a rule-based language interpreted by a generic analysis engine and of the UIMA Ruta Workbench, a development environment with additional tooling. Rules are sequentially applied and are composed of regular expressions of rule elements. The rule elements typically define the annotation type to be matched and an optional list of conditions and actions. The language provides a variety of diverse elements to elegantly solve arbitrary tasks. The rule matching supports overlapping alternatives and a coverage-based visibility. The following example illustrates the rule syntax:

```
(ANY{INLIST(MonthsList) -> Month} PERIOD? NUM{REGEXP(".{2,4}") -> Year}){-> Date};
```

This rule matches on any token present in an external dictionary *MonthsList* followed by an optional period and a number that contains two to four characters. If this pattern was recognized, then the actions create new annotations of the types *Month*, *Year* and *Date* for the corresponding matched segments. Following this, the rule identifies and annotates dates in the form of 'Dec. 2004", "July 85" or "11.2008". Rule scripts can additionally include and apply external components, or specify additional types. A detailed description of the UIMA Ruta language can be found in the documentation[5].

The UIMA Ruta Workbench is an Eclipse-based[6] development environment for the rule language. A screenshot of the Workbench's main perspective is depicted in Figure 1. Rule scripts are organized in UIMA Ruta projects and take advantage of the well-known features of Eclipse like version control

[2]http://www.alphaworks.ibm.com/tech/lrw

[3]https://code.google.com/p/zanzibar/

[4]https://sites.google.com/site/uimaregex/

[5]http://uima.apache.org/d/ruta-current/tools.ruta.book.html

[6]http://www.eclipse.org/

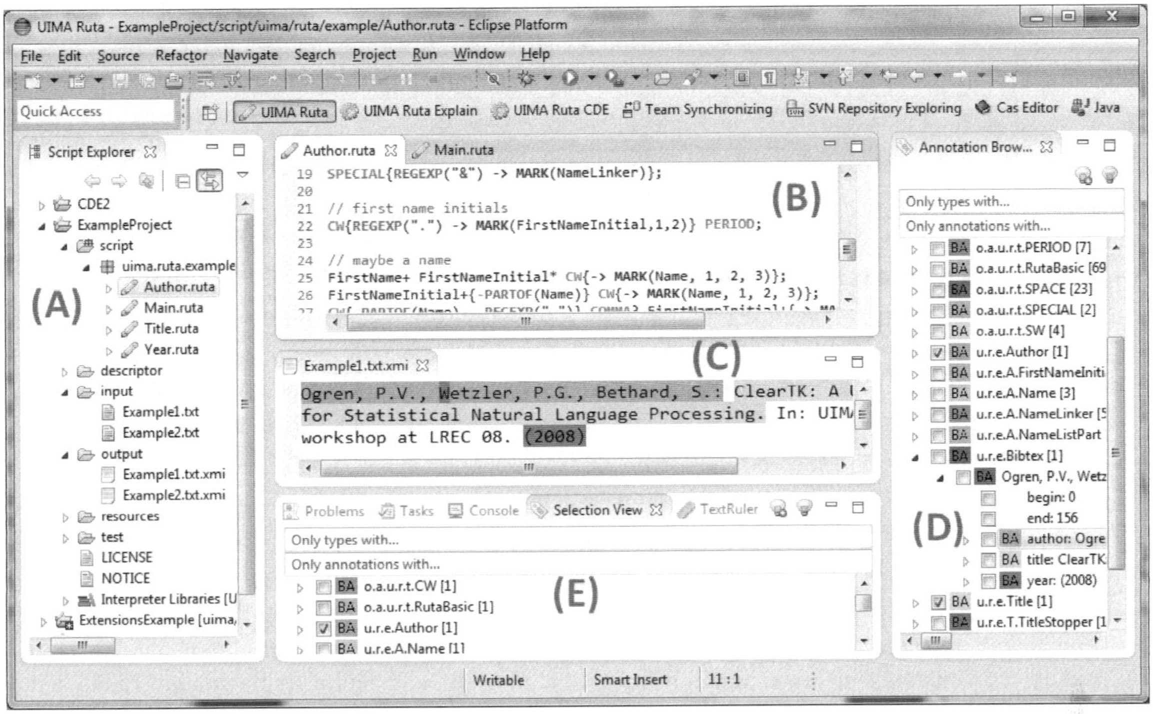

Figure 1: A selection of views in the UIMA Ruta Workbench: (A) Script Explorer with UIMA Ruta projects. Script files containing rules are indicated by the pencil icon. (B) Full-featured editor for specifying rules. (C) CAS Editor provided by UIMA for visualizing the results and manual creation of annotations. (D) Overview of annotations sorted by type. (E) Annotations overlapping the selected position in the active CAS Editor.

or search. The full featured editor for writing rules provides most of the characteristics known by editors for programming languages like instant syntax checking, syntactic and semantic highlighting, or context-sensitive auto-completion. An informative explanation of each step of the rule execution extended with profiling information helps to identify unintended behavior of the rules. The user is able to automatically evaluate the quality of rules on labeled documents and also on unlabeled documents using formalized background knowledge. Furthermore, the tools support pattern-based queries in collections of documents, semi-automatic creation of gold standards and different algorithms for supervised rule induction.

The rule language and the tooling are both extensible. The rule language can be enhanced with new actions, conditions, functions and even constructs that adapt aspects of the rule execution. Further functionality can be integrated by implementing supplementary analysis engines. The UIMA Ruta Workbench straightforwardly supports extensions due to its integration in Eclipse, e.g., new views can be added for improving specific development processes. Additional evaluation measures and rule learning algorithms are directly added by extension points. The Workbench also supports workspaces where the user develops interdependent Java and UIMA Ruta analysis engines simultaneously, and it seamlessly integrates components from Maven repositories.

The UIMA Ruta Workbench has been successfully utilized to develop diverse natural language applications. These include template-based information extraction in curricula vitae, segmentation of scientific references, or extraction of characters in novels, but also segmentation, chunking and relation extraction in clinical notes. Furthermore, the system is applied for feature extraction, creation of gold standards, and different pre- and post-processing tasks in combination with statistical models. The effectiveness of the Workbench can hardly be measured, but it is highlighted by the fact that several applications have been engineered in only a few hours of work.

4 Contents of Demonstration

The demonstration of the system concentrates on the general usage of the UIMA Ruta Workbench and how to develop rule-based analysis engines with it. We address the following use cases and aspects:

- **General rule engineering:** Simple examples are given for common tasks in UIMA Ruta, e.g., how to create new projects and script files, and how an initial set of rules is applied on a collection of documents. Several examples highlight the expressivity and effectiveness of the rule language.
- **Debugging erroneous rules:** Manual specification of rules is prone to errors. We will demonstrate the explanation component of the Workbench that facilitates the traceability of the rule matching and allows the identification of unintended behavior.
- **Definition of type systems and pipelines**: The UIMA Ruta language can be applied for textual definition of type systems and rule-based pipelines of arbitrary analysis engines, which enables rapid prototyping without switching tools.
- **Introspection of results:** The usage of the rule language as query statements allows the user to investigate different aspects of documents that have been annotated by arbitrary analysis engines, e.g., also based on statistical methods.
- **Quality assessment:** The automatic assessment of the analysis engines' quality is a central aspect in their development process. We demonstrate test-driven development using gold standard documents, and constraint-driven evaluation for unlabeled documents based on formalized background knowledge.
- **Document preprocessing:** The UIMA Ruta language can be applied for many tasks in the Workbench. These include different preprocessing steps like converting HTML files, anonymization, cutting paragraphs or rule-based document sorting.
- **Rule learning:** The provided rule induction algorithms based on boundary matching, extraction patterns and transformations are illustrated for simple examples.
- **Extension of the language:** Specific projects take advantage of specialized language elements. Extensions of the language and their seamless integration in the Workbench are shown with several examples.
- **Combinations with Java projects:** Some functionality can hardly be specified with rules, even with an extended language specification. Thus, examples provide insights how to make use of additional functionality implemented in Java.
- **Integration of external analysis engines:** Repositories like DKPro (Gurevych et al., 2007) or ClearTK (Ogren et al., 2008) provide a rich selection of well-known components for natural language processing. We demonstrate how these analysis engines and type systems can easily be integrated and how the user is able to specify rules based on the their results, e.g., for improving a part-of-speech tagger or for exploiting their annotations for relation extraction.
- **Semi-automatic annotation:** A semi-automatic process supported by rules can speed up the creation of gold documents. An exemplary use case will illustrate how the user can efficiently accept or reject the annotations created by rules.

A detailed description of these use cases will be available as part of the documentation of the project.

5 Conclusions

This demonstration presents the UIMA Ruta Workbench, a useful general-purpose tool for the UIMA community. The system helps to fill the gap of rule-based support in the UIMA ecosystem and is applicable for many different tasks and use cases. The user is optimally supported during the engineering process and is able to create complex and well-maintained applications as well as rapid prototypes. The UIMA Ruta Workbench is up-to-date unique concerning the combination of the provided features and tools, availability as open source, and integration in UIMA.

An interesting option for future work consists in making the functionality of UIMA Ruta and its tooling also available in web-based systems like the Argo UIMA platform (Rak et al., 2012).

Acknowledgements

This work was supported by the Competence Network Heart Failure, funded by the German Federal Ministry of Education and Research (BMBF01 EO1004), and is used for information extraction from medical reports and discharge letters.

References

Branimir Boguraev and Mary Neff. 2010. A Framework for Traversing dense Annotation Lattices. *Language Resources and Evaluation*, 44(3):183–203.

Laura Chiticariu, Rajasekar Krishnamurthy, Yunyao Li, Sriram Raghavan, Frederick R. Reiss, and Shivakumar Vaithyanathan. 2010. SystemT: An Algebraic Approach to Declarative Information Extraction. In *Proceedings of the 48th Annual Meeting of the Association for Computational Linguistics*, ACL '10, pages 128–137, Stroudsburg, PA, USA. Association for Computational Linguistics.

Laura Chiticariu, Vivian Chu, Sajib Dasgupta, Thilo W. Goetz, Howard Ho, Rajasekar Krishnamurthy, Alexander Lang, Yunyao Li, Bin Liu, Sriram Raghavan, Frederick R. Reiss, Shivakumar Vaithyanathan, and Huaiyu Zhu. 2011. The SystemT IDE: An Integrated Development Environment for Information Extraction Rules. In *Proceedings of the 2011 ACM SIGMOD International Conference on Management of Data*, SIGMOD '11, pages 1291–1294, New York, NY, USA. ACM.

Laura Chiticariu, Yunyao Li, and Frederick R. Reiss. 2013. Rule-based Information Extraction is Dead! Long Live Rule-based Information Extraction Systems! In *Proceedings of the 2013 Conference on Empirical Methods in Natural Language Processing*, pages 827–832, Seattle, Washington, USA, October. Association for Computational Linguistics.

Hamish Cunningham, Diana Maynard, and Valentin Tablan. 2000. JAPE: a Java Annotation Patterns Engine (Second Edition). Research Memorandum CS–00–10, Department of Computer Science, University of Sheffield, November.

Hamish Cunningham, Diana Maynard, Kalina Bontcheva, Valentin Tablan, Niraj Aswani, Ian Roberts, Genevieve Gorrell, Adam Funk, Angus Roberts, Danica Damljanovic, Thomas Heitz, Mark A. Greenwood, Horacio Saggion, Johann Petrak, Yaoyong Li, and Wim Peters. 2011. *Text Processing with GATE (Version 6).*

David Ferrucci and Adam Lally. 2004. UIMA: An Architectural Approach to Unstructured Information Processing in the Corporate Research Environment. *Natural Language Engineering*, 10(3/4):327–348.

David A. Ferrucci, Eric W. Brown, Jennifer Chu-Carroll, James Fan, David Gondek, Aditya Kalyanpur, Adam Lally, J. William Murdock, Eric Nyberg, John M. Prager, Nico Schlaefer, and Christopher A. Welty. 2010. Building Watson: An Overview of the DeepQA Project. *AI Magazine*, 31(3):59–79.

Iryna Gurevych, Max Mühlhäuser, Christof Müller, Jürgen Steimle, Markus Weimer, and Torsten Zesch. 2007. Darmstadt Knowledge Processing Repository Based on UIMA. In *Proceedings of the UIMA Workshop at GLDV*, Tübingen, Germany, April.

Peter Kluegl, Martin Toepfer, Philip-Daniel Beck, Georg Fette, and Frank Puppe. 2014. UIMA Ruta: Rapid Development of Rule-based Information Extraction Applications. *Natural Language Engineering*. submitted.

Philip V. Ogren, Philipp G. Wetzler, and Steven Bethard. 2008. ClearTK: A UIMA Toolkit for statistical Natural Language Processing. In *UIMA for NLP Workshop at LREC*.

Rafal Rak, Andrew Rowley, William Black, and Sophia Ananiadou. 2012. Argo: an Integrative, Interactive, Text Mining-based Workbench Supporting Curation. *Database*, 2012:bas010.

Guergana K. Savova, James J. Masanz, Philip V. Ogren, Jiaping Zheng, Sunghwan Sohn, Karin C. Kipper-Schuler, and Christopher G. Chute. 2010. Mayo clinical Text Analysis and Knowledge Extraction System (cTAKES): architecture, component evaluation and applications. *Journal of the American Medical Informatics Association*, 17(5):507–513, September.

Discourse Relations in the Prague Dependency Treebank 3.0

Jiří Mírovský, Pavlína Jínová, Lucie Poláková
Charles University in Prague, Faculty of Mathematics and Physics
Institute of Formal and Applied Linguistics
mirovsky|jinova|polakova@ufal.mff.cuni.cz

Abstract

The aim of the demo is threefold. First, it introduces the current version of the annotation tool for discourse relations in the Prague Dependency Treebank 3.0. Second, it presents the discourse relations in the treebank themselves, including new additions in comparison with the previous release. And third, it shows how to search in the treebank, with focus on the discourse relations.

1 Introduction

The Prague Dependency Treebank 3.0 (Bejček et al., 2013) is the newest version of the Prague Dependency Treebank series, succeeding versions 1.0 (PDT 1.0; Hajič et al., 2001), 2.0 (PDT 2.0; Hajič et al., 2006), 2.5 (PDT 2.5; Bejček et al., 2012) and Prague Discourse Treebank 1.0 (PDiT 1.0; Poláková et al., 2012, 2013). It is a corpus of Czech, consisting of almost 50 thousand sentences annotated mostly manually on three layers of language description: morphological, analytical (surface syntactic structure), and tectogrammatical (deep syntactic structure). On top of the tectogrammatical layer, explicitly marked discourse relations, both inter- and intra-sentential ones, have been annotated. The discourse annotation first appeared in PDiT 1.0, and it was corrected and updated for the newest release of the Prague Dependency Treebank, PDT 3.0.

In Section 2, we present the annotation tool for discourse relations in PDT 3.0. In Section 3, we briefly introduce principles of discourse annotation in PDT 3.0. Section 4 is dedicated to searching in PDT 3.0, focusing on searching for discourse relations.

2 The Annotation Tool

The primary format of PDT since version 2.0 is called PML (http://ufal.mff.cuni.cz/jazz/PML/). It is an abstract XML based format designed for annotation of linguistic corpora, especially treebanks. Data in the PML format can be browsed and edited in TrEd, a fully customizable tree editor (Pajas and Štěpánek, 2008). TrEd is written in Perl and can be easily customized to a desired purpose by extensions that are included into the system as modules. The TrEd extension for discourse annotation in PDT was first described in Mírovský et al. (2010). Here we summarize the main features of the tool, including additions that have been made since the previous version. Also the data format of discourse relations in PDT 3.0 has undergone several changes.

The data format and the tool for annotation of discourse in PDT allow for:

- **Creation of a link** between arguments of a relation; the link is depicted with a thick orange arrow between nodes representing the arguments (see Figure 2 below).
- **Exact specification of the extent** of the arguments of the relation; it takes advantage of the tree structure of the tectogrammatical layer and specifies the range of an argument as a set of (sub)trees; in unclear cases the argument can be defined as an under-specified sequence of trees starting (or newly also ending) at a given point in the data. In rare cases, an arbitrary set of individual nodes can be specified as an argument as well.

• **Assigning a connective** to the relation; the connective can be defined as a list of tectogrammatical nodes and, if needed, also by nodes from the lower (analytical) layer. Newly also extended connectives can be assigned to the relation, which is an addition required by the on-going annotation of so called AltLexes (alternative lexicalizations of connectives).
• **Setting additional information** to the relation (a type, a source, a comment etc.); newly also a flag for the AltLex can be indicated and also a flag for negation of a discourse type.
• **Assigning other discourse related information to nodes** at the tectogrammatical layer; article headings, table or figure captions and metatext can be indicated at the root node of the respective phrase.

3 Discourse Relations in PDT 3.0

Annotation of discourse relations in PDT 3.0 is inspired by the PDTB lexical approach of connective identification (Prasad et al., 2008) but it also takes advantage of the Prague tradition of dependency linguistics (see e.g. Sgall et al., 1986). While in PDTB approach, a list of possible discourse connectives was created and according to it, contexts for annotators were prepared, we only defined a connective theoretically and left annotators to go through the whole text and identify all such constructions with a connective function. In the first and second release of discourse annotation (PDiT 1.0 and PDT 3.0), only discourse relations indicated by overly present (explicit) discourse connectives, i.e. expressions like *but, however, as a result, even though* etc. have been annotated. Every discourse connective is thought of as a discourse-level predicate that takes two discourse units as its arguments. Only discourse relations connecting clausal arguments (with a predicate verb) have been annotated. The Prague discourse annotation also includes marking of list structures (as a separate type of discourse structure) and marking of smaller text phenomena like article headings, figure captions, metatext etc.

The annotation proceeded first manually for cases where the tectogrammatical layer did not allow for identifying a discourse relation automatically. Afterwards, using the information (mostly) from the tectogrammatical layer, we were able to identify and mark almost 10 thousand out of more than 12 thousand intra-sentential relations automatically – arguments (verbal phrases), types of relations and the connectives were identified using tree structures of the sentences, tectogrammatical functors (types of dependency or coordination), and morphological tags (details in Jínová et al., 2012).

The Prague discourse label set was inspired by the Penn sense tag hierarchy (Prasad et al., 2008) and by the tectogrammatical functors (Mikulová et al., 2005). The four main semantic classes, Temporal, Contingency, Contrast (Comparison) and Expansion are identical to those in PDTB but the hierarchy itself is only two-level (see Poláková et al., 2013). The third level is captured by the direction of the discourse arrow. Within the four classes, the types of relations partly differ from the Penn senses and go closer to Prague tectogrammatical functors and/or are a matter of language-specific distinctions. The annotators, unlike in the Penn approach, were not allowed to only assign the major class, they always had to decide for a specific relation within one of the classes.

PDT 3.0 brings an update of the discourse annotation released in PDiT 1.0. It has been enriched with several newly annotated (or not yet released) discourse-related phenomena, namely genre specification of the corpus texts (see Poláková et al., 2014), annotation of some type of rhematizers (or foculizing particles) as discourse connectives, and annotation of second relations (discourse relations with more than one semantic type). Also a new attribute discourse_special for several special roles of phrases has been introduced.

We newly annotated foculizing particles in structures with conjunction, to see how these particles cooperate with other types of connectives in discourse. Second relations were annotated in the data already before the PDiT 1.0 release but only in the annotator's comment, which did not become a part of the official release. In PDT 3.0, each second relation has been captured as an additional full-fledged relation with its own type and connective. It means that the arguments in question are connected with two arrows representing two discourse relations.

The newly introduced attribute discourse_special captures three special roles of the phrase represented by a node and its subtree; the possible values are: "heading" (article headings; replaces attribute is_heading from PDiT 1.0), "metatext" (text not belonging to the original newspaper text, produced during the creation of the corpus), and "caption" (for captions of pictures, graphs etc.).[1]

[1] Metatext and caption were also annotated already before the PDiT 1.0 release in the annotator's comment (but not published there).

4 Searching in PDT 3.0

For searching in PDT, a client-server based system called PML-TQ has been developed (PML-Tree Query; Pajas and Štěpánek, 2009). It belongs to the most powerful systems for searching in treebanks. The server part is implemented either as a relational database or as a system in a command-line version of TrEd (btred). The client part uses either the tree editor TrEd along with a PML-TQ extension or a web browser. The web browser client has however some limitations, so (in the demo) we focus on TrEd with the PML-TQ extension.

Queries in PML-TQ can be created both in a textual form and (in the TrEd client) in a graphical environment. The query language allows to define properties of tree nodes and relations among them, inside or between sentences and also across the layers of annotation. Negation on the tree structure and Boolean expressions over the relations can be used. Results of the corpus search can be viewed along with the context or processed with output filters to produce statistical tables. A detailed documentation can be found at http://ufal.mff.cuni.cz/pmltq/doc/pmltq_doc.html, in the demo we will offer an introduction to the principal parts of the language along with a set of illustrative examples, from the basic queries to more complex ones, respecting requests from the audience.

The following example shows how to search for a discourse relation. The query defines two tectogrammatical nodes (t-nodes) connected with a special "member" node that represents a discourse relation between the two nodes. The required type of the discourse relation can be specified at the member node, in this example it is set to "reason". The query also specifies that the start and target nodes of the relation are not from the same tree, i.e. it looks for an inter-sentential discourse relation of the semantic type "reason".

Textual form of the query:

```
t-node
[ !same-tree-as $t,
     member discourse
     [ discourse_type = "reason",
 target_node.rf t-node $t := [  ] ] ];
```

Graphical form of the query:

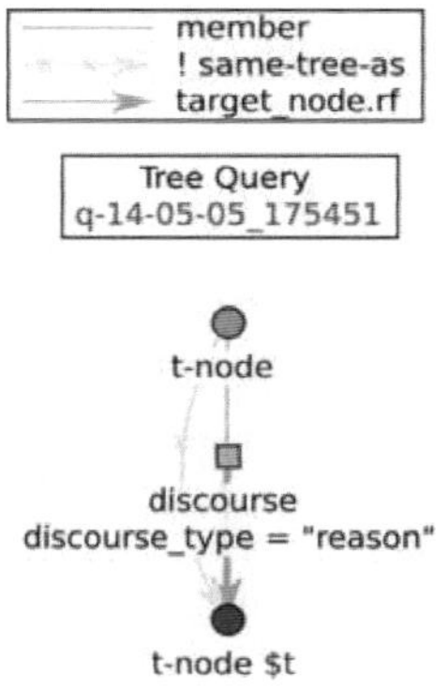

Figure 1: Graphical form of the query

The following two sentences represent one of the results of the query:

```
Pronikání do cizích počítačových systémů je podle našich zákonů beztrestné.
Policie tak jen bezmocně přihlíží, když v bankách řádí SLÍDILOVÉ.

[Infiltration of other computer systems is according to our laws not a criminal act.
Thus the police only helplessly watches, as SNOOPERS rage in banks.]
```

Figure 2 captures the tectogrammatical annotation of these two sentences, along with the discourse relation represented by the thick orange arrow connecting roots of the two respective propositions.
Results of queries in PML-TQ can be further processed using output filters. Thanks to an output filter, a result of a query does not consist of individual matching positions in the trees but of a tabular summary of all the matching positions, specified by the output filter.

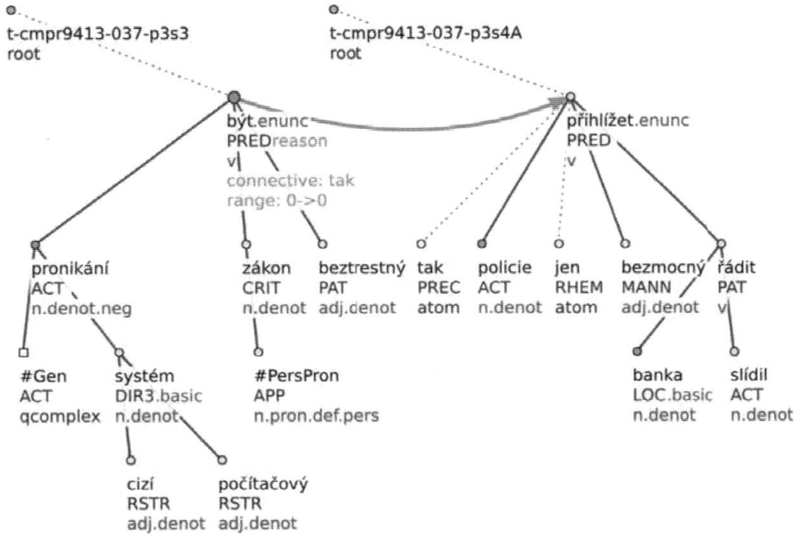

Figure 2: The tectogrammatical representation of the two result sentences of the query

If we modify the previous query by deleting the definition of the discourse type (`discourse_type = "reason"`), naming the member node (`$d :=`) and adding an output filter (the last line with prefix >>):

```
t-node
[ !same-tree-as $t,
     member discourse $d :=
         [ target_node.rf t-node $t := [  ] ] ];
>> for $d.discourse_type give $1, count() sort by $2 desc
```

...the query will search for all inter-sentential discourse relations in the data and – thanks to the output filter – produce the following distribution table of the discourse types, sorted in the descending order by the number of occurrences (only a few selected lines are printed here to save space):

opp	1,800
conj	1,389
reason	1,031
...	
grad	204
restr	172
explicat	130
...	

Table 1: (Selected) results of the output filter

5 Conclusion

A good annotation tool, well designed annotation guidelines, and a powerful search tool are necessary parts of a well managed project of any linguistic annotation. In the demo, we present all these parts for the current version of annotation of discourse relations in the Prague Dependency Treebank 3.0.

The PML as a data format, the annotation tool TrEd and the search system PML-TQ can be and have been extensively used for many other annotation tasks in PDT and also for many other treebanks, see for example a project of harmonizing various treebanks in HamleDT (Zeman et al., 2012).

Acknowledgment

The authors gratefully acknowledge support from the Grant Agency of the Czech Republic (projects P406/12/0658 and P406/2010/0875). This work has been using language resources developed, stored and distributed by the LINDAT/CLARIN project of the Ministry of Education, Youth and Sports of the Czech Republic (project LM2010013).

References

Bejček, Eduard, Hajičová, Eva, Hajič, Jan et al. (2013). *Prague Dependency Treebank 3.0.* Data/software, Charles University in Prague, MFF, ÚFAL. Available at: http://ufal.mff.cuni.cz/pdt3.0/.

Bejček, Eduard, Panevová, Jarmila, Popelka, Jan et al. (2012). *Prague Dependency Treebank 2.5.* Data/software, Charles University in Prague, MFF, ÚFAL. Available at: http://ufal.mff.cuni.cz/pdt2.5/.

Hajič, Jan, Vidová Hladká, Barbora, Panevová, Jarmila et al. (2001). *Prague Dependency Treebank 1.0* (Final Production Label). In: CDROM, CAT: LDC2001T10., ISBN 1-58563-212-0.

Hajič, Jan, Panevová, Jarmila, Hajičová, Eva et al. (2006). *Prague Dependency Treebank 2.0.* Software prototype, Linguistic Data Consortium, Philadelphia, PA, USA, ISBN 1-58563-370-4.

Jínová, Pavlína, Mírovský, Jiří, & Poláková, Lucie (2012). Semi-Automatic Annotation of Intra-Sentential Discourse Relations in PDT. In: *Proceedings of the Workshop on Advances in Discourse Analysis and its Computational Aspects (ADACA) at Coling 2012*, Mumbai, India, pp. 43-58.

Mikulová, Marie et al. (2005). *Annotation on the tectogrammatical layer in the Prague Dependency Treebank. The Annotation Guidelines.* Prague: UFAL MFF. Available at: http://ufal.mff.cuni.cz/pdt2.0/doc/manuals/en/t-layer/html/index.html.

Mírovský, Jiří, Mladová, Lucie, & Žabokrtský, Zdeněk (2010). Annotation Tool for Discourse in PDT. In: *Proceedings of the 23rd International Conference on Computational Linguistics (Coling 2010),* Tsinghua University Press, Beijing, China, ISBN 978-7-302-23456-2, pp. 9-12.

Pajas, Petr, & Štěpánek, Jan (2009). System for Querying Syntactically Annotated Corpora. In: *Proceedings of the ACL-IJCNLP 2009 Software Demonstrations*, Association for Computational Linguistics, Suntec, Singapore, ISBN 1-932432-61-2, pp. 33-36.

Pajas, Petr, & Štěpánek, Jan (2008). Recent Advances in a Feature-Rich Framework for Treebank Annotation. In: *Proceedings of the 22nd International Conference on Computational Linguistics (Coling 2008)*, Manchester, UK, ISBN 978-1-905593-45-3, pp. 673-680.

Poláková, Lucie, Jínová, Pavlína, & Mírovský, Jiří (2014). Genres in the Prague Discourse Treebank. In: *Proceedings of the Ninth International Conference on Language Resources and Evaluation (LREC 2014)*, Reykjavik, Iceland, ISBN 978-2-9517408-8-4, pp. 1320-1326.

Poláková, Lucie, Mírovský, Jiří, Nedoluzhko, Anna et al. (2013). Introducing the Prague Discourse Treebank 1.0. In: *Proceedings of the 6th International Joint Conference on Natural Language Processing,* Asian Federation of Natural Language Processing, Nagoya, Japan, ISBN 978-4-9907348-0-0, pp. 91-99.

Poláková, Lucie, Jínová, Pavlína, Zikánová, Šárka et al. (2012). *Prague Discourse Treebank 1.0.* Data/software, Charles University in Prague, MFF, ÚFAL. Available at: http://ufal.mff.cuni.cz/pdit/.

Prasad, Rashmi, Dinesh. Nikhil, Lee, Alan et al. (2008). The Penn Discourse Treebank 2.0. In: *Proceedings of the 6th International Conference on Language Resources and Evaluation (LREC 2008)*, Marrakech, Morocco.

Sgall, Petr, Hajičová, Eva, & Panevová, Jarmila (1986). *The Meaning of the Sentence in Its Semantic and Pragmatic Aspects.* Dordrecht: Reidel Publishing Company and Prague: Academia.

Zeman, Daniel, Mareček, David, Popel, Martin et al. (2012). HamleDT: To Parse or Not to Parse? In: *Proceedings of the 8th International Conference on Language Resources and Evaluation (LREC 2012*, European Language Resources Association, İstanbul, Turkey, ISBN 978-2-9517408-7-7, pp. 2735-2741.

Lightweight Client-Side Chinese/Japanese Morphological Analyzer Based on Online Learning

Masato Hagiwara **Satoshi Sekine**
Rakuten Institute of Technology, New York
215 Park Avenue South, New York, NY
{masato.hagiwara, satoshi.b.sekine}@mail.rakuten.com

Abstract

As mobile devices and Web applications become popular, lightweight, client-side language analysis is more important than ever. We propose Rakuten MA, a Chinese/Japanese morphological analyzer written in JavaScript. It employs an online learning algorithm SCW, which enables client-side model update and domain adaptation. We have achieved a compact model size (5MB) while maintaining the state-of-the-art performance, via techniques such as feature hashing, FOBOS, and feature quantization.

1 Introduction

Word segmentation (WS) and part-of-speech (PoS) tagging, often jointly called morphological analysis (MA), are the essential component for processing Chinese and Japanese, where words are not explicitly separated by whitespaces. There have been many word segmentater and PoS taggers proposed in both Chinese and Japanese, such as Stanford Segmenter (Tseng et al., 2005), zpar (Zhang and Clark, 2011), MeCab (Kudo et al., 2004), JUMAN (Kurohashi and Nagao, 1994), to name a few. Most of them are intended for server-side use and provide limited capability to extend or re-train models. However, as mobile devices such as smartphones and tablets become popular, there is a growing need for client based, lightweight language analysis, and a growing number of applications are built upon lightweight languages such as HTML, CSS, and JavaScript. Techniques such as domain adaptation and model extension are also becoming more important than ever.

In this paper, we present Rakuten MA, a morphological analyzer entirely written in JavaScript based on online learning. We will be releasing the software as open source before the COLING 2014 conference at `https://github.com/rakuten-nlp/rakutenma`, under Apache License, version 2.0. It relies on general, character-based sequential tagging, which is applicable to any languages and tasks which can be processed in a character-by-character basis, including WS and PoS tagging for Chinese and Japanese. Notable features include:

1. JavaScript based — Rakuten MA works as a JavaScript library, the de facto "lingua franca" of the Web. It works on popular Web browsers as well as node.js, which enables a wide range of adoption such as smartphones and Web browser extensions. Note that TinySegmenter[1] is also entirely written in JavaScript, but it does not support model re-training or any languages other than Japanese. It doesn't output PoS tags, either.
2. Compact — JavaScript-based analyzers pose a difficult technical challenge, that is, the compactness of the model. Modern language analyzers often rely on a large number of features and/or dictionary entries, which is impractical on JavaScript runtime environments. In order to address this issue, Rakuten MA implements some notable techniques. First, the features are character-based and don't rely on dictionaries. Therefore, while it is inherently incapable of dealing with words which are longer than features can capture, it may be robust

[1] http://chasen.org/~taku/software/TinySegmenter/

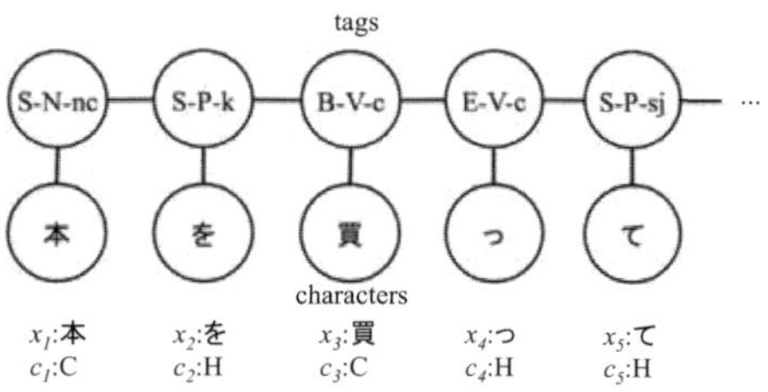

Figure 1: Character-based tagging model

Feature	Description
$x_{i-2}, x_{i-1}, x_i, x_{i+1}, x_{i+2}$	char. unigrams
$x_{i-2}x_{i-1}, x_{i-1}x_i, x_ix_{i+1}, x_{i+1}x_{i+2}$	char. bigrams
$c_{i-2}, c_{i-1}, c_i, c_{i+1}, c_{i+2}$	type unigrams
$c_{i-2}c_{i-1}, c_{i-1}c_i, c_ic_{i+1}, c_{i+1}c_{i+2}$	type bigrams

Table 1: Feature Templates Used for Tagging

x_i and c_i are the character and the character type at i^a.

[a] Each feature template is instantiated and concatenated with possible tags. Character type bigram features were only used for JA. In CN, we built a character type dictionary, where character types are simply all the possible tags in the training corpus for a particular character.

to unknown words compared with purely dictionary-based systems. Second, it employs techniques such as feature hashing (Weinberger et al., 2009), FOBOS (Duchi and Singer, 2009), and feature quantization, to make the model compact while maintaining the same level of analysis performance.

3. Online Learning — it employs a modern online learning algorithm called SCW (Wang et al., 2012), and the model can be incrementally updated by feeding new instances. This enables users to update the model if errors are found, without even leaving the Web browser or node.js. Domain adaptation is also straightforward. Note that MeCab (Kudo et al., 2004), also supports model re-training using a small re-training corpus. However, the training is inherently a batch, iterative algorithm (CRF) thus it is hard to predict when it finishes.

2 Analysis Model and Compact Model Representation

Base Model Rakuten MA employs the standard character-based sequential tagging model. It assigns combination of position tags[2] and PoS tags to each character (Figure 1). The optimal tag sequence $\boldsymbol{y}^*$ for an input string x is inferred based on the features $\phi(y)$ and the weight vector $\boldsymbol{w}$ as $\boldsymbol{y}^* = \arg\max_{y \in Y(x)} \boldsymbol{w} \cdot \phi(y)$, where $Y(x)$ denotes all the possible tag sequences for x, via standard Viterbi decoding. Table 1 shows the feature template sets.

For training, we used soft confidence weighted (SCW) (Wang et al., 2012). SCW is an online learning scheme based on Confidence Weighted (CW), which maintains "confidence" of each parameter as variance Σ in order to better control the updates. Since SCW itself is a general classification model, we employed the structured prediction model (Collins, 2002) for WS.

The code snippet in Figure 2 shows typical usage of Rakuten MA in an interactive way. Lines starting with "//" and ">" are comments and user input, and the next lines are returned results. Notice that the analysis of バラクオバマ大統領 "President Barak Obama" get better as the model observes more instances. The analyzer can only segment it into individual characters when the model is empty ((1) in the code), whereas WS is partially correct after observing the first 10 sentences of the corpus ((2) in the code). After directly providing the gold standard, the result (3) becomes perfect.

We used and compared the following three techniques for compact model representations:

Feature Hashing (Weinberger et al., 2009) applies hashing functions h which turn an arbitrary feature $\phi_i(y)$ into a bounded integer value v, i.e., $v = h(\phi_i(y)) \in R$, where $0 \leq v < 2^N$, (N = hash size). This technique is especially useful for online learning, where a large, growing number of features such as character/word n-grams could be observed on the fly, which the model would otherwise need to keep track of using flexible data structures such as trie, which could make training slower as the model observes more training instances. The negative effect of hash collisions to the performance is negligible because most collisions are between rare features.

[2] As for the position tags, we employed the SBIEO scheme, where S stands for a single character word, BIE for beginning, middle, and end of a word, respectively, and O for other positions.

```
// initialize with empty model
> var r = new RakutenMA({});

// (1) first attempt, failed with separate chars.
> r.tokenize("バラクオバマ大統領").toString()
"バ,,ラ,,ク,,オ,,バ,,マ,,大,,統,,領,"

// train with first 10 sentences in a corpus
> for (var i = 0; i < 10; i ++)
>   r.train_one( rcorpus[i] );

// the model is no longer empty
> r.model
Object {mu: Object, sigma: Object}

// (2) second attempt -> getting closer
> r.tokenize("バラクオバマ大統領").toString()
"バラク,N-nc,オバマ,N-pn,大,,統,,領,Q-n"

// retrain with an answer
// return object suggests there was an update
> r.train_one([["バラク","N-np"],
...     ["オバマ","N-np"],["大統領","N-nc"]]);
Object {ans: Array[3], sys: Array[5], updated: true}

// (3) third attempt
> r.tokenize("バラクオバマ大統領").toString()
"バラク,N-np,オバマ,N-np,大統領,N-nc"
```

Figure 2: Rakuten MA usage example

Chinese	Prec.	Rec.	F	Japanese	Prec.	Rec.	F
Stanford Parser	97.37	93.54	95.42	MeCab+UniDic	99.15	99.61	99.38
zpar	91.18	92.36	91.77	JUMAN	**88.55	**83.06	**85.72
Rakuten MA	92.61	92.64	92.62	KyTea	*80.57	*85.02	*82.73
				TinySegmenter	*86.93	*85.19	*86.05
				Rakuten MA	96.76	97.30	97.03

Table 2: Segmentation Performance Comparison with Different Systems
* These systems use different WS criteria and their performance is shown simply for reference. ** We postprocessed JUMAN's WS result so that the WS criteria are closer to Rakuten MA's.

Forward-Backward Splitting (FOBOS) (Duchi and Singer, 2009) is a framework to introduce regularization to online learning algorithms. For each training instance, it runs unconstrained parameter update of the original algorithm as the first phase, then solves an instantaneous optimization problem to minimize a regularization term while keeping the parameter close to the first phrase. Specifically, letting $w_{t+\frac{1}{2},j}$ the j-th parameter after the first phrase of iteration t and λ the regularization coefficient, parameter update of FOBOS with L1 regularization is done by: $w_{t+1,j} = \text{sign}\left(w_{t+\frac{1}{2},j}\right)\left[\left|w_{t+\frac{1}{2},j}\right| - \lambda\right]_+$. The strength of regularization can be adjusted by the coefficient λ. In combining SCW and FOBOS, we retained the confidence value Σ of SCW unchanged.

Feature Quantization simply multiplies float numbers (e.g., 0.0165725659236262) by M (e.g., 1,000) and round it to obtain a short integer (e.g., 16). The multiple M determines the strength of quantization, i.e., the larger the finer grained, but the larger model size.

3 Experiments

We used CTB 7.0 (Xue et al., 2005) for Chinese (CN), and BCCWJ (Maekawa, 2008) for Japanese (JA), with 50,805 and 60,374 sentences, respectively. We used the top two levels of BCCWJ's PoS tag hierarchy (38 unique tags) and all the CTB PoS tags (38 unique tags). The average decoding time was 250 millisecond per sentence on Intel Xeon 2.13GHz, measured on node.js. We used precision (Prec.), recall (Rec.), and F-value (F) of WS as the evaluation metrics, averaged over 5-fold cross validation. We ignored the PoS tags in the evaluation because they are especially difficult to compare across different systems with different PoS tag hierarchies.

Comparison with Other Analyzers First, we compare the performance of Rakuten MA with other word segmenters. In CN, we compared with Stanford Segmenter (Tseng et al., 2005) and zpar (Zhang and Clark, 2011). In JA, we compared with MeCab (Kudo et al., 2004), JUMAN (Kurohashi and Nagao, 1994), KyTea (Neubig et al., 2011), and TinySegmenter.

Table 2 shows the result. Note that, some of the systems (e.g., Stanford Parser for CN and MeCab+UniDic for JA) use the same corpus as the training data and their performance is unfairly high. Also, other systems such as JUMAN and KyTea employ different WS criteria, and their performance is unfairly low, although JUMAN's WS result was postprocessed so that

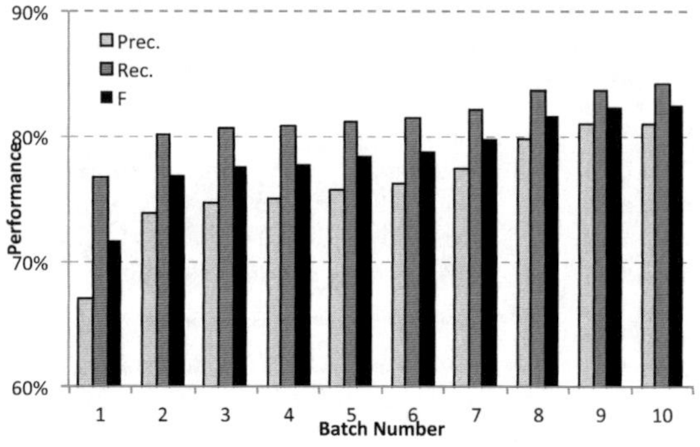

Figure 3: Domain Adaptation Result for CN

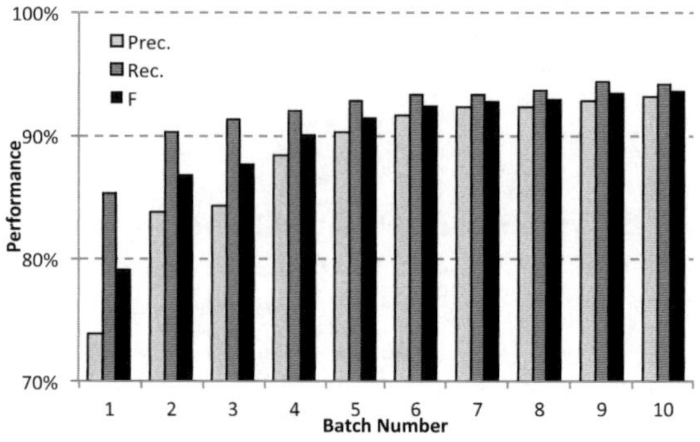

Figure 4: Domain Adaptation Result for JA

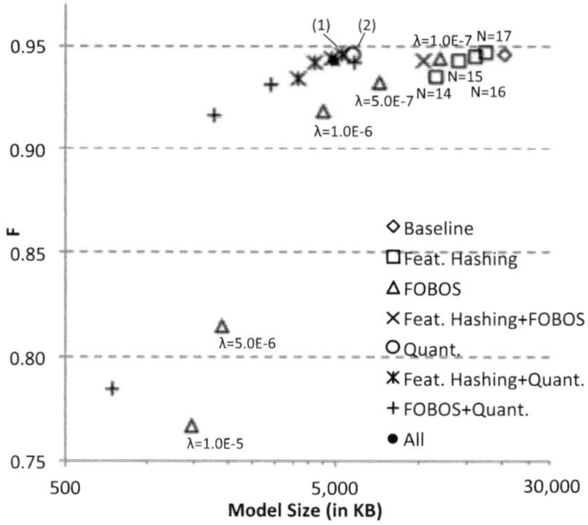

Figure 5: Model Comparison

it gives a better idea how it compares with Rakuten MA. We can see that Rakuten MA can achieve WS performance comparable with the state-of-the-art even without using dictionaries.

Domain Adaptation Second, we tested Rakuten MA's domain adaptation ability. We chose e-commerce as the target domain, since it is a rich source of out-of-vocabulary words and poses a challenge to analyzers trained on newswire text. We sampled product titles and descriptions from Rakuten Taiwan[3] (for CN, 2,786 sentences) and Rakuten Ichiba[4] (for JA, 13,268 sentences). These collections were then annotated by human native speakers in each language, following the tagging guidelines of CTB (for CN) and BCCWJ (for JA).

We divided the corpus into 5 folds, then used four of them for re-training and one for testing. The re-training data is divided into "batches," consisting of mutually exclusive 50 sentences, which were fed to the pre-trained model on CTB (for CN) and BCCWJ (for JA) one by one.

Figure 3 and 4 show the results. The performance quickly levels off after five batches for JA, which gives an approximated number of re-training instances needed (200 to 300) for adaptation. Note that adaptation took longer on CN, which may be attributed to the fact that Chinese WS itself is a harder problem, and to the disparity between CTB (mainly news articles in mainland China) and the adaptation corpus (e-commerce text in Taiwan).

[3] `http://www.rakuten.com.tw/`. Note that Rakuten Taiwan is written in Taiwanese traditional Chinese. It was converted to simplified Chinese by using Wikipedia's traditional-simplified conversion table `http://svn.wikimedia.org/viewvc/mediawiki/trunk/phase3/includes/ZhConversion.php`. Still, having large Taiwan specific vocabulary poses additional challenges for domain adaptation.

[4] `http://www.rakuten.co.jp/`

Compact Model Representation Third, we consider the three techniques, and investigate how these techniques affect the trade-off between WS performance and the model size, which is measured by the feature trie byte size in raw JSON format[5].

Figure 5 shows the scatter plot of F-value vs model size in KB, since we are rather interested in the trade-off between the model size and the performance. The baseline is the raw model without any techniques mentioned above. Notice that the figure's x-axis is in log scale, and the upper left corner in the figure corresponds to better trade-off (higher performance with smaller model size). We can observe that all the three techniques can reduce the model size to some extent while keeping the performance at the same level. In fact, these three techniques are independent from each other and can be freely combined to achieve better trade-off. If we limit strictly the same level of performance compared to the baseline, feature hashing (17bit hash size) with quantization (Point (1) in the figure) seems to achieve the best trade-off, slightly *outperforming* the baseline (F = 0.9457 vs F = 0.9455 of the baseline) with the model size of as little as one fourth (5.2MB vs 20.6MB of the baseline). It is somewhat surprising to see that feature quantization, which is a very simple method, achieves relatively good performance-size trade-off (Point (2) in the figure).

4 Conclusion

In this paper, we proposed Rakuten MA, a lightweight, client-side morphological analyzer entirely written in JavaScript. It supports online learning based on the SCW algorithm, which enables quick domain adaptation, as shown in the experiments. We successfully achieved a compact model size of as little as 5MB while maintaining the state-of-the-art performance, using feature hashing, FOBOS, and feature quantization. We are planning to achieve even smaller model size by adopting succinct data structure such as wavelet tree (Grossi et al., 2003).

Acknowledgements

The authors thank Satoko Marumoto, Keiji Shinzato, Keita Yaegashi, and Soh Masuko for their contribution to this project.

References

Michael Collins. 2002. Discriminative training methods for hidden Markov models: theory and experiments with perceptron algorithms. In *Proc. of the EMNLP 2002*, pages 1–8.

John Duchi and Yoram Singer. 2009. Efficient online and batch learning using forward backward splitting. *Journal of Machine Learning Research*, 10:2899–2934.

Roberto Grossi, Ankur Gupta, and Jeffrey Scott Vitter. 2003. High-order entropy-compressed text indexes. In *Prof. of SODA 2003*, pages 841–850.

Taku Kudo, Kaoru Yamamoto, and Yuji Matsumoto. 2004. Applying conditional random fields to Japanese morphological analysis. In *Proceedings of EMNLP*, pages 230–237.

Sadao Kurohashi and Makoto Nagao. 1994. Improvements of Japanese morphological analyzer JUMAN. In *Proceedings of the International Workshop on Sharable Natural Language Resources*, pages 22–38.

Kikuo Maekawa. 2008. Compilation of the Kotonoha-BCCWJ corpus (in Japanese). *Nihongo no kenkyu (Studies in Japanese)*, 4(1):82–95.

Graham Neubig, Yosuke Nakata, and Shinsuke Mori. 2011. Pointwise prediction for robust, adaptable japanese morphological analysis. In *Proceedings of ACL-HLT*, pages 529–533.

Huihsin Tseng, Pichuan Chang, Galen Andrew, Daniel Jurafsky, and Christopher Manning. 2005. A conditional random field word segmenter. In *Fourth SIGHAN Workshop on Chinese Language Processing*.

Jialei Wang, Peilin Zhao, and Steven C. Hoi. 2012. Exact soft confidence-weighted learning. In *Proc. of ICML 2012*, pages 121–128.

Kilian Weinberger, Anirban Dasgupta, Josh Attenberg, John Langford, and Alex Smola. 2009. Feature hashing for large scale multitask learning. In *Proc. of ICML 2009*, pages 1113–1120.

Naiwen Xue, Fei Xia, Fu-dong Chiou, and Marta Palmer. 2005. The penn Chinese treebank: Phrase structure annotation of a large corpus. *Natural Language Engineering*, 11(2):207–238.

Yue Zhang and Stephen Clark. 2011. Syntactic processing using the generalized perceptron and beam search. *Computational Linguistics*, 37(1):105–151.

---

[5]We used one fifth of the Japanese corpus BCCWJ for this experiment. Parameter λ of FOBOS was varied over $\{1.0 \times 10^{-7}, 5.0 \times 10^{-7}, 1.0 \times 10^{-6}, 5.0 \times 10^{-6}, 1.0 \times 10^{-5}\}$. The hash size of feature hashing was varied over $14, 15, 16, 17^6$. The multiple of feature quantization M is set to $M = 1000$.

MultiDPS – A multilingual Discourse Processing System

Daniel Alexandru Anechitei
"Al. I. Cuza" University of Iasi
Faculty of Computer Science
16, General Berthelot St., 700483, Iasi, Romania
daniel.anechitei@info.uaic.ro

Abstract

[1]This paper presents an adaptable online Multilingual Discourse Processing System (MultiDPS), composed of four natural language processing tools: named entity recognizer, anaphora resolver, clause splitter and a discourse parser. This NLP Meta System allows any user to run it on the web or via web services and, if necessary, to build its own processing chain, by incorporating knowledge or resources for each tool for the desired language. In this paper is presented a brief description for each independent module, and a case study in which the system is adapted to five different languages for creating a multilingual summarization system.

1 Introduction

This paper describes a multilingual discourse processing system (MultiDPS) consisting in four different modules: Named Entity Recognizer (NER), Anaphora Resolver (AR), Clause Splitter (CS), Discourse Parser (DP), and for the summarization scope, the proper summarizer (SUM). This system can run online via web services such that it can be accessed from any programming environment and the architecture allows each tool to be individually trained. Each task, except for discourse parsing, MultiDPS's component tools combines machine learning techniques with heuristics to learn from a manually created corpus (a gold corpus of discourse trees is very difficult to obtain due to the complexity of the task). The complexity of the processing tasks (reaching to discourse analysis) and the multilingual capabilities, make MultiDPS an important system in the field of natural language processing.

2 System Design

The MultiDPS architecture includes two main parts as it can be seen in Figure **1**.

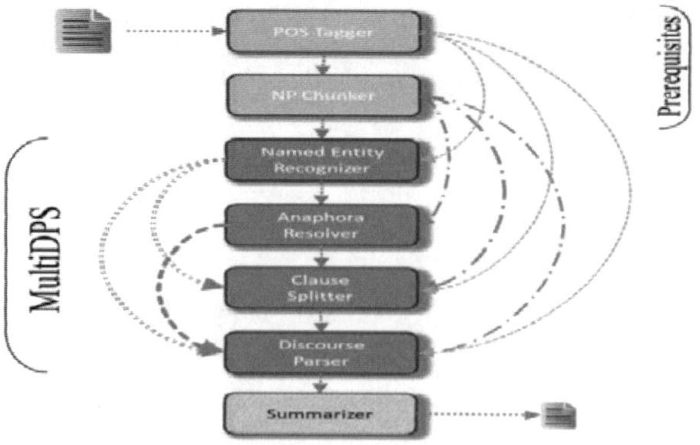

Figure 1: The MultiDPS's component modules and supported workflows

The Prerequisite part includes usually known basic NLP tools and it is a primary step for obtaining the input for MultiDPS. The system consists of four different modules which will be discussed in detail in the next sections. All modules implement a language independent vision in which the algorithm is separated from linguistic details. Each phase and the output of each module is an input for a next phase, not necessarily the immediately next one, as it is depicted in Figure **1** (dotted arrows suggest different paths that the system supports). Depending on individual needs or on the existence of specific resources (manual annotated corpora for a specific language), different language processing chains can be created. The entire system is designed in such a way that each individual module brings an extra annotation to the text therefore, when building a processing chain, some modules can be skipped.

2.1 Named Entity Recognizer

Named Entity Recognition (NER) is a computational linguistic task that seeks to classify sequences of words in predefined categories. In this approach the categories are organized under four top level classes (PERSON, LOCATION, ORGANIZATION and MISC) and a total of nine subclasses.

In order to identify the type of entities a voting system is implemented, being meant to decide between different heuristics, which use automatically calibrated weights for different features, where high scores are given for the entities within gazetteers. Examples of features are: context bi/tri grams for different classes; appearance of a definite article; partial matches with gazetteers or within the same text.

2.2 Anaphora Resolution

The AR module used in MultiDPS is based on the work done in Anechitei et al (2013), and improved by adding a classifier, to predict whether there is a relation between each pair of noun phrases, resulting in a hybrid approach. Examples of features used to decide if there is a co-referential chain between two noun phrases are: number agreement, gender agreement, and morphological description, implementing on the head noun; similarity between the two noun phrases, both at lemma level and text level implemented on the head noun and also on the entire noun phrase; condition if the two noun phrases belong to the same phrase or not.

If the matching score given by the two methods is greater than an automatically computed threshold, then the actual noun phrase is added to already existing chain of referential expressions attached to the noun phrase, and all the features are copied onto the list of features of the new referential expression. If there is no previous noun phrase, for which the matching score to be greater than the threshold, then a new co-referential chain is created containing only the actual noun phrase along with its features.

2.3 Clause Splitter

A clause is a grammatical unit comprising a predicate and an explicit or implied subject, and expresses a proposition. For the present work, the delimitation of clauses follows the work done in Anechitei et al (2013) and starts from the identification of verbs and verb compounds. Verb compounds are sequences of more than one verb in which one is the main verb and the others are auxiliaries ("is writing", "like to read"). Examples of features used to build the model of compound verbs are: distance between the verbs; the existence of punctuation or markers between them; the lemma and the morphological description of the verbs, etc.

The semantics of the compound verbs makes it necessary to take the whole construction together not putting boundary in the interior, so that the clause does not lose its meaning. Clause boundaries are looked between verbs and compound verbs which are considered the pivots of clauses. The exact location of a boundary is, in many cases, best indicated by discourse markers. A discourse marker is a word, or a group of words, that also have the function to indicate a rhetorical relation between two clauses. The features used to build the marker's model are: the lemma and the context of the marker expressed as configurable length sequences of POS tags and the distance from the verb in front of it.

When markers are missing, boundaries can still be indicated by statistical methods, trained on explicit annotations. The weights of the features are tuned like in previous examples, by running the calibration system on the manual annotated corpora and creating the models using *MaxEnt*[1] library.

---

[1] The Maximum Entropy Framework: http://maxent.sourceforge.net/about.html

2.4 Discourse Parser

The approach to discourse parsing implemented in MultiDPS follows the one described in Anechitei et al (2013) and is a symbolic approach rooted on (Marcu, 1999). The generated discourse trees put in evidence only the nuclearity of the nodes, while the name of relations is ignored. The discourse parser adopts an incremental policy in developing the trees and it is constrained by two general principles, well known in discourse parsing: sequentiality of the terminal nodes (Marcu, 2000) and attachment restricted to the right frontier (Cristea, 2005). The algorithm involves a *generate-rank-evaluate* method by generating a forest of developing trees at each step, followed by heuristics for ranking and evaluating the trees. The heuristics are suggested by both Veins Theory (Cristea et al, 1998) and Centering Theory (Grosz et al, 1995). The aim of these heuristics is to assign scores to the developing trees and also to master the exponential explosion of the developing structure.

2.5 The Summarizer

For the summarization purpose, the discourse structure gives more information than properly needed. The summary is achieved by trimming unimportant clauses/sentences on the basis of the relative saliency, cohesion and coherence properties. For each discourse unit, a score is attached and reflects the properties mentioned above. Each component of MultiDPS contributes to the calculation of this score.

3 Implementation of the modules

The main idea behind the system architecture is that, if a module is fuelled with appropriate language resources, it can be put to work on any language. For the Romanian language, the input for MultiDPS is obtained using a deep noun phrase chunker (Simionescu, 2011) and for the English language using the Stanford Parser (Socher et al, 2013). All the resources (manually annotated corpora for English and Romanian) are available for download.

The clear benefit of this system architecture using web services is that if an improvement is made in a certain module, the results will be propagated through the others, without the need of human intervention. Figure **2** illustrates the web interface for the discourse parser, where the XML annotations are mapped in a visual mode.

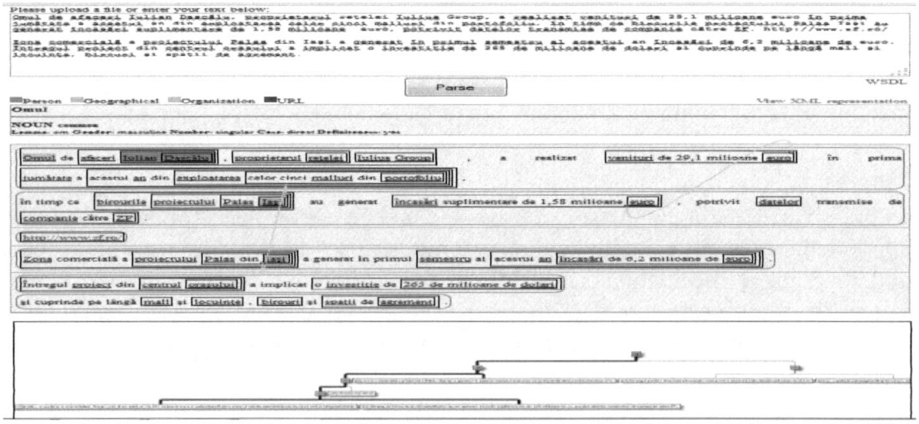

Figure 2: View of the Discourse Parser web application that illustrates all annotations.

In addition to the web applications and the core of the system (each module can be used as a library), what is made available is a wide range of free additional tools like online annotation services and calibration systems for each individual module. MultiDPS was easily adapted for other languages where there was input provided for the system entry and training corpus for each module.

4 Experiments and results

In this paper I present the results obtained after combining all the modules to create a multilingual summarization system. The results were obtained after attending an international workshop on summarization (Kubina et al., 2013), where the objective of each participant was to compute a maximum

250 words summary for each document for at least two of the dataset languages (30 documents per language). The submitted summaries were evaluated using ROUGE metric (Lin, 2004) and presented in the next table, where the oracle in the table represents the "perfect summary":

Language	System							
	baseline	s1	s2	s3	s4	s5	s6	oracle
bg	0.2854	**0.3190**	0.2955	0.2969	0.2974			0.3966
de	0.2529	**0.3414**	0.3198	0.3341	0.3203			0.3675
el	0.2899	**0.3229**	0.2777	0.2747	0.2698			0.3775
en	0.4113	0.3273	0.2781	0.2799	0.2765	**0.3638**	0.3411	0.5554
ro	0.3125	**0.3337**	0.29048	0.3006	0.2985			0.4361

Table 1: ROUGE-1 average for all five languages

(Bulgarian, German, Greek, English and Romanian)

Nevertheless, the results are encouraging for this complex system (**s1** is the id of the system presented in this paper).

5 Conclusions

MultiDPS's strength is manifested through its online availability and the existence of the online services for creating corpora for each module. Moreover, considering that the results obtained by putting together all the modules are similar for different languages, the system can be regarded as having language-wide validity.

Reference

Barbara J. Grosz, Aravind K. Joshi and Scott Weinstein. 1995. *Centering: A framework for modeling the local coherence of discourse*. Computational Linguistics, 21(2), pages 203–226.

Chin-Yew Lin. 2004. *Rouge: A package for automatic evaluation of summaries*. In Proceedings of the ACL Workshop on Text Summarization Branches Out, Barcelona, Spain.

Dan Cristea, Nancy Ide, Laurent Romary. 1998. *Veins theory: A model of global discourse cohesion and coherence*. In Proceedings of the 17th international conference on Computational linguistics, pages 281-285, Montreal.

Dan Cristea. 2005. *The Right Frontier Constraint Holds Unconditionally*. In Proceedings of the Multidisciplinary Approaches to Discourse (MAD'05), Chorin/Berlin, Germany.

Daniel A. Anechitei, Dan Cristea, Ioannidis Dimosthenis, Eugen Ignat, Diman Karagiozov, Svetla Koeva, Mateusz Kopeć, Cristina Vertan. 2013. *Summarizing Short Texts Through a Discourse-Centered Approach in a Multilingual Context*. In Neustein, A., Markowitz, J.A. (eds.), Where Humans Meet Machines: Innovative Solutions to Knotty natural Language Problems. Springer Verlag, Heidelber/New York.

Daniel Marcu. 1999. *Discourse trees are good indicators of importance in text*. In I. Mani and M. Maybury (eds.), Advances in Automatic Text Summarization, pages 123-136, The MIT Press.

Daniel Marcu. 2000. *The Theory and Practice of Discourse Parsing and Summarization*. The MIT Press. Cambridge, Massachusetts.

Jeff Kubina, John M. Conroy, Judith D. Schleisinger. 2013. *ACL 2013 MultiLing Pilot Overview*. In Proceedings of MultiLing 2013 Workshop on Multilingual Multi-document Summarization, Sofia, Bulgaria, pages 29-38, workshop in conjunction with the 51st Annual Meeting of the Association for Computational Linguistics (ACL 2013).

Radu Simionescu. 2011. *Romanian Deep Noun Phrase Chunking Using Graphical Grammar Studio*. In Proceedings of The International Conference on Resources and tools for Romanian Language.

Richard Socher, John Bauer, Christopher D. Manning, Andrew Y. Ng. 2013. *Parsing with Compositional Vector Grammars*. In Proceedings of ACL.

Sanskrit Linguistics Web Services

Gérard Huet
Inria Paris-Rocquencourt
gerard.huet@inria.fr

Amba Kulkarni
University of Hyderabad
apksh@uohyd.ernet.in

Abstract

We propose to demonstrate a collection of tools for Sanskrit Computational Linguistics developed by cooperating teams in the general setting of Web services. These services offer a systematic architecture integrating multilingual lexicons, morphological generation and analysis, segmentation and parsing, and interlink with the Sanskrit Library digital repository. They may be used as distributed Internet services, or installed as local tools on individual users workstations.

1 Community building

Sanskrit is the primary culture-bearing language of India, with a continuous production of literature in all fields of human endeavour over the course of four millennia. It benefited from a strong linguistics tradition, established from early times, and notably from the grammar composed by Pāṇini around the fourth century B.C.E., and commented since by innumerable grammatical treatises. This fairly complete descriptive apparatus took a prescriptive character, resulting in a constrained evolution of the language within its official grammar, leading to its stability as a semi-formal language. On the other hand, multiple styles of writing treatises, commentaries, and even poetry, led to a variety of specific dialects, both in prose and in versified form.

The efforts towards developing tools for the computational treatment of Sanskrit have been steadily progressing both at national as well as international level. A Sanskrit Computational Linguistics consortium funded by the Indian Government coordinates the development of consistent tools within 7 research institutes. In 2007, the first of a series of International Sanskrit Computational Linguistics Symposia was organized in Paris with the aim of gathering a community of teams sharing ideas as well as linguistic resources, and developing inter-operable software. These symposia have benefited the computer scientists from the grammatical expertise of the traditional scholars, while the traditional scholars could see the practical applications of the thousand of years old theories.

Within this general effort, specific tools were developed at Inria in Paris and University of Hyderabad for the analysis of Sanskrit texts, designed as inter-communicating Web services. A specific human-machine interface was developed, allowing annotation experts to produce tagged tree banks for the Sanskrit Library, a digital TEI-conformant repository of Sanskrit corpus. This joint work was presented at COLING-2012 (Goyal et al., 2012). We herein propose to demonstrate the current functionalities of this software platform.

2 Architecture of components

It was deemed counter-productive to attempt to build a monolithical rigid system, and we turned rather to developing on various sites independent components, communicating with each other as Web services interchanging XML data. This allows freedom of programming languages and environments, operating systems, and even linguistic resources. This also permits greater flexibility of independent versioning of the components. Furthermore, HTML and client-side scripting provide a standardized solution to a common user interface, with easy multilingual display through Unicode.

Currently the system supports several lexicon resources. A specific core lexicon, the Sanskrit Heritage dictionary (Huet, 2004), has been developed as the seed resource for morphological databases. Digitalized versions of the Monier-Williams (Monier-Williams et al., 1999) and the Apte dictionaries are being progressively integrated by semi-automatic alignment. Amarakośa, the oldest thesaurus of Sanskrit, has also been digitalized (Nair and Kulkarni, 2010), providing the ontological information following the Indian tradition.

A number of components use the Zen Computational Linguistics Toolkit[1], a systematic functional programming library of finite-state tools. It handles lexicon management, phonological computation, morphology generation (both generative and inflexional), and segmentation. The segmentation component is specially important, in view of sandhi. Sanskrit text is represented as the result of phonetic smoothing, whose efficient inversion is problematic. An original solution to sandhi analysis was developed (Huet, 2005; Huet, 2006).

Morphological databanks are produced mechanically from the core dictionary stems, informed with their production parameters. Sharing techniques give highly compressed data structures loadable dynamically in process memory, eschewing the use of costly database technology. The morphological treatment processes are not strictly speaking Pāṇinian, but it is possible to relate them precisely to Pāṇinian derivations (Goyal and Huet, 2012). Independently, databanks issued from the Sanskrit traditional repositories have been digitalized (Bharati et al., 2006) and linked to the Aṣṭādhyāyī simulator which generates the nominal forms following the Pāṇinian process (Goyal et al., 2009). Lemma alignment algorithms permit inter-operability of these various resources, seen as plug-in components.

Segmentation leads to morphological tagging, a complete but much over-generating process. A typical sentence may have billions of possible analyses. A graphical user-interface, providing a fully shared view of all segmentations, has been developed (Huet and Goyal, 2013). It is designed to be very fast, and to allow human annotators easy inspection of the segment features. Experiments with semi-automatic annotation of parts of the Sanskrit Library[2] validated the approach.

A deterministic tabulated dependency parser has been designed (Kulkarni, 2013). The application of local constraints at an early stage and stacking of intermediate results along dynamic programming yield fast results. The graphical user-interface of the segmenter is adapted to the parser in order to show the shared view of all possible solutions in a compact form.

Annotated corpus statistics are being used to build the language and grammar models for various tasks. An experimental version of a segmenter (Kumar et al., 2010) is developed that constraints the sequence of constituents by a language model and uses the split model based on the empirical data of sandhi rules for splitting. These empirical models may further be used to build weighted finite state automaton to prioritize the solutions.

3 Salient novel features

The segmentation algorithm uses a novel approach to finite state technology, through Effective Eilenberg machines (Huet and Razet, 2008). Although Sanskrit has huge literature, only a negligible part of it has been tagged for various levels of analyses. Thus use of statistical techniques or machine learning is almost ruled out. While machines are good at syntactic analysis, for semantic compatibility of solutions we still depend on human assistance. This calls for a suitable interface which can represent billions of solutions with all relevant linguistic details

[1]`http://yquem.inria.fr/~huet/ZEN/`

[2]`http://sanskritlibrary.org`

to be displayed on a screen. This requirement led us to develop a tabulated display interface, using efficiently a compact shared representation of solutions, presenting an ergonomical solution to human assistance. This interface was also further adapted to display all possible sentential parses in a compact tabular format for choosing the correct parse.

A new technology of forms alignment, indexed by their morphological production history ("unique naming"), allows uniform access to various dictionaries, despite possibly conflicting homophony partitions.

The consistently structured core lexical repository, together with lexicon alignment, allows the automatic production of derived human-readable dictionaries under the Babyloo/Stardict/Goldendict formats, with consistent hypertext linking to grammatical processes.

Some requirements of Sanskrit computational tools are very specific. Sanskrit has a vast literature spreading over several knowledge domains. Most of the important Sanskrit literature is already translated into several languages. In spite of this, scholars want to have access to original sources, and thus development of the computational tools with convenient user interfaces that allow seamless connectivity to and from the lexical resources, generation engines and analysis tools becomes meaningful. Further, the availability of Aṣṭādhyāyī, an almost complete grammar for Sanskrit, also puts demands on the developers to authenticate the inverse process of analysis by the generative rules of grammars. These considerations have resulted in the development of suitable interfaces linking various resources and tools through Web services.

4 Software engineering and deployment issues

The Web services approach allows independent development of components, seen as XML transducers keeping a history of interactions through the argument structure of the CGI invocations. This allows independent development, archiving and distribution of modules developed in C, PERL, Ocaml, Python, Java, Javascript, etc.

Parametrization of the various platform interconnections allows for distributed use through Internet, as well as local use on workstations. Extreme programming methodology allows for agile development with high frequency releasing and a fast user feedback.

The software, as well as linguistic resources, are available under open-source licences.

5 Demonstration scenario

The tools will be demonstrated on a few typical sentences, showing various usages of the software. The first presentation will demonstrate the Sanskrit Heritage segmenter on an input sentence. It will show how to select a segmentation solution using the graphical interface, then the way to refine the solution using the dependency parser of the Hyderabad Sanskrit Computational Linguistics analyser, in order to get its dependency structure. A dual presentation will start from the Hyderabad analyser, using the Heritage segmenter as a front end. Finally it will be shown how to access the analyser tools from marked-up corpus in the Sanskrit library. Settings allow switching between the various lexicons, and displaying grammatical information either in romanized Western style, or in *Devanāgarī* traditional Indian style. The demo will also include linking to actual Pāṇinian derivation process to ensure precision in the analysis. If time permits, the Goldendict versions of the lexicons will be shown, informed with grammatical information.

Acknowledgement

The Inria 'Sanskrit Heritage' platform benefited from important contributions of Pawan Goyal, notably in its graphical interface. We wish also to thank Peter Scharf for his cooperation on the Sanskrit Library interface. Various components of the software at University of Hyderabad were developed with support from TDIL Programme, DeitY, Government of India for the project 'Development of Sanskrit computational toolkit and Sanskrit-Hindi Machine Translation system' with contributions from Sivaja Nair, Anil Kumar, Karunakar, Devanand Shukl and Pavankumar.

References

Akshar Bharati, Amba Kulkarni, and V. Sheeba. 2006. Building a wide coverage Sanskrit morphological analyser: A practical approach. First National Symposium on Modeling and Shallow Parsing of Indian Languages, IIT Mumbai.

Pawan Goyal and Gérard Huet. 2012. Completeness analysis of a Sanskrit reader. In *Proceedings, 5th International Symposium on Sanskrit Computational Linguistics*. DK Publisher.

Pawan Goyal, Amba Kulkarni, and Laxmidhar Behera. 2009. Computer simulation of *Aṣṭādhyāyī*: Some insights. In Gérard Huet, Amba Kulkarni, and Peter Scharf, editors, *Sanskrit Computational Linguistics 1 & 2*, pages 139–161. Springer-Verlag LNAI 5402.

Pawan Goyal, Gérard Huet, Amba Kulkarni, Peter Scharf, and Ralph Bunker. 2012. A distributed platform for Sanskrit processing. In *24th International Conference on Computational Linguistics (COLING), Mumbai*.

Gérard Huet and Pawan Goyal. 2013. Design of a lean interface for Sanskrit corpus annotation. In *Proceedings, ICON13, Hyderabad*.

Gérard Huet and Benoît Razet. 2008. Computing with relational machines. ICON'2008 tutorial.

Gérard Huet. 2003. Towards computational processing of Sanskrit. In *International Conference on Natural Language Processing (ICON)*.

Gérard Huet. 2004. Design of a lexical database for Sanskrit. In *Workshop on Enhancing and Using Electronic Dictionaries, COLING 2004*. International Conference on Computational Linguistics.

Gérard Huet. 2005. A functional toolkit for morphological and phonological processing, application to a Sanskrit tagger. *J. Functional Programming*, 15,4:573–614.

Gérard Huet, 2006. *Themes and Tasks in Old and Middle Indo-Aryan Linguistics, Eds. Bertil Tikkanen and Heinrich Hettrich*, chapter Lexicon-directed Segmentation and Tagging of Sanskrit, pages 307–325. Motilal Banarsidass, Delhi.

Gérard Huet. 2007. Shallow syntax analysis in Sanskrit guided by semantic nets constraints. In *Proceedings of the 2006 International Workshop on Research Issues in Digital Libraries*, New York, NY, USA. ACM.

Amba Kulkarni and Devanand Shukl. 2009. Sanskrit morphological analyser: Some issues. *Indian Linguistics*, 70(1-4):169–177.

Amba Kulkarni, Sheetal Pokar, and Devanand Shukl. 2010. Designing a constraint based parser for Sanskrit. In G N Jha, editor, *Proceedings of the 4th International Sanskrit Computational Linguistics Symposium*. Springer-Verlag LNAI 6465.

Amba Kulkarni. 2013. A deterministic dependency parser with dynamic programming for Sanskrit. In *Proceedings of the Second International Conference on Dependency Linguistics (DepLing 2013)*, pages 157–166, Prague, August. Charles University Matfyzpress, Prague, Czech Republic.

Anil Kumar, Vipul Mittal, and Amba Kulkarni. 2010. Sanskrit compound processor. In G N Jha, editor, *Proceedings of the International Sanskrit Computational Linguistics Symposium*. Springer-Verlag LNAI 6465.

Vipul Mittal. 2010. Automatic sanskrit segmentizer using finite state transducers. In *Proceedings of the ACL 2010 Student Research Workshop*, pages 85–90, Uppsala, Sweden, July. Association for Computational Linguistics.

M. Monier-Williams, E. Leumann, and C. Cappeller. 1999. *A Sanskrit-English Dictionary: Etymological And Philologically Arranged With Special Reference To Cognate Indo-European Languages*. Asian Educational Services.

Sivaja S. Nair and Amba Kulkarni. 2010. The knowledge structure in Amarakośa. In G N Jha, editor, *Proceedings of the International Sanskrit Computational Linguistics Symposium*. Springer-Verlag LNAI 6465.

Peter Scharf and Malcolm Hyman. 2009. *Linguistic Issues in Encoding Sanskrit*. Motilal Banarsidass, Delhi.

S.C. Vasu. 1980. *The Aṣṭādhyāyī of Pāṇini*. Motilal Banarsidass.

TICCLops: Text-Induced Corpus Clean-up as online processing system

Martin Reynaert
TiCC - Tilburg University and CLST - Radboud Universiteit Nijmegen
The Netherlands
reynaert@uvt.nl

Abstract

We present the 'online processing system' version of Text-Induced Corpus Clean-up, a web service and application open for use to researchers. The system has over the past years been developed to provide mainly OCR error post-correction, but can just as fruitfully be employed to automatically correct texts for spelling errors, or to transcribe texts in an older spelling into the modern variant of the language. It has recently been re-implemented as a distributable and scalable software system in C++, designed to be easily adaptable for use with a broad range of languages and diachronical language varieties. Its new code base is now fit for production work and to be released as open source.

1 Introduction

The spelling and OCR-error correction system Text-Induced Corpus Clean-up[1] (TICCL) we gradually developed in prior projects is now TICCLops (TICCL online processing system). TICCLops is a fully operational web application and RESTful web service. This is thanks to the Computational Linguistics Application Mediator (CLAM), more fully described in our companion paper (van Gompel and Reynaert, 2014). CLAM comes with its own extensive documentation and is maintained at GitHub[2]. CLAM and TICCLops are the result of a project in the initial phase of the CLARIN-NL programme, a Dutch initiative in the wider European CLARIN framework. The project TICCLops ran in 2010. The new version of TICClops described here is the result of project @PhilosTEI[3], which now runs in the final phase of the CLARIN-NL programme.

TICCL is a later reincarnation of TISC (Text-Induced Spelling Correction) which was developed as part of the author's PhD work (Reynaert, 2005). TICCL extends some of the ideas explored in TISC to the often graver and sometimes different types of errors present in digital texts as produced by machines, in contrast to texts produced by humans. Human errors are commonly ascribed to mechanical failure as in typing, dubbed 'typos', or to cognitive causes (not knowing, failure to recall, ...) dubbed 'cognitive errors'. In contrast, machines' text digitization errors may have a plethora of causes. Their combined main effect in text digitised by means of e.g. Optical Character Reading (OCR) is nevertheless inaccurate text – even if the system in the final analysis faithfully managed to reproduce the original human typesetter's lapse. For this reason, we think OCR post-correction is an essential step in the process of overall quality enhancement of digital libraries. Also, with more and more diachronical texts becoming available digitally, more and more researchers are interested in further linguistically enriching them. To this end many wish to automatically obtain a modernised version of the texts in order not to have to adapt their synchronic linguistic annotation tools to the diachronic texts. This, too, is a use TICCL may fruitfully be put to.

---

[1]TICCL is now set to be released under GPL v.3. Please see: http://ticclops.uvt.nl

[2]https://github.com/proycon/clam/ Its documentation can also be found at: http:/ilk.uvt.nl/clam

[3]http://axiom.vu.nl/PhilosTEI.html

2 TICCL

In this section we briefly describe the heavy-duty version of TICCL geared at offline production work. We have recently described the separate C++ modules that make up the current TICCL (Reynaert, 2014). TICCL is now meant to be easily adaptable to a new language or language variety. This is achieved by first deriving the alphabet for the language from an appropriate source. To this end we currently recommend the available Aspell dictionaries in their expanded form, if the user has no other lexicon at his disposal. Such an expanded list is converted by the TICCL helper module TICCL-lexstat into a character frequency list. Characters are ranked descendingly according to their observed frequency in the dictionary. One may then decide that some characters do not really belong to the language, i.e. are infrequently present and due to loan words having been incorporated in the lexicon. A good example from the German Aspell dictionary is the character 'ñ', derived from the 7 expanded word forms for the Spanish loan word 'Señor'. By means of a frequency threshold infrequent characters for one's language can be virtually neutralized: they will still be handled by TICCL, but incorporating them as-is would simply enlarge the search space unnecessarily. This is because TICCL will perform an exhaustive lookup of alle possible character combinations up to the Levenshtein or edit limit one specifies. Each additional character retained unnecessarily in the language's alphabet would result in many thousands additional lookups having to be performed. Based on the set of characters retained for the language, TICCL-lexstat next produces the list of all possible character confusions given the chosen Levenshtein distance or LD.

A core element of TICCL, TICCL-indexer, is a purely numerical step and is in large part what allows TICCL to scale to very large corpora sizes. Based on 'anagram hashing' (Reynaert, 2010) it affords fast efficient identification of all typographical near-neighbours for the words types in a corpus. For each anagram value in the character confusion list TICCL-indexer collects the values in the corpus hash that when summed with the particular character confusion list value give a hit on another value in the anagram hash. It thus builds an index to all word pairs displaying all the possible confusions given the LD limit. This means we perform an exhaustive lookup for all possible character confusions regardless of where they occur in the word forms represented by the corpus hash. The output of TICCL-indexer can be reconstructed as a full Spellnet in the terms of (Choudhury et al., 2007), i.e. a full graph of all the word forms in the lexicon and the corpus linked by an edit distance of at most the LD imposed. TICCL-indexer represents the character confusion approach to spelling correction as introduced in (Reynaert, 2010). We describe an equivalent to the focus word approach discussed in the same paper in the next paragraph.

Most books have a vocabulary which is far smaller than that present in an extended lexicon for the particular language. Building the full Spellnet over both resources would therefore be overkill in terms of processing performed, time required and superfluous variant pairs output. We have therefore produced a new implementation which for smaller corpora is far quicker in so far that it searches for variants only for those word types actually present in the text to be corrected. This module is called TICCL-indexerNT. It can be invoked to use several processor threads, i.e. to work in a distributed fashion.

The decision whether to use TICCL-indexer rather than TICCL-indexerNT might be taken on an informed basis by comparing the number of character confusion lookups to be performed given the LD one wants to work to with the number of word types actually present in the corpus to be corrected. The character confusion approach, for an alphabet of 38 characters, amounts to 275,651 character confusion values and therefore lookups given LD 2. Very few single books have this amount of word types. For single book size correction jobs the use of TICCL-indexerNT is therefore indicated. This module is then what is invoked when TICCLops runs.

3 TICCLops

The aim of the TICCLops system is to make TICCL available to researchers whose text correction needs are modest, whose personal computer facilities may perhaps be insufficient to run the full system and whose computer skills are based more on Graphical User Interfaces rather than command-line environments.

TICCL is geared to automatically correct large corpora. Recent evaluations on about 10.000 Dutch books (Reynaert, 2014) have shown that the extra lexical information the system derives from the corpus to be corrected effectively helps it to better perform its task. TICCLops, the TICCL 'online processing system' is however not meant for production work on massive digitized text collections. It is oriented more towards helping users to improve the lexical quality of e.g. a single book for which they have obtained an OCRed version.

The system has been designed to be user-adaptable. This is first and foremost expressed in the facilities it offers to work with different languages. In its simplest form, adapting TICCLops to a new language would involve uploading a lexicon for the language and have the system derive a language specific alphabet from the lexicon. The user has the option of imposing a character frequency threshold. The lexicon might well be e.g. a list of the expanded word forms available for almost 100 languages in open source for the spelling checker Aspell[4].

TICCL is highly modular. It may be halted after each main processing step if one so desires, to be restarted from the point it left off at the user's convenience. Only the very first and last corpus processing steps require FoLiA XML (van Gompel and Reynaert, 2013). The major first processing step is converting the text extracted from FoLiA XML into a corpus frequency list, which simply lists all the word types and their observed frequencies in the corpus. This means that the user has the option of not actually submitting his texts to the online service. This one may well not be able or be inclined to do for e.g. copyright or privacy reasons. In this case it is possible to simply upload a frequency list one has obtained by one's own means. Alternatively, the user may have his texts converted to FoLiA XML. The system has conversion facilities from plain text, Alto and Page XML and hOCR HTML, i.e. the major OCR output formats. If the corpus is in FoLiA XML, the user has the option of performing language classification on it, at the paragraph level. This is performed by FoLiA-langcat, typically before the corpus frequency list is built by the module FoLiA-stats. Given mixed language texts, one then has the option of correcting only the paragraphs in a particular language and to not deal with the others.

The web application actually shields the user from the further processing steps. One may as well log off and just wait to be notified e.g. by email that the process has run. In practice, however, this should not require more than a few minutes given a single book input.

3.1 Running TICCLops

After logging in to the system, see Figure 1, the first thing a user is required to do is to specify a 'project name', i.e. in fact create a repository for his input files and for the system's output files. Next, the users are presented with the main interface page. Here, one is able to upload the input files for one's (OCR post-)correction or transcription project. These can be e.g. OCRed book pages in FoLiA format or the frequency list derived by the users from the corpus they want to have corrected. The users may further upload their own lexicon or opt to use one of the default lexicons available.

Next, the user may specify some system parameters. For all these the most reliable defaults have already been specified. We briefly describe them here. A drop-down list allows the user to specify the language of the input corpus, by default this is Dutch, but most European languages are available. In so far as it is not advisable to let TICCL work on very short words, a limit in lower character length needs next to be specified. For this the default is 6 characters, with lower settings the system may become less precise. The LD to be imposed on the retrieved Correction Candidates or CCs is by default 2. The default number of CCs that will be output at the end of the variant identification and retrieval phase of the correction process is 5 CCs. Optionally this may be set to one, e.g. when the user wants to go for fully-automatic spelling correction (where only the best-first ranked CC is in fact relevant). Alternatively, this may be set to maximally 33 CCs – with a sensible range of in-between values – in case the user intends to present these to human annotators in e.g. a crowd sourcing setting aimed at corpus correction. Please see Figure 2.

Only if the input was FoLiA XML has the user the option of letting TICCL edit his corpus on the basis of the list of ranked CCs produced and output. If this option is activated, TICCL will create copies of the OCR layer paragraph elements and in these replace identified variants with their best-first ranked

[4] `ftp://ftp.gnu.org/gnu/aspell/dict/0index.html`

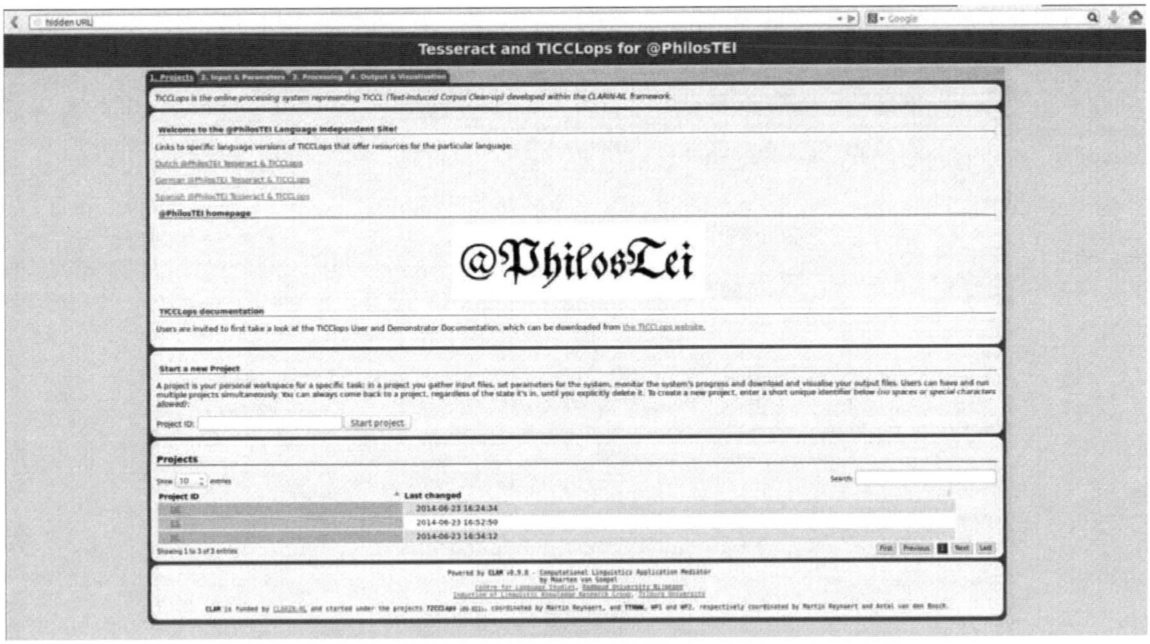

Figure 1: The @PhilosTEI start-up screen offering the user access to the specific language demonstrators, the @PhilosTEI website, the user manual, as well as the option to start a new project or visit one of the previous projects run by the system.

CC. The edited paragraph elements are identified by the attribute 'TICCL'. It will further create string elements for the user-specified number of CCs and insert them. These string elements are identified as correction 'suggestion'.

3.2 Related work

To the best of our knowledge there are no other systems geared at fully automatically performing correction of isolated non-words (whether typos or OCR errors). The open-source spelling checker Aspell can be set to automatically replace supposed errors in the text by its best-first ranked CC. However this is likely to lower the accuracy of the text rather then raise it as is shown by the evaluation results presented in (Reynaert, 2005) for both English and Dutch.

A newly open-sourced system produced by German colleagues is PoCoTo (Post Correction Tool) (Vobl et al., 2014). It is geared at interactive correction of e.g. a digitised book and shares with TICCL that it takes into account information derived from the whole book in the correction process. The correction process adapts to the text to be corrected on the basis of both text and error profiles derived from the text. It seems oriented primarily to the quite possibly very large numbers of systematic errors occurring in the text. TICCL uses as input only the electronic OCRed text version, also aiming for non-systematic errors, which may well account for a large proportion of the actual number of errors in an OCRed text. PoCoTo has an edge in that it also derives useful information from the text images that were used for the actual OCRing. An evaluative comparison of the respective strengths and potential weaknesses of both systems should be enlightening.

4 Conclusion

We have presented an overview of the CLAM-based web service and application TICCLops. This is an online instantiation of Text-Induced Corpus Clean-up not geared at large scale production work on massive digital text collections, but rather at the more modest needs of perhaps individual researchers who want to enhance the quality or modernise the spelling of single manuscripts or digitised books.

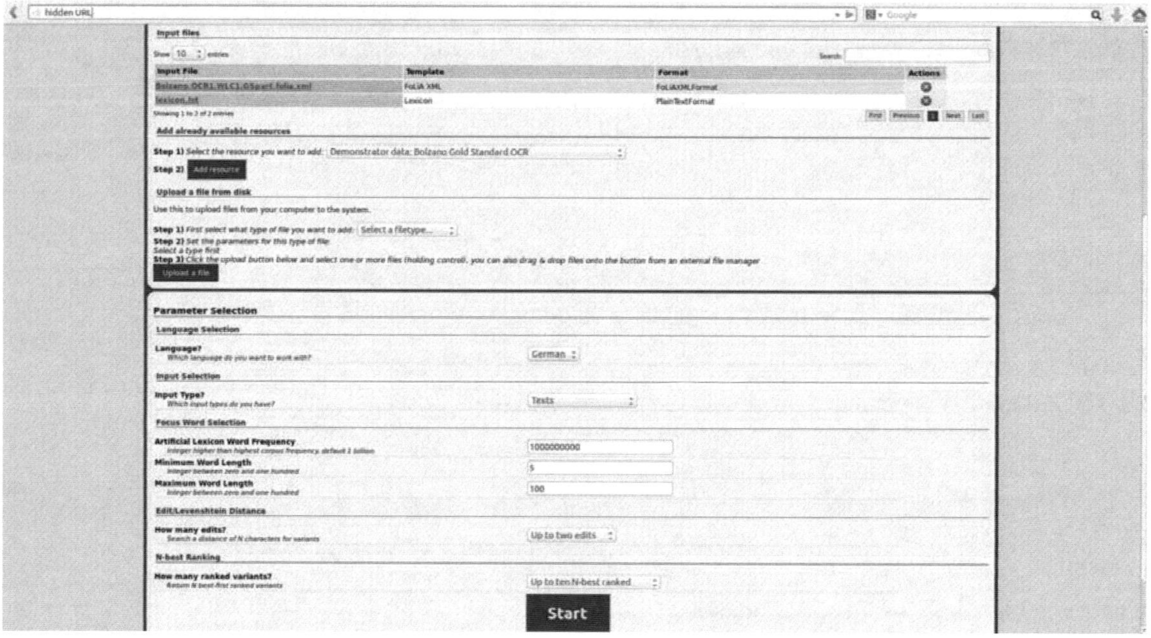

Figure 2: Having started a new project, the user has loaded the necessary input files, set some system parameters or accepted their most sensible defaults, and is now ready to run by a simple mouse click on the START button..

Acknowledgements

The author, Martin Reynaert, and TiCC senior scientific programmer Ko van der Sloot gratefully acknowledge support from CLARIN-NL in projects @PhilosTEI (CLARIN-NL-12-006) and OpenSoNaR (CLARIN-NL-12-013). The author further acknowledges support from NWO in project Nederlab.

References

Monojit Choudhury, Markose Thomas, Animesh Mukherjee, Anupam Basu, and Niloy Ganguly. 2007. How difficult is it to develop a perfect spell-checker? A cross-linguistic analysis through complex network approach. *Proceedings of the second workshop on TextGraphs: Graph-based algorithms for natural language processing*, pages 81–88.

Martin Reynaert. 2005. *Text-induced spelling correction*. Ph.D. thesis, Tilburg University.

Martin Reynaert. 2010. Character confusion versus focus word-based correction of spelling and OCR variants in corpora. *International Journal on Document Analysis and Recognition*, 14:173–187. 10.1007/s10032-010-0133-5.

Martin Reynaert. 2014. Synergy of Nederlab and @PhilosTEI: diachronic and multilingual Text-Induced Corpus Clean-up. In *Proceedings of the Sixth International Language Resources and Evaluation (LREC'14)*, Reykjavik, Iceland. ELRA.

Maarten van Gompel and Martin Reynaert. 2013. FoLiA: A practical XML Format for Linguistic Annotation - a descriptive and comparative study. *Computational Linguistics in the Netherlands Journal*, 3.

Maarten van Gompel and Martin Reynaert. 2014. CLAM: Quickly deploy NLP command-line tools on the web. In *this volume*. COLING 2014.

Thorsten Vobl, Annette Gotscharek, Ulrich Reffle, Christoph Ringlstetter, and Klaus Schulz. 2014. PoCoTo - An Open Source System for Efficient Interactive Postcorrection of OCRed Historical Texts. In *Proceedings of Datech 2014*. ACM.

Trameur: A Framework for Annotated Text Corpora Exploration

Serge Fleury
Sorbonne Nouvelle – Paris 3
SYLED-CLA2T, EA2290
75005 Paris, France
serge.fleury@univ-paris3.fr

Maria Zimina
Paris Diderot – Sorbonne Paris Cité
CLILLAC-ARP, EA 3967
75205 Paris, cedex 13, France
maria.zimina@eila.univ-paris-diderot.fr

Abstract

Corpus resources with complex linguistic annotations are becoming increasingly important in the work of language specialists. They often need to perform extensive corpus research, including Natural Language Processing (NLP), statistical modelling and data visualisation. Our software system, called Trameur, aims at making these analyses possible within a single graphical user interface. It relies upon a specific data modelling framework presented in this paper.

1 Introduction

Treebanks, or parsed text corpora that annotate syntactic or semantic sentence structure, are widely appreciated in language studies. These corpora are getting more and more complex and consist of several layers of annotations. Such multifaceted data collections present many challenges for the development of specific NLP (Natural Language Processing) tools, statistical modelling and data visualisation techniques. In terms of statistical text analysis, most research has been carried out using either unannotated texts or tagged texts, annotated with parts of speech only (Lebart et al., 1998). As for corpora with richer annotations such as clauses, grammatical functions and dependency links, recent research projects have been focused on the development of treebank querying methods with fast search algorithms (Cunningham et al., 2002; Mírovský and Ondruška, 2002; Götze and Dipper, 2006). However, for annotated corpus analysis, it is often necessary to precisely locate different types of linguistic schemes under study, with simultaneous access to multiple corpus layers and their interactions statistics.

To face these challenges, we develop an integrated system for statistical analysis of annotated text data called Trameur (Fleury, 2013a). Trameur manages multiple layers of linguistic annotations and allows statistical exploration of complex linguistic features and embedded dependency relations. Additionally, Trameur incorporates advanced NLP processing and text mapping features. This framework has been developed to allow multiple corpus analyses within a single graphical user interface, accessible to any corpus linguist, without extensive programing skills and knowledge of statistical modelling tools.

2 Corpus research with Trameur

Trameur was successfully tested for monolingual text processing within several research projects in corpus linguistics and discourse analysis (Branca-Rosoff et al., 2012; Née et al., 2012). On-going research demonstrates its potential for processing parallel and comparable text data in distant languages (Zimina and Fleury, 2014).

2.1 Data structures for annotated text processing

Several software packages dedicated to multi-level text processing apply pipeline architecture to support reproducible analyses of text annotations stored in specific formats (Eberle et al., 2012; Eckart et al., 2012). We provide here a description of the specific data structures used by Trameur (text segmentation, partition, statistical tables, etc.) to implement incremental textual resources for treebanks.

In Trameur, a formal representation of text segmentation relies upon two systems of units: text containers and contents (or items) (Fleury, 2013a). Text containers reflect the structure of different corpus parts, while contents represent systems of textual units (lexemes, graphemes, etc.) and their frequency variations which can be examined on a statistical basis. Based on computerized procedures, the systems of containers and contents allow automatic counts in the form of large statistical tables. These tables can be further processed by quantitative methods to detect salient points of statistical distribution in the corpus and build the premises of variation analysis.

Containers and contents are essential elements of double-tracking text segmentation process: (1) Cutting text into containers (parts, textual zones, sections, chapters, paragraphs, sentences, etc.) allows creating a system of text spans that can be further compared on a quantitative basis. (2) Text segmentation into items (or contents) isolates distinct textual units within a text corpus. This text segmentation is closely interconnected with the other two operations: annotation of items (attributing a distinct tag, such as lemma or grammatical category, to each isolated item), and typing of isolated items (judged similar because of their intrinsic nature or on the basis of corpus annotations). Thus, each segmented text is a succession of isolated items that can always be reunited to restore the initial text sequence. Each item is further attached to a given type.

After text segmentation in Trameur, the items are numbered to create a system of coordinates, where each item is spotted by its corresponding sequence number. In Trameur, this system is called Thread (in French: *trame*). The same system of coordinates is used to define and locate text spans (or textual zones) formed by a series of consecutive items between positions x_1 and x_2, or by a certain number of textual zones of this type. The definition of a Thread allows describing various systems of textual zones corresponding to the text containers (corpus parts, sections, chapters, paragraphs, sentences, etc.). The descriptions of the containers are united within a specific data structure called Frame.

The Thread/Frame structure allows defining Selection as any object corresponding to the selected subset of Thread items used in the corpus exploration. There are several types of Selection: (1) Selection corresponding to the contents (certain Thread items, such as occurrences of the same token, lemma, or items corresponding to the same regular expression operated on one or several annotation levels); (2) Selection corresponding to certain containers (textual zones, paragraphs, sections, etc.) composed of contiguous item sequences, selected according to their positions in the text; (3) Selection resulting from highlighting operations performed by a human expert on the basis of some complex criteria, possibly difficult to describe on a formal basis; (4) A textual zone discovered following the results of a statistical calculation; (5) A sub-set of textual units selected following a statistical calculation that highlights a specific distribution of items (contents) within a corpus.

The following demonstration of these principles is based on a data sample from the Rhapsodie corpus of spoken French annotated for prosody and syntax (Gerdes et al., 2012). The data file is available online in tabular form and can be displayed in a spreadsheet.[1] The data set used in this demonstration comes from Rhapsodie v1 micro-syntax annotations. This first release is limited to 13 annotations.[2] The corpus data is structured as follows: all Rhapsodie texts are first identified by codes (column 1). Each text is further divided into separate units (column 2) and segmented into tokens (column 3). The remaining columns display linguistic annotations of the tokens, including microsyntax (rection, dependency and constituancy) (Fleury, 2013b).

Figure 1 shows the Rhapsodie data set transformed from the spreadsheet format into a Trameur base file using regular expressions. The data structure is composed of two parts: (1) a Thread, which is a list of items with position identifiers; (2) a Frame, which is a list of corpus partitions defined on the Thread. Each partition has a name and a list of named constituents identified through their first and

[1] The Rhapsodie corpus is available for download from: `http://www.projet-rhapsodie.fr`

[2] Rhapsodie v3 is the latest online release with micro-syntax, macro-syntax and prosody annotations. It is currently under study in a number of on-going research projects that will be revealed in forthcoming publications.

last token positions on the Thread. Thus, each annotated token from the Rhapsodie corpus becomes an item identified by its position on the Thread.

Dependency relations among items are annotated as follows: RELATION(TARGET), where: RELATION is a character string corresponding to the name of the relation; TARGET is a numerical value of the position identifier on the Thread (see Figure 1). All linguistic annotations from the Rhapsodie sample file are preserved in the Trameur base file. These annotations can be displayed and edited in the graphical user interface (see Figure 2): a-00001:Token, a-00002 Lemma, a-00003 P.O.S, a-00004 Mode, a-00005 Tense, a-00006 Person, a-00007 Number, a-00008 Gender, a-00009 Type_rection(Gov_rection), a-00010 Type_para(Gov_para), a-00011 Type_inher(Gov_inher), a-00012 Type_junc(Gov_junc), a-00013 Type_junc-inher(Gov_junc-inher).


```
<item type="delim" pos="46"><f> </f><c>BLANK</c><l>BLANK</l><a>-</a><a>-</a><a>-</a><a>-</a><a>-</a><a>-</a><a>-</a><a>-</a><a>-</a><a>-</a></item>
<item type="forme" pos="47"><f>lance</f><c>B_V</c><l>lancer</l><a>indicative</a><a>present</a><a>3</a><a>sg</a><a>-</a><a>ROOT</a><a>-</a><a>-</a><a>-</a><a>-
</a></item>
<item type="delim" pos="48"><f> </f><c>BLANK</c><l>BLANK</l><a>-</a><a>-</a><a>-</a><a>-</a><a>-</a><a>-</a><a>-</a><a>-</a><a>-</a><a>-</a></item>
<item type="forme" pos="49"><f>un</f><c>B_D</c><l>un</l><a>-</a><a>-</a><a>-</a><a>sg</a><a>masc</a><a>DEP(51)</a><a>-</a><a>-</a><a>-</a><a>-</a></item>
<item type="delim" pos="50"><f> </f><c>BLANK</c><l>BLANK</l><a>-</a><a>-</a><a>-</a><a>-</a><a>-</a><a>-</a><a>-</a><a>-</a><a>-</a><a>-</a></item>
<item type="forme" pos="51"><f>appel</f><c>B_N</c><l>appel</l><a>-</a><a>-</a><a>-</a><a>sg</a><a>masc</a><a>OBJ(47)</a><a>-</a><a>-</a><a>-</a><a>-</a></item>
<item type="delim" pos="52"><f> </f><c>BLANK</c><l>BLANK</l><a>-</a><a>-</a><a>-</a><a>-</a><a>-</a><a>-</a><a>-</a><a>-</a><a>-</a><a>-</a></item>   Thread

<p n="D2013 " d="58359" f="59730" nd="85" nf="86"/>
<p n="M2006 " d="1" f="2086" nd="1" nf="2"/>
<p n="M0015 " d="40347" f="40514" nd="59" nf="60"/>
<p n="M0022 " d="60079" f="60554" nd="89" nf="90"/>
<p n="M0010 " d="33229" f="33372" nd="41" nf="42"/>   Frame
```


Figure 1: Rhapsodie data in a Trameur base file.

2.2 Exploration of dependency relations

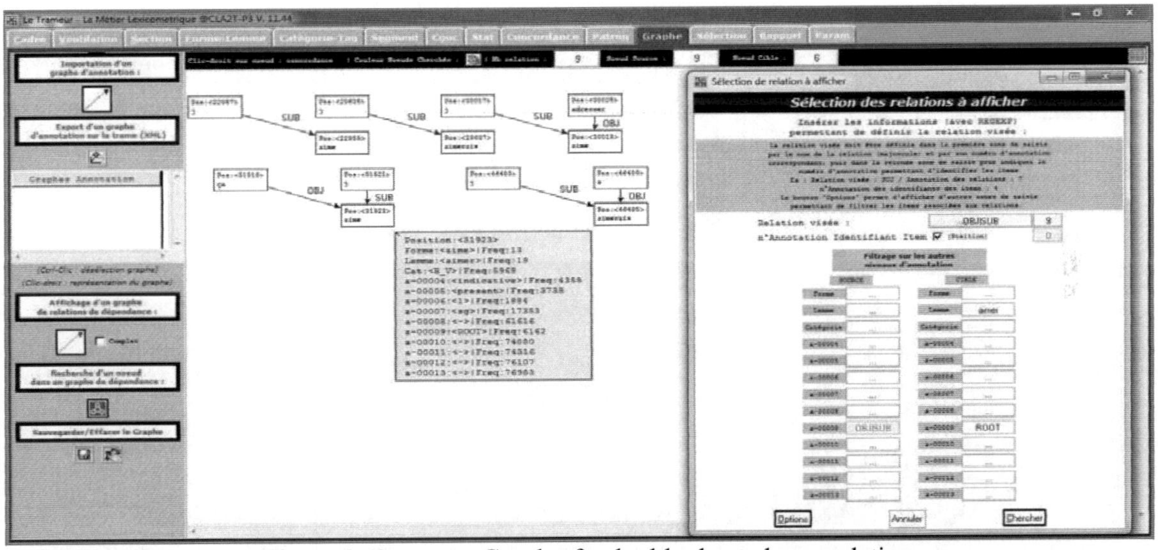

Figure 2: Trameur. Graph of a double dependency relation.

Dependency relations emerging from linguistic annotations can be explored, filtered and displayed using dependency graphs, text maps with context return, concordances, co-occurrence statistics, etc. All these features with related screenshots are presented in the on-line user guide.[3]

Figure 2 displays a sample graph of a double dependency relation from Rhapsodie. It is set by the regular expression `OBJ|SUB` (OBJ or SUB), where the relation target for the lemma is "aimer" and the annotation n°9 Type_rection(Gov_rection) is ROOT. For each item in context, a pop-up window displays all annotation levels with corresponding tags (or "no tag" signs <—>) and their frequencies (Freq) on a given annotation level.

Figure 3 displays the nodes of the same graph in a concordance window. A selection tool is used to highlight annotation n°3 in concordance lines (value = `B_adv`).

[3] Trameur (user guide): `http://www.tal.univ-paris3.fr/trameur/leMetierLexicometrique.htm`

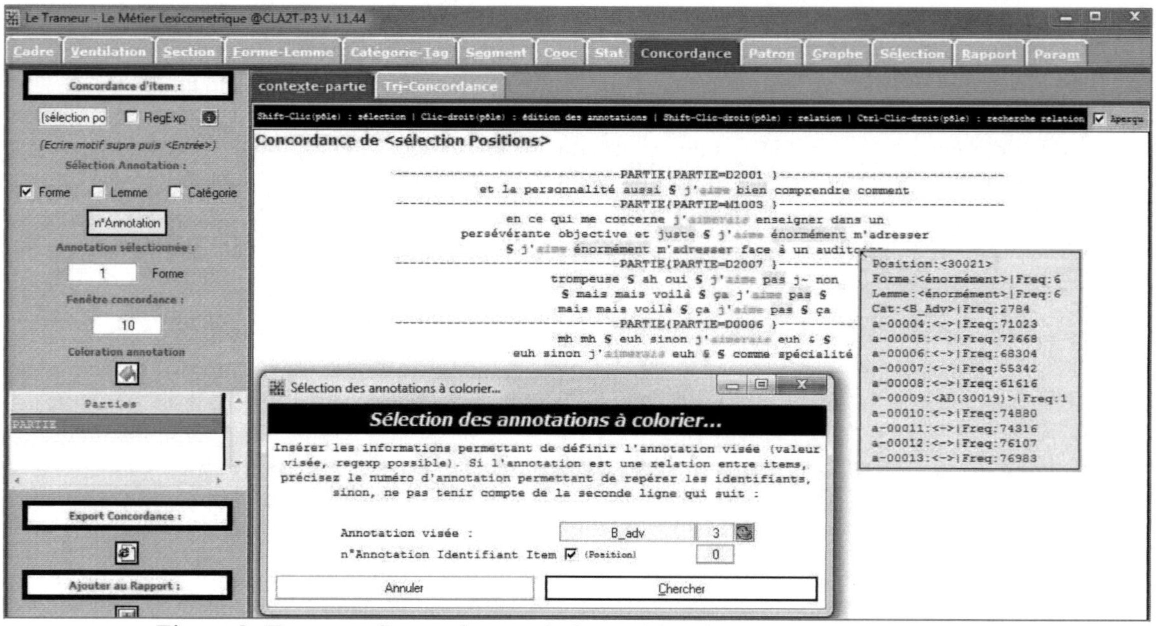

Figure 3: Trameur. Concordance window with selected dependency relations.

Figure 4 displays a co-occurrence graph for the lemma “vouloir” constrained by the dependency RELATION set by the regular expression `SUB|AD` (SUB or AD).

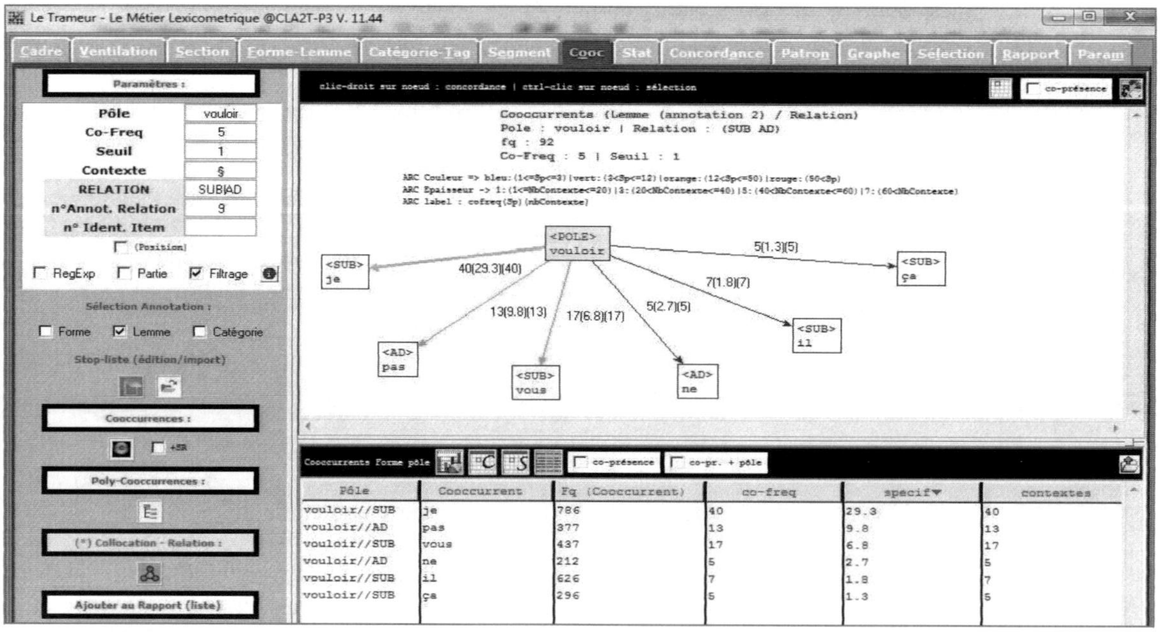

Figure 4: Trameur. Co-occurrence graph constrained by selected dependency relations.

3 Conclusion

Trameur is a tool for exploration of complex multi-layer linguistic corpora with different annotations. It is built upon a Thread/Frame data model using XML. The software is distributed with a graphical user interface. A reference package for Windows is available for free download from the official website: `http://www.tal.univ-paris3.fr/trameur`.

Several other systems have been already developed for processing annotated corpora, for example: PDT2.0[4], GATE[5], ANNIS[6], Macaon[7]. However, the novelty of Trameur consists in expanding a multi-layered data model to all stages of corpus exploration, including text mapping features and statistical analysis of dependency relations within a single graphical user interface.

Following this integrated approach, Trameur can be used, for example, to build complex linguistic units, analyse their dependency relations and reveal their characteristic attractions using text statistics.

In Trameur, quantitative analyses are applied to textual resources, built upon a Thread and an evolutionary Frame. These analyses can progressively enrich these resources with new text divisions or annotations, without deleting previous information. Following this approach, it becomes possible to implement incremental textual resources for treebanks.

It is the use of the Thread/Frame data model implemented in Trameur that allows different combinations of analyses when processing multifaceted linguistic annotations. We believe that this evolutionary framework offers new perspectives for corpus research.

References

Sonia Branca-Rosoff, Serge Fleury, Florence Lefeuvre and Mat Pires. 2012. *Discours sur la ville. Corpus de Français Parlé Parisien des années 2000 (CFPP 2000). Sorbonne nouvelle – Paris 3*. Online publication: `http://cfpp2000.univ-paris3.fr/CFPP2000.pdf`

Hamish Cunningham, Diana Maynard, Kalina Bontcheva and Valentin Tablan. 2002. *GATE: A Framework and Graphical Development Environment for Robust NLP Tools and Applications. Proceedings of the 40th Anniversary Meeting of the Association for Computational Linguistics (ACL'02)*. Philadelphia, July 2002.

Kurt Eberle, Kerstin Eckart, Ulrich Heid and Boris Haselbach, 2012. *A Tool/Database Interface for Multi-Level Analyses. Proceedings of the eighth conference on International Language Resources and Evaluation (LREC 2012)*. Istanbul (Turkey), May 2012.

Kerstin Eckart, Arndt Riester and Katrin Schweitzer, 2012. *A Discourse Information Radio News Database for Linguistic Analysis. Linked Data in Linguistics*. Springer.

Serge Fleury. 2013a. *Le Trameur. Propositions de description et d'implémentation des objets textométriques. Sorbonne nouvelle – Paris 3*. Online publication: `http://www.tal.univ-paris3.fr/trameur/trameur-propositions-definitions-objets-textometriques.pdf`

Serge Fleury. 2013b. *Annotations Rhapsodie pour le Trameur. Sorbonne nouvelle – Paris 3*. Online publication: `http://www.tal.univ-paris3.fr/trameur/bases/rhapsodie2trameur.pdf` (v1 base) `http://www.tal.univ-paris3.fr/trameur/bases/rhapsodie2trameur-v3.pdf` (v3 base)

Kim Gerdes, Sylvain Kahane, Anne Lacheret, Arthur Truong and Paola Pietrandrea. 2012. *Intonosyntactic data structures: The Rhapsodie treebank of spoken French. Proceedings of the Linguistic Annotation Workshop, COLING 2012*. Jeju, Republic of Korea, July 2012.

Michael Götze and Stefanie Dipper. 2006. *ANNIS: Complex Multilevel Annotations in a Linguistic Database. Proceedings of the 5th Workshop on NLP and XML: Multi-Dimensional Markup in Natural Language Processing (NLPXML-2006)*. Trento (Italy), April 2006.

Ludvic Lebart, André Salem and Lisette Barry. 1998. *Exploring Textual Data*. Kluwer Academic Publishers.

Jiří Mírovský and Roman Ondruška. 2002. *NetGraph System: Searching through the Prague Dependency Treebank. Prague Bulletin of Mathematical Linguistics*, 77, MFF UK, Prague, Czech Republic, Prague, 2002.

Emilie Née, Erin MacMurray and Serge Fleury. 2012. *Textometric Explorations of Writing Processes: A Discursive and Genetic Approach to the Study of Drafts. Journées internationales d'Analyse statistique des Données Textuelles (JADT 2012)*. Liège (Belgium), June 2012.

Maria Zimina and Serge Fleury. 2014. *Approche systémique de la résonance textuelle multilingue. Journées internationales d'Analyse statistique des Données Textuelles (JADT 2014)*. Paris, June 2014.

[4] PDT (The Prague Dependency Treebank 2.0): `ufal.mff.cuni.cz/pdt2.0/`

[5] GATE (General Architecture for Text Engineering): `http://gate.ac.uk/gate/`

[6] ANNIS (ANNotation of Information Structure): `http://www.sfb632.uni-potsdam.de/annis/`

[7] MACAON Project: `http://macaon.lif.univ-mrs.fr`

TweetGenie: Development, Evaluation, and Lessons Learned

Dong Nguyen[1] **Dolf Trieschnigg**[1] **Theo Meder**[2]
(1) Human Media Interaction, University of Twente, Enschede, The Netherlands
(2) Meertens Institute, Amsterdam, The Netherlands
{d.nguyen,d.trieschnigg}@utwente.nl, theo.meder@meertens.knaw.nl

Abstract

TweetGenie is an online demo that infers the gender and age of Twitter users based on their tweets. TweetGenie was able to attract thousands of visitors. We collected data by asking feedback from visitors and launching an online game. In this paper, we describe the development of TweetGenie and evaluate the demo based on the received feedback and manual annotation. We also reflect on practical lessons learned from launching a demo for the general public.

1 Introduction

The language use of speakers is related to variables such as the speaker's gender and age (Eckert, 1997; Eckert and McConnell-Ginet, 2013). Systems that can automatically predict such variables have been receiving increasing attention. They enable more fine-grained analyses of trends by profiling the involved users. They also support sociolinguistics research by shedding light on the link between variables such as gender and age, and the language use of speakers.

In this paper, we describe TweetGenie (www.tweetgenie.nl), a website that allows visitors to enter public Dutch Twitter accounts. The system predicts gender and age of the users behind the entered accounts based on the 200 most recent tweets. Due to press attention from various media outlets, we were able to attract a large number of visitors. In comparison to previous gender and age prediction systems that have been evaluated with carefully constructed datasets, we are the first to evaluate the performance of such a system 'in the wild'.

We first discuss the development of TweetGenie (Section 2). Next, we study the launch and TweetGenie's spread through social media, based on log data of the first week after the launch (Section 3). We then evaluate TweetGenie based on collected feedback (Section 4) and reflect on practical issues we encountered while launching an online demo for the general public (Section 5). We end with a conclusion (Section 6).

2 TweetGenie

In this section we describe the development and setup of TweetGenie.

Goals The original research (Nguyen et al., 2013) was carried out to support analyses of trends and to study sociolinguistic aspects of language use. By launching a public demo of this research, we aimed to 1) test the system on a large-scale 'in the wild' 2) collect data, and 3) demo the project to interested people. Unlike most demos of NLP research, the target audience of this demo was the '*general public*'. For example, we aimed for a simple and attractive interface, and released a press announcement to reach a large audience.

Model TweetGenie was developed based on the research and dataset described in (Nguyen et al., 2013) and predicts the gender and age of Dutch Twitter users based on the 200 most recent tweets. First, unigrams and bigrams are extracted from the tweets using the tokenization tool by O'Connor et al. (2010). This feature representation was chosen, because it is fast and unigrams have shown to perform already very well (Nguyen et al., 2013). We then trained logistic (for gender prediction) and linear (for age prediction) regression models (Pedregosa et al., 2011) with L2 regularization.

Setup TweetGenie is available at www.tweetgenie.nl. After a visitor enters a public Twitter account, a results page is shown (see Figure 1 for a screenshot). The results page shows the predicted age (in years), the gender, and a gender 'score' indicating how strong the prediction was (based on $\mathbf{x}^\top\boldsymbol{\beta}$ with $\mathbf{x}$ being the features and $\boldsymbol{\beta}$ the estimated parameters). In addition, an option is available to share their results page on Twitter.

An overview of the components is shown in Figure 3. The first webserver hosts the frontend. A MySQL database is used to keep track of the progress of each prediction, and to store logs and feedback received by users. A second webserver is used to retrieve the data from Twitter and perform the predictions.

Feedback To collect data and improve the system, users are encouraged to provide feedback on the predictions. On the page with the automatic prediction (Figure 1), users have the option to enter the correct age and confirm whether the gender prediction was correct.

Online Game We also developed an online game to study how humans perform on the task. Figure 2 shows a screenshot of the interface. Players are shown 20-40 tweets per Twitter user and have to guess the gender and age of the Twitter users behind the tweets. After each guess, players receive feedback in various ways (the correct gender and age, the predictions by the automatic system, and the average guesses by other players). The data collected proved to be valuable: using the data, we reflected on the task of inferring gender and age from tweets and the limitations of current systems (Nguyen et al., 2014).

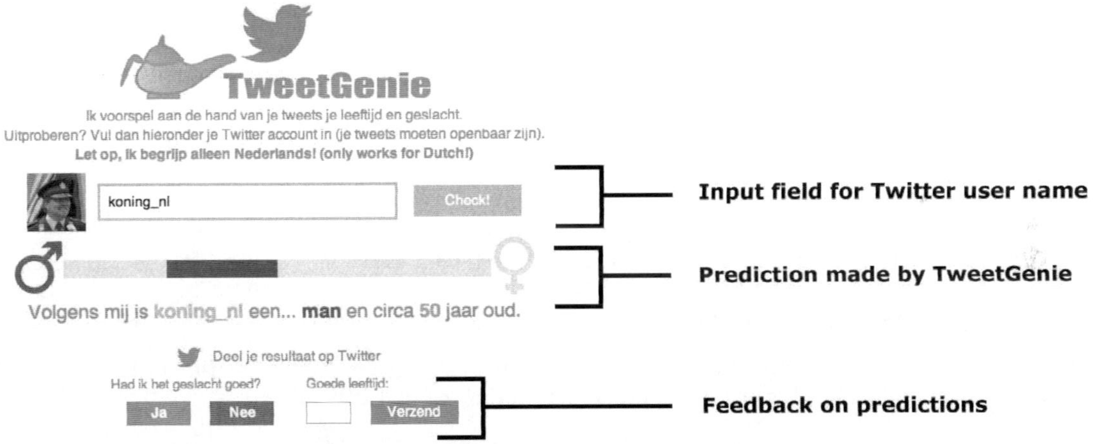

Figure 1: Screenshot prediction interface

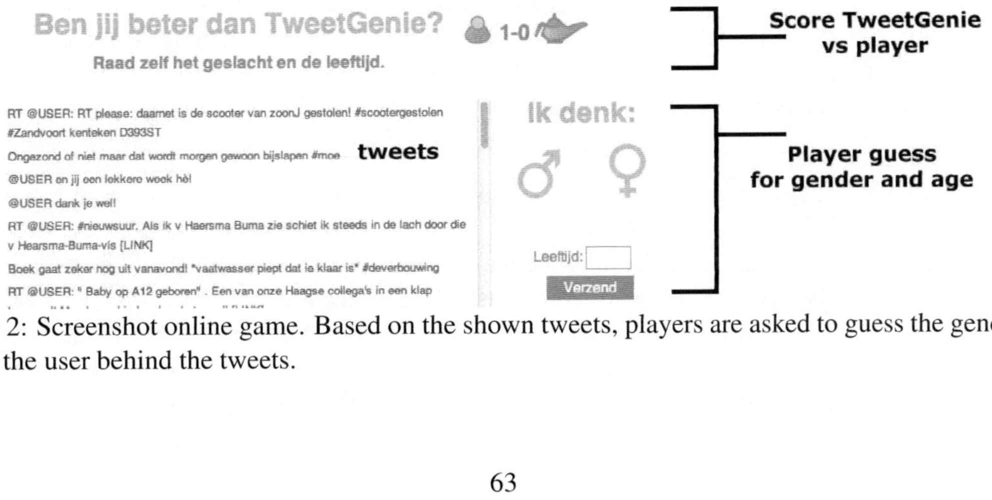

Figure 2: Screenshot online game. Based on the shown tweets, players are asked to guess the gender and age of the user behind the tweets.

3 Launching TweetGenie

TweetGenie was launched on May 13, 2013 at around 11.30 AM. To reach a large audience, a press statement was released and messages were posted on social media networks. In this section, we analyze the data in the first week after the launch.

Figure 3 shows the number of entered Twitter users and the number of tweets mentioning TweetGenie in the first week after the launch. The number of tweets and the number of users entered follow similar trends. We observe a high peak in the beginning, but it also rapidly decreases over time. The system was asked to make a prediction 87,818 times and 9,291 tweets were posted with the word 'TweetGenie'. 1,931 of these tweets were created using the tweet sharing function of TweetGenie. The observed sentiment was mostly positive. If TweetGenie made an incorrect prediction, most people joked about it (e.g. '**grin* I just became 13 years younger without plastic chirurgy #tweetgenie*'). The game was played often as well, a guess was made 31,414 times.

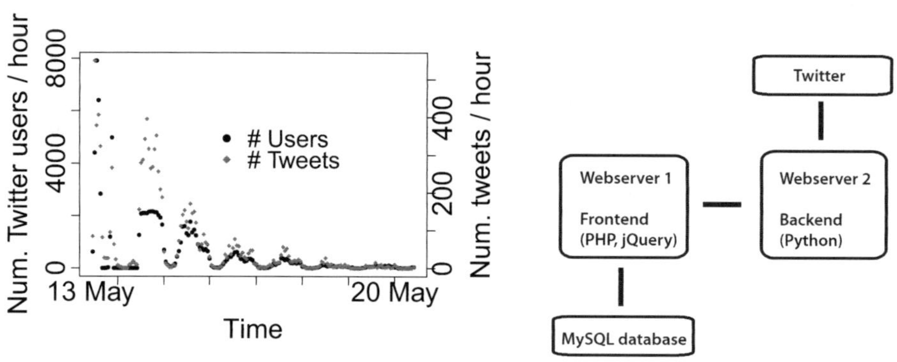

(a) Entered users and tweets per hour (b) Architecture

Figure 3: Overview of the system

4 Evaluation

We evaluate the system in two ways, 1) using the feedback from users, and 2) using manual annotation.

4.1 Evaluation Based on User Feedback

Visitors were encouraged to give feedback on the predictions of TweetGenie. In the first week, we received feedback on the gender of 16,563 users and on the age of 17,034 users.

Reliability We randomly sampled 150 Twitter users for which we received feedback on both the gender and age. We checked the feedback of these users by visiting their Twitter profiles. If the feedback seemed plausible based on the profile, we assumed the feedback was correct (i.e. we did not visit any other social media profiles to find the exact age). The results are shown in Table 1. We find that 90% of the feedback appears to be correct. Only a small fraction (4%) of the feedback was incorrect, this could be deliberate or due to sloppiness. The remaining feedback was on Twitter accounts of non-Dutch users (e.g. English, German, French), or accounts that did not represent a person (e.g. a sports team, animal, multiple persons).

Accuracy We calculate the performance based on the 135 users for who we received correct feedback. We find that the users who gave feedback are *not* representative of the general Dutch Twitter population (Nguyen et al., 2013). The users are older than average (the age distribution is shown in Figure 4). There are more older males, and more younger females using Twitter in the Netherlands (Nguyen et al., 2013), and as a consequence the number of males (60.7%) is higher than the number of females (39.3%).

Based on this dataset, we find that the accuracy of the gender predictions was 94%. The Mean Absolute Error (MAE) for the age predictions is 6.1 years, which is higher than reported in (Nguyen et al., 2013).

Feedback	Frequency	Percentage
Correct	135	90%
Incorrect	6	4%
Not a Dutch account	5	3.33%
Not a person	4	2.67%

Table 1: Statistics feedback reliability

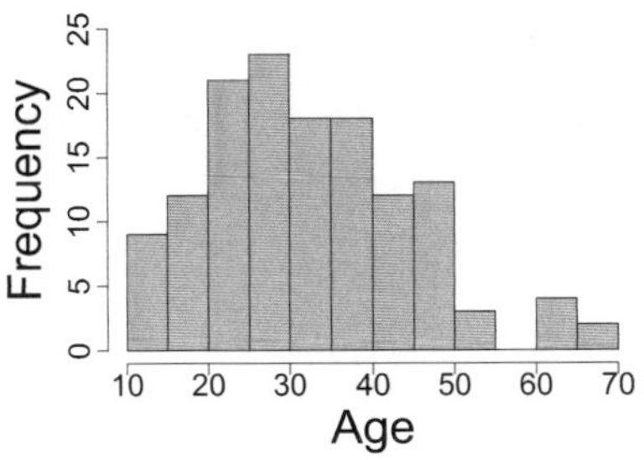

Figure 4: Age distribution feedback

However, this can be explained by the observation that relatively many older Twitter users give feedback, and as discussed in (Nguyen et al., 2013), automatic age predictions for older Twitter users are less accurate.

4.2 Evaluation Based on Manual Annotation

We also evaluated the system by manually annotating 50 users that were randomly sampled from the entered users in the logs. We did not include accounts that were not Dutch or did not represent individual persons. If feedback was available for a Twitter user, we used the provided feedback (after a manual check). Otherwise, we manually annotated the gender and age using all available information (e.g. social media profiles, websites). The gender was correctly predicted for 82% of the users, which is lower than measured in the evaluation based on the user feedback (Section 4.1). The Mean Absolute Error (MAE) is 6.18 years, which is in line with the observed MAE based on the user feedback.

Our analyses confirm that users for who feedback was available are *not* representative of all users who were entered in the system. Of the sampled 50 entered users, the fraction of males and females is almost equal (52% and 48%) compared to 60.7% and 30.9% in Section 4.1. The number of users who were less than 20 years old (15) is similar to the number of users in the range of > 20 and ≤ 30 years (17), while in Section 4.1 the fraction of users below 20 years is smaller. Thus, less feedback was received for younger Twitter users.

In line with the analysis in Section 4.1, we find that relatively many older Twitter users were entered into TweetGenie compared to a more representative set of Dutch Twitter users (Nguyen et al., 2013).

5 Lessons Learned

We learned many lessons from launching a demo for the general public.

1) *Test all components of the demo.* While developing the system, we focused mostly on ensuring that the backend would be able to handle the number of visitors. However, after the demo went online, problems arose at the frontend due to the visitor load. This was solved by only allowing a fixed number of visitors at the same time. We also did not test the interface for non-Dutch visitors. Only later we found out that the automatically translated version contained serious errors: international visitors were misled that the model worked on English tweets.

2) *The distribution of users trying out the demo might not correspond to the distribution in the development dataset.* While we extensively evaluated the system on a carefully constructed, representative dataset (Nguyen et al., 2013), the numbers in this paper's evaluation are lower. Users who were entered into the system were not representative of the Dutch Twitter population: relatively more older Twitter users were entered in the system, leading to more errors in the automic age prediction.

3) *A demo is a good opportunity to collect data.* Many visitors were willing to provide feedback or participated in the online game. Data collected through the online game has been used to study the task of inferring gender and age in more depth (Nguyen et al., 2014). Manual analysis of the feedback in this paper revealed that almost all of the feedback appears to be genuine. Further research is needed to study how the feedback on the automatic predictions can be used to improve the prediction models.

6 Conclusion

In this paper we discussed TweetGenie, an online system that infers the gender and age of Twitter users based on tweets alone. We collected much feedback from the users, but also found that users who provided feedback are not representative of all the entered users. We demonstrated that besides being a valuable tool for user profiling, TweetGenie also appeals to the general public.

Acknowledgements

This research was supported by the Royal Netherlands Academy of Arts and Sciences (KNAW) and the Netherlands Organization for Scientific Research (NWO), grants IB/MP/2955 (TINPOT) and 640.005.002 (FACT).

References

P. Eckert and S. McConnell-Ginet. 2013. *Language and gender.* Cambridge University Press.

P. Eckert. 1997. *Age as a sociolinguistic variable.* The handbook of sociolinguistics. Blackwell Publishers.

D. Nguyen, R. Gravel, D. Trieschnigg, and T. Meder. 2013. "How old do you think I am?": A study of language and age in Twitter. In *Proceedings of ICWSM 2013.*

D. Nguyen, D. Trieschnigg, A. S. Doğruöz, R. Gravel, M. Theune, T. Meder, and F.M.G. de Jong. 2014. Why gender and age prediction from tweets is hard: Lessons from a crowdsourcing experiment. In *Proceedings of COLING 2014.*

B. O'Connor, M. Krieger, and D. Ahn. 2010. TweetMotif: exploratory search and topic summarization for Twitter. In *Proceedings of ICWSM 2010.*

F. Pedregosa, G. Varoquaux, A. Gramfort, V. Michel, B. Thirion, O. Grisel, M. Blondel, P. Prettenhofer, R. Weiss, V. Dubourg, J. Vanderplas, A. Passos, D. Cournapeau, M. Brucher, M. Perrot, and E. Duchesnay. 2011. Scikit-learn: Machine learning in Python. *Journal of Machine Learning Research*, 12:2825–2830.

A Sentence Judgment System for Grammatical Error Detection

Lung-Hao Lee [1,2], Liang-Chih Yu[3,4], Kuei-Ching Lee[1,2],
Yuen-Hsien Tseng[1], Li-Ping Chang[5], Hsin-Hsi Chen[2]
[1]Information Technology Center, National Taiwan Normal University
[2]Dept. of Computer Science and Information Engineering, National Taiwan University
[3]Dept. of Information Management, Yuen Ze University
[4]Innovation Center for Big Data and Digital Convergence, Yuen Ze University
[5]Mandarin Training Center, National Taiwan Normal University
lcyu@saturn.yzu.edu.tw, {lhlee, johnlee, lchang, samtseng}@ntnu.edu.tw, hhchen@ntu.edu.tw

Abstract

This study develops a sentence judgment system using both rule-based and n-gram statistical methods to detect grammatical errors in Chinese sentences. The rule-based method provides 142 rules developed by linguistic experts to identify potential rule violations in input sentences. The n-gram statistical method relies on the n-gram scores of both correct and incorrect training sentences to determine the correctness of the input sentences, providing learners with improved understanding of linguistic rules and n-gram frequencies.

1 Introduction

China's growing global influence has prompted a surge of interest in learning Chinese as a foreign language (CFL), and this trend is expected to continue. This has driven an increase in demand for automated IT-based tools designed to assist CFL learners in mastering the language, including so-called MOOCs (Massive Open Online Courses) which allows huge numbers of learners to simultaneously access instructional opportunities and resources. This, in turn, has driven demand for automatic proofreading techniques to help instructors review and respond to the large volume of assignments and tests submitted by enrolled learners.

However, whereas many computer-assisted learning tools have been developed for use by students of English as a Foreign Language (EFL), support for CFL learners is relatively sparse, especially in terms of tools designed to automatically detect and correct Chinese grammatical errors. For example, while Microsoft Word has integrated robust English spelling and grammar checking functions for years, such tools for Chinese are still quite primitive. In contrast to the plethora of research related to EFL learning, relatively few studies have focused on grammar checking for CFL learners. Wu et al. (2010) proposed relative position and parse template language models to detect Chinese errors written by US learner. Yu and Chen (2012) proposed a classifier to detect word-ordering errors in Chinese sentences from the HSK dynamic composition corpus. Chang et al. (2012) proposed a penalized probabilistic First-Order Inductive Learning (pFOIL) algorithm for error diagnosis. In summary, although there are many approaches and tools to help EFL learners, the research problem described above for CFL learning is still under-explored. In addition, no common platform is available to compare different approaches and to promote the study of this important issue.

This study develops a sentence judgment system using both rule-based and *n*-gram statistical methods to detect grammatical errors in sentences written by CFL learners. Learners can input Chinese sentences into the proposed system to check for possible grammatical errors. The rule-based method uses a set of rules developed by linguistic experts to identify potential rule violations in input sentences.

The *n*-gram statistical method relies on the *n*-gram scores of both correct and incorrect training sentences to determine the correctness of the input sentences. The system helps learners develop an improved understanding of both linguistic rules and *n*-gram frequencies. In addition, the proposed system can also be incorporated into online CFL MOOC platforms to help assess and/or score the numbers of assignments and tests.

2 A Sentence Judgement System

Figure 1 shows the user interface of the sentence judgment system, which can be accessed at http://sjf.itc.ntnu.edu.tw/demo/. Learners can submit single or multiple sentences through the textbox shown in the upper part of Fig. 1. Each input sentence is pre-processed for word segmentation and part-of-speech tagging, and then passed to both the rule-based and *n*-gram statistical methods for grammatical error detection. Finally, an input sentence will be marked as incorrect (⊗) if both methods detect grammatical errors. Otherwise, it will be marked as correct (✓). In addition to the decision information, the explanation of the matched rules and *n*-gram frequencies are also presented for reference, as shown in the bottom part of Fig. 1. For instance, the following sentence is marked as incorrect:

我 從 這裡 走 往 北
(I from here go towads north.)

The rule-based method shows a rule violation is detected and explains that a preposition (e.g., "往" (towards)) cannot be used after a verb (e.g., "走" (go)). The *n*-gram frequencies also shows that the the frequency of the bigram "走 往" (go towards) is relative low. The following subsections describe in detail the pre-processing, rule-based method, and *n*-gram statistical method.

2.1 Pre-processing

Chinese is written without word boundaries. As a result, prior to the implementation of most Natural Language Processing (NLP) tasks, texts must undergo automatic word segmentation. Automatic Chinese word segmenters are generally trained by an input lexicon and probability models. However, it usually suffers from the unknown word (i.e., the out-of-vocabulary, or OOV) problem. In this study, a corpus-based learning method is used to merge unknown words to tackle the OOV problem (Chen and Ma, 2002). This is followed by a reliable and cost-effective POS-tagging method to label the segmented words with parts-of-speech (Tsai and Chen, 2004). For example, take the Chinese sentence "歐巴馬是美國總統" (Obama is the president of the USA). It was segmented and tagged in the form of "POS:Word" sequence shown as follows: Nb:歐巴馬 SHI:是 Nc:美國 Na:總統. Among these words, the translation of a foreign proper name "歐巴馬" (Obama) is not likely to be included in a lexicon and therefore is extracted by the unknown word detection mechanism. In this case, the special POS tag 'SHI' is a tag to represent the be-verb "是".

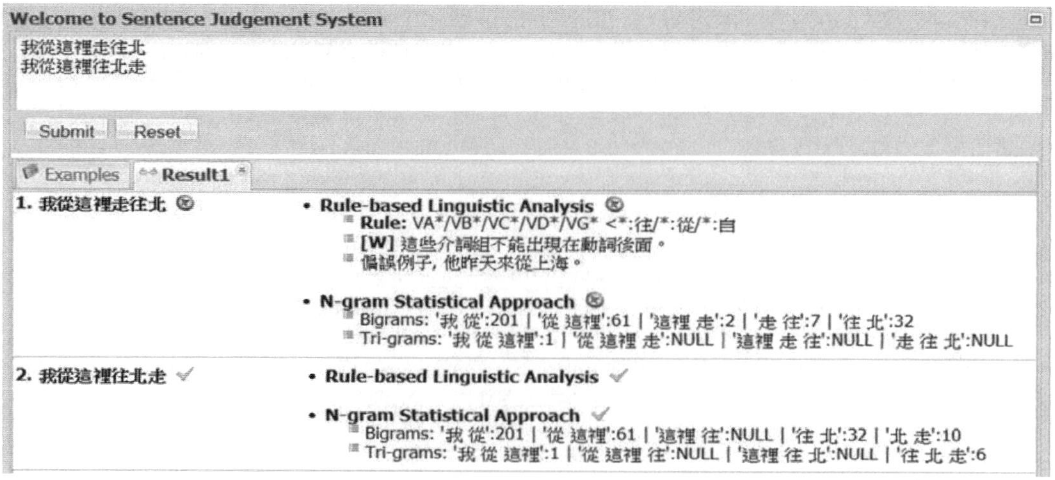

Figure 1. Screenshot of the sentence judgement system.

2.2 Rule-based Linguistic Analysis

Several symbols are used to represent the syntactic rules to facilitate the detection of errors embedded in Chinese sentences written by CFL learners: (1) "*" is a wild card, with "Nh*" denoting all subordinate tags of "Nh", *e.g.*, "Nhaa," "Nhab," "Nhac," "Nhb," and "Nhc". (2) "-" means an exclusion from the previous representation, with "N*-Nab-Nbc" indicating that the corresponding word should be any noun (N*) excluding countable entity nouns (Nab) and surnames (Nbc). (3) "/" means an alternative (i.e., "or"), where the expression "一些/這些/那些" (some/these/those) indicates that one of these three words satisfies the rule. (4) The rule mx{W1 W2} denotes the mutual exclusivity of the two words W1 and W2. (5) "<" denotes the follow-by condition, where the expression "Nhb < Nep" means the POS-tag "Nep" follows the tag "Nhb" that can exist several words ahead of the "Nep".

Using such rule symbols, we manually constructed syntactic rules to cover errors that frequently occur in sentences written by CFL learners. We adopted the "Analysis of 900 Common Erroneous Samples of Chinese Sentences" (Cheng, 1997) as the development set to handcraft the linguistic rules with syntactic information. If an input sentence satisfies any syntactic rule, the system will report the input as suspected of containing grammatical errors, creating a useful tool for autonomous CFL learners.

2.3 N-gram Statistical Analysis

Language modeling approaches to grammatical error detection are usually based on a score (log probability) output by an *n*-gram model trained on a large corpus. A sentence with grammatical errors usually has a low *n*-gram score. However, choosing an appropriate threshold to determine whether a sentence is correct is still a nontrivial task. Therefore, this study proposes the use of *n*-gram scores of correct and incorrect sentences to build the respective correct and incorrect statistical models for grammatical error detection. That is, a given sentence is denoted as incorrect (i.e., having grammatical errors) if its probability score output by the statistical model of incorrect sentences (i.e., the incorrect model) is greater than that of correct sentences (i.e., the correct model).

To build the incorrect and correct statistical models, a total of 19,080 sentences with grammatical errors were extracted from the HSK dynamic composition corpus. These sentences were then manually corrected. An *n*-gram (n= 2 and 3) language model was then built from the Sinica corpus released by the Association for Computational Linguistics and Chinese Language Processing (ACLCLP) using the SRILM toolkit (Stolcke, 2002). The trained language model was used to assign an *n*–gram score for each correct and incorrect sentence, which were then used to build the respective correct and incorrect models based on a normal probability density function (Manning and Schütze, 1999). Both models can then be used to evaluate each test sentence by transforming its *n*-gram score into a probability score to determine whether the sentence is correct or not.

3 Performance Evaluation

The test set included 880 sentences with grammatical errors generated by CSL learners in the NCKU Chinese Language Center, and the corresponding 880 manually corrected sentences. For the rule-based approach, a total of 142 rules were developed to identify incorrect sentences. For the n-gram statistical approach, both bi-gram and tri-gram language models were used for the correct and incorrect statistical models. In addition to precision, recall, and F1, the false positive rate (FPR) was defined as the number of correct sentences incorrectly identified as incorrect sentences divided by the total number of correct sentences in the test set.

Table 1 shows the comparative results of the rule-based and *n*-gram statistical approaches to grammatical error detection. The results show that the rule-based approach achieved high precision, low recall and low FPR. Conversely, the *n*-gram-based approach yielded low precision, high recall and high FPR. In addition, the tri-gram model outperformed the bi-gram model for all metrics. Given the different results yielded by the rule-based and *n*-gram statistical approaches, we present different combinations of these two methods for comparison. The "OR" combination means that a given sentence is identified as incorrect by only one of the methods, while the "AND" combination means that a given sentence is identified as incorrect by both methods. The results show that the "OR" combination yielded better recall than the individual methods, and the "AND" combination yielded better precision and FPR than the individual methods. Thus, the choice of methods may depend on application requirements or preferences

Method	Precision	Recall	F1	False Positive Rate
Rule	0.857	0.224	0.356	0.038
2-gram	0.555	0.751	0.638	0.603
3-gram	0.585	0.838	0.689	0.595
Rule OR 2-gram	0.500	1.000	0.667	1.000
Rule OR 3-gram	0.502	1.000	0.668	0.993
Rule AND 2-gram	0.924	0.083	0.153	0.007
Rule AND 3-gram	0.924	0.083	0.153	0.007

Table 1. Comparative results of the rule-based and *n*-gram statistical approaches.

Many learner corpora exist for EFL for use in machine learning, including the International Corpus of Learner English (ICLE) and Cambridge Learner Corpus (CLC). But collecting a representative sample of authentic errors from CFL learners poses a challenge. In addition, English and Chinese grammars are markedly different. In contrast to syntax-oriented English language, Chinese is discourse-oriented, with meaning often expressed in several clauses to make a complete sentence. These characteristics make syntactic parsing difficult, due to long dependency between words in a clause or across clauses in a sentence. These difficulties constrain system performance.

4 Conclusions

This study presents a sentence judgment system developed using both rule-based and *n*-gram statistical methods to detect grammatical errors in sentences written by CFL learners. The system not only alerts learners to potential grammatical errors in their input sentences, but also helps them learn about linguistic rules and *n*-gram frequencies. The major contributions of this work include: (a) demonstratingg the feasibility of detecting grammatical errors in sentences written by CFL learners, (b) developing a system to facilitate autonomous learning among CFL learners and (c) collecting real grammatical errors from CFL learners for the construction of a Chinese learner corpus.

Acknowledgments

This research was partially supported by Ministry of Science and Technology, Taiwan under the grant NSC102-2221-E-155-029-MY3, NSC 102-2221-E-002-103-MY3, and the "Aim for the Top University Project" sponsored by the Ministry of Education, Taiwan.

Reference

Andreas Stolcke. 2002. SRILM – An extensible language modeling toolkit. *Proceedings of ICSLP'02*, pages 901-904.

Chi-Hsin Yu and Hsin-Hsi Chen. 2012. Detecting word ordering errors in Chinese sentences for learning Chinese as a foreign language. *Proceedings of COLING'12,* pages 3003-3018.

Christopher D. Manning and Hinrich Schütze. 1999. *Foundations of Statistical Natural Language Processing.* MIT Press. Cambridge, MA.

Chung-Hsien Wu, Chao-Hung Liu, Matthew Harris and Liang-Chih Yu. 2010. Sentence correction incorporating relative position and parse template language model. *IEEE Transactions on Audio, Speech, and Language Processing*, 18(6):1170-1181.

Keh-Jiann Chen and Wei-Yun Ma. 2002. Unknown word extraction for Chinese documents. *Proceedings of COLING'02,* pages 169-175.

M. Cheng. 1997. Analysis of 900 Common Erroneous Samples of Chinese Sentences - for Chinese Learners from English Speaking Countries (in Chinese). Beijing, CN: Sinolingua.

Ru-Ying Chang, Chung-Hsien Wu, and Philips K. Prasetyo. 2012. Error diagnosis of Chinese sentences using inductive learning algorithm and decomposition-based testing mechanism. *ACM Transactions on Asian Language Information Processing*, 11(1):Article 3.

Yu-Fang Tsai and Keh-Jiann Chen. 2004. Reliable and cost-effective pos-tagging. *International Journal of Computational Linguistics and Chinese Language Processing*, 9(1):83-96.

CLAM: Quickly deploy NLP command-line tools on the web

Maarten van Gompel
Centre for Language Studies (CLS)
Radboud University Nijmegen
proycon@anaproy.nl

Martin Reynaert
CLS, Radboud University Nijmegen
TiCC, Tilburg University
reynaert@uvt.nl

http://proycon.github.io/clam

Abstract

In this paper we present the software CLAM; the Computational Linguistics Application Mediator. CLAM is a tool that allows you to quickly and transparently transform command-line NLP tools into fully-fledged *RESTful* webservices with which automated clients can communicate, as well as a generic webapplication interface for human end-users.

1 Introduction

In the field of Natural Language Processing, tools often come in the form of command-line tools aimed at UNIX-derived systems. We consider this good practice in line with the UNIX philosophy (McIlroy et al., 1978) which states, amongst others, that programs should 1) do one thing and do it well, and 2) expect the output of one program to be the input of another. This can be rephrased as the *Rule of Modularity*: write programs consisting of simple parts, connected by well-defined interfaces (Raymond, 2004).

Programs operating at the command-line offer such modularity, making them ideally suitable for integration in a wide variety of workflows. However, the command-line may not be the most suitable interface for non-specialised human end-users. Neither does it by itself facilitate usage over network unless explicit server functionality has been programmed into the application. Human end-users often want a Graphical User Interface (GUI), a special instance of which is a Web User Interface. Yet for automated clients operating over a network, such an interface is a cumbersome barrier, and these instead prefer a properly formalised webservice interface. CLAM offers a solution to this problem, when all there is is a simple NLP command-line tool.

CLAM finds application in areas where people want to make their software available to a larger public, but a command-line interface is not sufficient. Setting up your tool may be complicated, especially if there are many dependencies or the target audience does not use Linux machines. CLAM is ideally suited for quick demo purposes, or for integration into larger workflow systems. It removes the burden from the software developer (you) to have to implement a server mode and build a GUI or web-interface, thus saving precious time.

2 System architecture

The Computational Linguistics Application Mediator (CLAM) is a tool that wraps around your command-line interface and allows you to very quickly and transparently turn your program into **1)** a *RESTful* (Fielding, 2000) webservice with which automated clients can communicate, as well as **2)** a generic web user interface for human end-users. Just like an actual clam is a shell around the animal that inhabits it, which most onlookers never see directly, CLAM wraps around your sofware, providing extra functionality and hardening it through its built-in security mechanism. You do not need to modify your original software in any way, it is always taken as a given, you merely need to describe it.

An NLP command-line tool can usually be described in terms of *input files*, *output files* and parameters influencing its run. Parameters may either be *global parameters*, pertaining to the system as a whole, or *local parameters* which act as *metadata* for specific input files. File formats are never dictated by CLAM itself, but are up to the service provider to define.

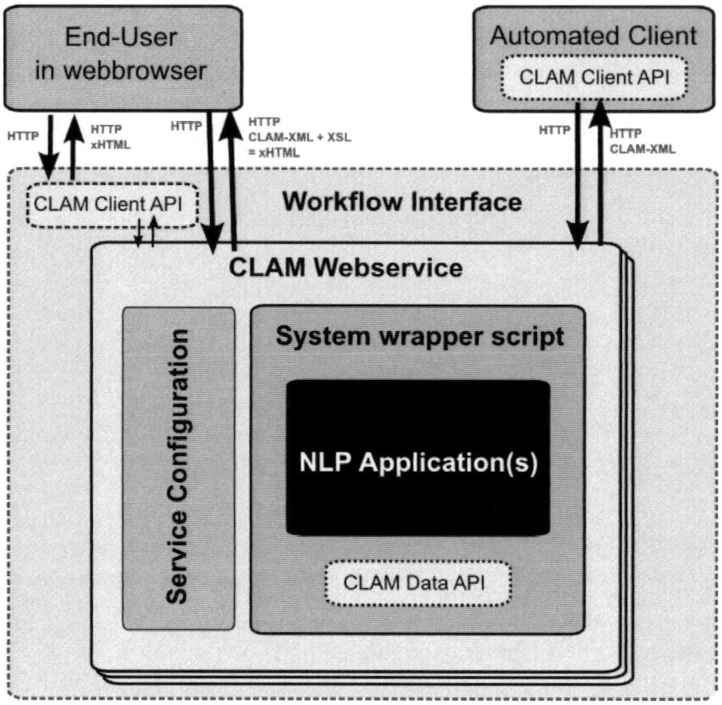

Figure 1: Schematic overview of the CLAM architecture

CLAM discerns three *states*, which also reflect the stages in which the end-user or automated client interacts with the system

1. The system is ready to accept files for input and input parameters
2. The system is running
3. The system is done and the output files are offered for presentation/download.

Any tool that can be described in these terms can be used with CLAM. The system has been designed specifically to work with software that may take quite some time to process or runs large batches. Stage two therefore is not confined to lasting mere seconds as is custom in web-based applications, but may last as long as hours, days, or any duration that the end-user is willing to wait. Also, end-users need not maintain a connection to the server. Human end-users may close their browser and return at will, and automated clients simply poll the system's status with a certain interval.

You are not limited to just a single run of your system; you may set it up to allow upload and processing of multiple files and run them in batch fashion. This approach is common in processing text files for purposes such as tokenisation or any form of tagging.

In order for CLAM to turn a command-line tool into a webservice, developers are expected to provide two things in addition to the actual tool:

1. **Service configuration** - This specifies everything there is to know about your application, it defines what the input will be, what the output will be, and what parameters the system may take. Input and output are always in the form of files, adhering to whatever format you desire. The web user interface, however, also optionally offers a text field for users to create files on the fly.

2. **System wrapper script** - This is a small script that CLAM will invoke to start your system. It acts as the glue between CLAM and your actual application and may do some necessary interpretation and transformation of parameters to suit the command-line interface of your application.

A generic client for communicating with the webservice is already provided, more specific clients can be written using the CLAM API (Python) to greatly facilitate development. The architecture of CLAM is schematically visualised in Figure 1.

CLAM is a multi-user system, although out-of-the-box it simply uses an "anonymous" user and requires no authentication. Each user can create an arbitrary number of *projects*. One project corresponds to one run of the system, which may be one large batch depending on how you configure your service. Users can always return to earlier projects and inspect input files and output files, until they explicitly delete the project.

2.1 Service Configuration

In the service configuration file, you specify precisely what kind of input goes into the system, and what kind of output goes out: this results in a deterministic and thus predictable webservice. With any input and output files, arbitrary metadata can be associated. For input files, metadata is created from parameters that can be set by users, these are rendered as input fields in the web interface. You can specify how this metadata is carried over to output files. Additionally, as part of the metadata, provenance data is generated for all output files. These are both stored in a simple and straightforward XML format.

All these definitions are specified in so-called *profiles*. A profile defines *input templates* and *output templates*. These can be seen as "slots" for certain filetypes and their metadata. A small excerpt of a profile for a simple translation system with some associated metadata is shown in Figure 2. A full discussion of its syntax goes beyond the scope of this paper, but is explained at length in the manual.

```
Profile(InputTemplate('maininput', PlainTextFormat,
  "Translator input: Plain-text document",
  StaticParameter(
    id='encoding',name='Encoding',description='The character encoding of the file',
    value='utf-8'
  ),
  ChoiceParameter(
    id='language',name='Language',description='The language the text is in',
    choices=[('en','English'),('nl','Dutch'),('fr','French')]),
  ),
  extension='.txt',
  multi=True
), OutputTemplate('translationoutput', PlainTextFormat,
    "Translator output: Plain-text document",
    CopyMetaField('encoding','maininput.encoding')
    SetMetaField('language','de'),
    removeextension='.txt',
    extension='.translation',
    multi=True
))
```

Figure 2: An excerpt of a fictitious *profile* for a simple translation system from English, Dutch or French to German. The attribute `multi=True` states that multiple files of this type may be submitted during a single run

Global parameters to the system are specified independently of any profiles. Consider a global parameter that would indicate whether or not want the fictitious translation system seen in Figure 2 to be case-sensitive, and take a look at the following example[1]:

```
PARAMETERS =  [
  ('Translation parameters', [
        BooleanParameter(id='casesensitive',name='Case Sensitivity',
        description='Enable case sensitive behaviour?')
])]
```

[1]Parameters are always grouped into named groups, "Translation parameters" is just the label of the group here

2.2 System Wrapper

Communication between CLAM and your command-line tool proceeds through a system wrapper script. The service configuration file defines what script to call and what variables, pre-defined by CLAM, to pass to it:

```
COMMAND = "mywrapper.py $DATAFILE $OUTPUTDIRECTORY"
```

This is then executed whenever a user runs a project. It is the job of the system wrapper script to invoke your actual application.

There are two main means of communicating the parameters to the system wrapper: one is to make use of the data file (`$DATAFILE`), which is an XML file that contains all input parameters. It can be parsed and queried effortlessly using the CLAM API, provided you write your wrapper script in Python. The other way, more limited, is to specify parameter flags for your global parameters[2] in the service configuration, and simply let CLAM pass all global parameters as arguments on the command line:

```
COMMAND = "mywrapper.pl $INPUTDIRECTORY $OUTPUTDIRECTORY $PARAMETERS"
```

By passing the input directory, the system wrapper script can simply look for its input files there.

3 Extensions

CLAM can be extended by developers in several ways. One is to write *viewers*, which take care of the visualisation of output files for a specific file format, and are used by the web user interface. Viewers may be implemented as internal Python modules, or you can link to any external URL which takes care of the visualisation. Another extension is *converters*, these allow users to upload an input file in one file type and have it automatically converted to another. Converters for PDF and Word to plain text are already provided through third party tools.

4 Technical Details

CLAM is written in Python (2.6 or 2.7), (van Rossum, 2007). It comes with a built-in HTTP server for development purposes, allowing you to quickly test and adjust your service. Final deployment can be made on common webservers such as Apache, Nginx or lighthttpd through the WSGI mechanism. The service configuration file itself is by definition a Python file calling specific configuration directives in the CLAM API. The system wrapper script may be written in any language, but Python users benefit as they can use the CLAM API which makes the job easier. Projects and input files are stored in a simple directory structure on disk, allowing your tool easy access. No database server is required.

The webservice offers a *RESTful* interface (Fielding, 2000), meaning that the HTTP verbs `GET`, `POST`, `PUT` and `DELETE` are used on URLs that represent resources such as projects, input files, output files. The web application is implemented as a client-side layer on the webservice. It is presented through XSL transformation (Clark, 1999) of the webservice XML output.

User authentication is implemented in the form of HTTP Digest Authentication, which ensures that the password is sent in encrypted form over the network even with servers where HTTPS is not used. HTTPS support is not present in CLAM itself but can be configured in the encompassing webserver. The underlying user database can be specified either directly in the service configuration file or in a table in a Mysql database, but it is fairly easy to replace this and communicate with another external database of your choice instead. There is also support for propagating credentials from another authentication source such as Shibboleth[3], allowing for integrating with single-sign-on scenarios. Implementation of OAuth2[4] will follow in a later version.

CLAM is open-source software licensed under the GNU Public License v3. Both the software as well as the documentation can be obtained through the CLAM website at github: `http://proycon.github.io/clam`.

[2] caveat: this does not work for local parameters, i.e. parameters pertaining to files

[3] `http://shibboleth.net`

[4] `http://oauth.net/2/`

5 Related Work

As far as we know, the only tool comparable to CLAM is Weblicht (Hinrichs et al., 2010). Both tools are specifically designed for an NLP context. CLAM, however, is of a more generic and flexible nature and may also find easier adoption in other fields.

When it comes to data formats, Weblicht commits to a specific file format for corpus data. CLAM leaves file formats completely up to the service providers, although it does come, as a bonus, with a viewer for users of FoLiA (van Gompel and Reynaert, 2013).

Weblicht is Java-based whereas CLAM is Python-based, which tends to be less verbose and more easily accessible. System wrapper scripts can be written in any language, and service configuration files simply consist of directives that require virtually no Python knowledge.

All in all CLAM offers a more lightweight solution than Weblicht, allowing webservices to be set up more easily and quicker. Nevertheless, CLAM offers more power and flexibility in doing what it does: wrapping around command-line tools, its webservice specification is more elaborate than that of Weblicht. On the other hand, CLAM deliberately does not go as far as Weblicht and does not offer a complete chaining environment, which is what Weblicht is. In this we follow the aforementioned UNIX philosophy of doing one thing well and one thing only. Service chaining certainly remains possible and CLAM provides all the information to facilitate it, but it is left to other tools designed for the task. CLAM has been successfully used with Taverna (Hull et al., 2006) in the scope of the CLARIN-NL project "TST Tools for Dutch as Webservices in a Workflow" (Kemps-Snijders et al., 2012).

Acknowledgements

CLAM support and development is generously funded by CLARIN-NL (Odijk, 2010), and is being used by various projects in the Dutch & Flemish NLP communities, whose feedback and support have contributed to its success.

References

J. Clark. 1999. XSL transformations (XSLT) version 1.0. Technical report, 11.

R. T. Fielding. 2000. *Architectural Styles and the Design of Network-based Software Architectures. Doctoral dissertation.* University of California, Irvine.

M. Hinrichs, T. Zastrow, and E. W. Hinrichs. 2010. Weblicht: Web-based LRT services in a Distributed eScience Infrastructure. In Nicoletta Calzolari, Khalid Choukri, Bente Maegaard, Joseph Mariani, Jan Odijk, Stelios Piperidis, Mike Rosner, and Daniel Tapias, editors, *LREC*. European Language Resources Association.

D. Hull, K. Wolstencroft, R. Stevens, C. Goble, M. R. Pocock, P. Li, and T. Oinn. 2006. Taverna: a tool for building and running workflows of services. *Nucleic Acids Res*, 34(Web Server issue):729–732, July.

M. Kemps-Snijders, M. Brouwer, J.P. Kunst, and T. Visser. 2012. Dynamic web service deployment in a cloud environment. In Nicoletta Calzolari, Khalid Choukri, Thierry Declerck, Mehmet Ugur Dogan, Bente Maegaard, Joseph Mariani, Jan Odijk, and Stelios Piperidis, editors, *LREC*, pages 2941–2944. European Language Resources Association (ELRA).

M. D. McIlroy, E. N. Pinson, and B. A. Tague. 1978. Unix time-sharing system forward. *The Bell System Technical Journal*, 57(6, part 2):p.1902.

J. Odijk. 2010. The CLARIN-NL project. In *Proceedings of the Seventh International Conference on Language Resources and Evaluation, LREC-2010*, pages 48–53, Valletta, Malta.

E. S. Raymond. 2004. The Art of Unix Programming.

M. van Gompel and M. Reynaert. 2013. FoLiA: A practical XML Format for Linguistic Annotation - a descriptive and comparative study. *Computational Linguistics in the Netherlands Journal*, 3.

G. van Rossum. 2007. Python programming language. In *USENIX Annual Technical Conference*. USENIX.

CRAB 2.0: A text mining tool for supporting literature review in chemical cancer risk assessment

Yufan Guo[1], **Diarmuid Ó Séaghdha**[1], **Ilona Silins**[2], **Lin Sun**[1], **Johan Högberg**[2], **Ulla Stenius**[2], **Anna Korhonen**[1]

[1] Computer Laboratory, University of Cambridge, UK
[2] Institute of Environmental Medicine, Karolinska Institutet, Stockholm, Sweden

Abstract

Chemical cancer risk assessment is a literature-dependent task which could greatly benefit from text mining support. In this paper we describe CRAB – the first publicly available tool for supporting the risk assessment workflow. CRAB, currently at version 2.0, facilitates the gathering of relevant literature via PubMed queries as well as semantic classification, statistical analysis and efficient study of the literature. The tool is freely available as an in-browser application.

1 Introduction

Biomedical text mining addresses the great need to access information in the growing body of literature in biomedical sciences. Prior research has produced useful tools for supporting practical tasks such as literature curation and development of semantic databases, among others (Chapman and Cohen, 2009; Harmston et al., 2010; Simpson and Demner-Fushman, 2012; McDonald and Kelly, 2012). In this paper we describe a tool we have built to aid literature exploration for the task of chemical risk assessment (CRA). The need for assessment of chemical hazards, exposures and their corresponding health risks is growing, as many countries have tightened up their chemical safety rules. CRA work requires thorough review of available scientific data for each chemical under inspection, much of which can be found in scientific literature (EPA, 2005). Since the scientific data is highly varied and well-studied chemicals may have tens of thousands of publications (e.g. to date PubMed contains 23,665 articles mentioning phenobarbital), the task can be extremely time consuming when conducted via conventional means (Korhonen et al., 2009). As a result, there is interest among the CRA community in text mining tools that can aid and streamline the literature review process.

We have developed CRAB, an online system that supports the entire process of literature review for cancer risk assessors. It is the first and only NLP system that serves this need. CRAB contains three main components:

1. **Literature search** with PubMed integration
2. **Semantic classification** of abstracts with summary visualisation
3. **Literature browsing** with markup of information structure

These components are described further in Section 2 below. Version 2.0 of CRAB is freely available as an in-browser application; see Section 4 for access information.

2 System description

2.1 Literature search

The first step for the user is to retrieve a collection of scientific articles relevant to their need, e.g., all articles with abstracts that contain the name of a given chemical. The CRAB 2.0 search page (Figure 1) allows the user to directly query the MEDLINE database of biomedical abstracts. The search query

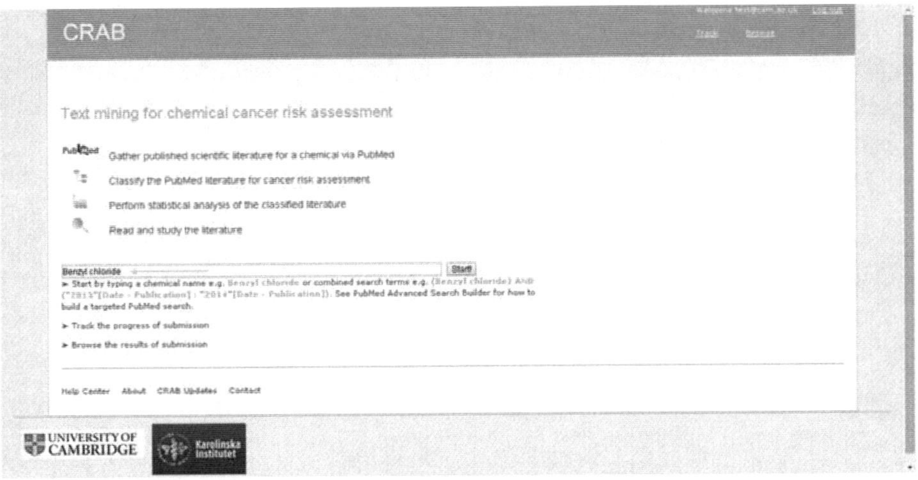

Figure 1: The CRAB 2.0 search interface

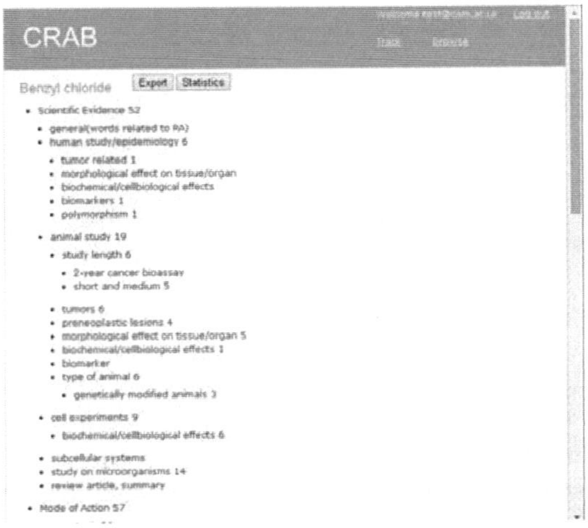

(a) Taxonomy view

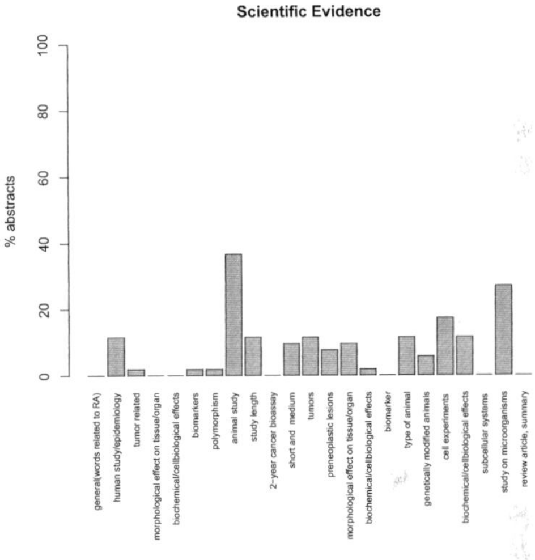

(b) Histogram view

Figure 2: The CRAB 2.0 classification component

is sent, and the results received, using the E-Utilities web service provided by the National Center for Biotechnology Information.[1] This query interface supports PubMed Advanced Search, facilitating complex Boolean queries.

2.2 Semantic classification

The document collection returned by the PubMed web service is passed in XML format to a semantic classifier that annotates each abstract with 42 binary labels indicating the presence/absence of concepts relevant to CRA. These concepts are organised hierarchically in two main taxonomies: (1) kinds of scientific evidence used for CRA (e.g., *human studies*, *animal studies*, *cell experiments*, *biochemical/cell biological effects*); (2) the carcinogenic modes of action indicated by the evidence (e.g., *genotoxic*, *nongenotoxic/indirect genotoxic*, *cell death*, *inflammation*, *angiogenesis*). The underlying classifier is a support vector machine (SVM) trained on a dataset of 3,078 manually annotated abstracts. Features used by the SVM include lexical n-grams, character n-grams and MeSH concepts. For more details on the concept taxonomies, training corpus and classifier see Korhonen et al. (2012).

[1] http://www.ncbi.nlm.nih.gov/books/NBK25501/

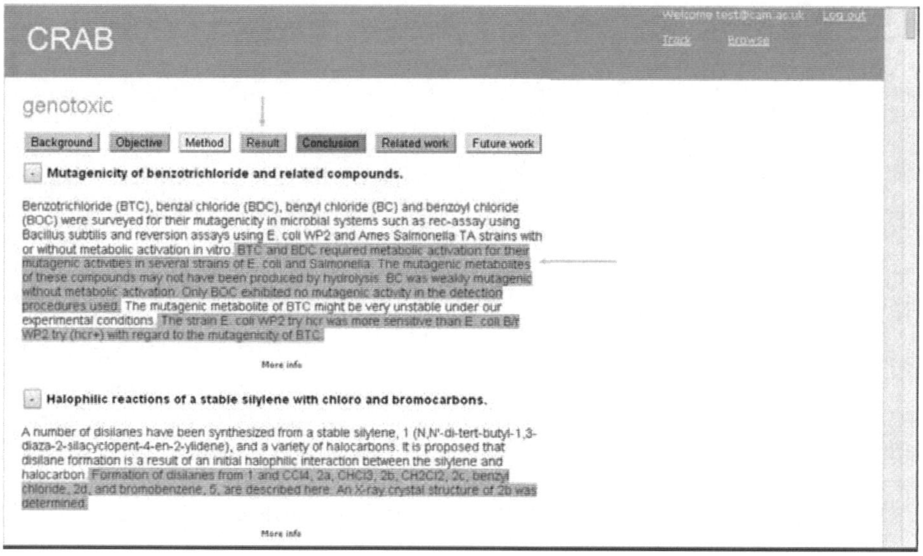

Figure 3: The CRAB 2.0 information structure component

Once each abstract in the retrieved collection has been classified, the user is presented with a summary of counts for each concept (Figure 2a). In a user study, risk assessors found this summary very useful for obtaining a broad overview of the literature, identifying groups of chemicals with similar toxicological profiles and identifying data gaps (Korhonen et al., 2012). The user can also request a histogram visualisation (Figure 2b), which is produced through a call to the statistical software R.[2]

2.3 Literature browsing

The risk assessment workflow involves close reading of relevant abstracts to identify specific information about methods, experimental details, results and conclusions. While it is not feasible to automate this process, we have shown that automatic markup and visualisation of abstracts' information structure can accelerate it considerably (Guo et al., 2011). The model of information structure incorporated in CRAB 2.0 is based on *argumentative zoning* (Teufel and Moens, 2002; Mizuta et al., 2006; Teufel, 2010), whereby the text of a scientific abstract (or article) is segmented into blocks of sentences that carry a specific rhetorical function and combine to communicate the argument the authors wish to convey to the reader. The markup scheme used in our system labels each sentence with one of seven categories: *background*, *objective*, *method*, *result*, *conclusion*, *related work* and *future work* (Guo et al., 2010). The CRAB system incorporates preprocessing (lemmatisation, POS tagging, parsing) with the C&C toolkit[3] and information structure markup with an SVM classifier that labels sentences according to a combination of lexical, syntactic and discourse features (Guo et al., 2011). The classifier has been trained on an annotated dataset of 1,000 CRA abstracts (Guo et al., 2010).

The automatic information structure markup is used to support browsing of the set of abstracts assigned a label of interest by the semantic classifier; e.g., the user can inspect all abstracts labelled *genotoxic* (Figure 3). Each information structure category is highlighted in a different colour and the user can select a single category to focus on. To our knowledge, CRAB 2.0 is the first publicly available online tool that provides information structure analysis of biomedical literature.

3 Evaluation

Intrinsic cross-validation evaluations of the semantic taxonomy classifier and information structure classifier show high performance: 0.78 macro-averaged F-score (Korhonen et al., 2012) and 0.88 accuracy (Guo et al., 2011), respectively. Furthermore, user-based evaluation in the context of real-life CRA has

[2] `http://www.r-project.org/`

[3] `http://svn.ask.it.usyd.edu.au/trac/candc`

produced promising results. (Korhonen et al., 2012) showed that the concept distributions produced by our classifier confirmed known properties of chemicals without human input. Guo et al. (2011) found that integrating information structure visualisation in abstract browsing helped risk assessors to find relevant information in abstracts 7-8% more quickly.

4 Use

CRAB 2.0 is freely available as an in-browser application at `http://omotesando-e.cl.cam.ac.uk/CRAB/request.html`. New users can register an id and password to allow them to store and retrieve data from previous sessions. Alternatively, they can use an anonymous guest account (id `guest@coling`, password `guest@coling`).

5 Conclusion

We have presented Version 2.0 of CRAB, the first NLP tool for supporting the workflow of literature review for cancer risk assessment. CRAB meets a real, specialised need and is already being used to improve the efficiency of CRA work. Although currently focused on cancer, CRAB can be easily adapted to other health risks provided with the appropriate taxonomy and annotated data for machine learning. In the future, the tool can be developed further in various ways, e.g. to support submissions in other formats than PubMed XML; to take into account journal impact factors, number of citations and cross references to better organize the literature; and to offer enriched statistical analysis of classified literature.

Acknowledgements

This work was supported by the Royal Society, Vinnova and the Swedish Research Council.

References

Wendy W. Chapman and K. Bretonnel Cohen. 2009. Current issues in biomedical text mining and natural language processing. *Journal of Biomedical Informatics*, 42(5):757–759.

EPA. 2005. Guidelines for carcinogen risk assessment. US Environmental Protection Agency.

Yufan Guo, Anna Korhonen, Maria Liakata, Ilona Silins, Lin Sun, and Ulla Stenius. 2010. Identifying the information structure of scientific abstracts: An investigation of three different schemes. In *Proceedings of BioNLP-10*, Uppsala, Sweden.

Yufan Guo, Anna Korhonen, Ilona Silins, and Ulla Stenius. 2011. Weakly supervised learning of information structure of scientific abstracts: Is it accurate enough to benefit real-world tasks in biomedicine? *Bioinformatics*, 27(22):3179–3185.

Nathan Harmston, Wendy Filsell, and Michael P.H. Stumpf. 2010. What the papers say: Text mining for genomics and systems biology. *Human Genomics*, 5(1):17–29.

Anna Korhonen, Ilona Silins, Lin Sun, and Ulla Stenius. 2009. The first step in the development of text mining technology for cancer risk assessment: Identifying and organizing scientific evidence in risk assessment literature. *BMC Bioinformatics*, 10:303.

Anna Korhonen, Diarmuid Ó Séaghdha, Ilona Silins, Lin Sun, Johan Högberg, and Ulla Stenius. 2012. Text mining for literature review and knowledge discovery in cancer risk assessment and research. *PLoS ONE*, 7(4):e33427.

Diane McDonald and Ursula Kelly. 2012. The value and benefit of text mining to UK further and higher education. Report 811, JISC.

Yoko Mizuta, Anna Korhonen, Tony Mullen, and Nigel Collier. 2006. Zone analysis in biology articles as a basis for information extraction. *International Journal of Medical Informatics*, 75(6):468–487.

Matthew S. Simpson and Dina Demner-Fushman. 2012. Biomedical text mining: A survey of recent progress. In Charu C. Aggarwal and ChengXiang Zhai, editors, *Mining Text Data*. Springer.

Simone Teufel and Marc Moens. 2002. Summarizing scientific articles: Experiments with relevance and rhetorical status. *Computational Linguistics*, 28(4):409–445.

Simone Teufel. 2010. *The Structure of Scientific Articles: Applications to Citation Indexing and Summarization*. CSLI Publications, Stanford, CA.

Nerdle: Topic-Specific Question Answering Using Wikia Seeds

Umar Maqsud, **Sebastian Arnold**, **Michael Hülfenhaus** and **Alan Akbik**
Database Systems and Information Management Group
Technische Universität Berlin
Einsteinufer 17, 10587 Berlin, Germany

Abstract

The WIKIA project maintains wikis across a diverse range of subjects from areas of popular culture. Each wiki consists of collaboratively authored content and focuses on a particular topic, including franchises such as "Star Trek", "Star Wars" and "The Simpsons". In this paper, we investigate the use of such wikis to create Question-Answering (QA) systems for a given topic. Our key idea is to use a wiki as seed to gather large amounts of relevant text and to use semantic role labeling (SRL) methods to extract N-ary facts from this data. By applying our method to very large amounts of topically focused text, we propose to address the coverage issues that have been noted for QA systems built using such techniques. To illustrate the strengths and weaknesses of the proposed approach, we make a Web demonstrator of our system publicly available; it provides a *QA view* that enables users to pose natural language questions to the system and that visualizes how questions are interpreted and matched to answers. In addition, the demonstrator provides a *graph exploration view* in which users can directly browse the fact base in order to inspect the scope of the extracted information.

1 Introduction

The WIKIA project operates the largest network of collaboratively authored wikis, consisting of over 390.000 wikis on subjects such as games, entertainment and lifestyle, and is available online at *www.wikia.com*. Each wiki is focused on one particular topic and may consist of tens of thousands of pages of text content. Such data, we argue, provides a unique opportunity for extracting structured relational data confined to one domain of interest.

In this paper, we investigate such an approach; our overall goal is to automatically create Question Answering (QA) systems that are "experts" in one field of interest. Our key idea is to use wikis as seeds to a focused crawler to gather as much text as possible for a given topic. The more text we can gather, the greater the chance that we can address coverage issues that related works in QA have noted: Phenomena such as coreferences, synonyms and paraphrasing may negatively affect a QA systems ability to find answers to questions that are phrased differently from occurrences in text (Fader et al., 2013; Ravichandran and Hovy, 2002). By gathering large amounts of topically relevant text and by employing semantic role labeling (SRL) as a means for fact extraction and representation (Shen and Lapata, 2007), our hypothesis is that we can sidestep many of these issues.

The main purpose of this demonstration is therefore to illustrate and discuss in how far a direct application of SRL to domain-specific text can be employed to create a QA system. To this end, we make publicly available a Web demonstrator of a QA system on three topics of popular culture, namely the "Star Trek", "Star Wars" and "The Simpsons" franchises. Our system, named NERDLE, supports eight types of questions, examples of which are given in Table 1. The fact base on these topics is gathered with our proposed approach. The demonstrator offers two views that highlight different aspects of the system: The *QA view* allows users to pose natural language questions and visualizes how questions are

	STAR TREK	THE SIMPSONS	STAR WARS
WHO	Who attacked the Enterprise?	Who is Homer's father?	Who destroyed the Death Star?
WHERE	Where was Picard born?	Where was Homer born?	Where was the Death Star destroyed?
WHEN	When did James Kirk die?	When was Homer born?	When was Vader killed?
HOW	How did James Kirk die?	How does Homer work?	How did Luke destroy the Death Star?
WHOM	Whom did the Klingons attack?	Whom does Homer know?	Whom did Luke Skywalker attack?
WHAT	What are Klingons?	What does Bart think?	What is the Rebel Alliance?
WHY	Why was Voyager destroyed?	Why was Homer sad?	Why does Luke Skywalker die?
WHICH	Which captain was born on Earth?	Which food critic was born in Springfield?	Which Jedi attacked the Death Star?

Table 1: The eight question types currently supported by our system and example questions for each of the three topics.

interpreted and how they are matched to answers. The *graph exploration view* enables users to directly browse the fact base in order to inspect the scope of the extracted information.

In the following sections, we briefly describe our method for using WIKIA to gather text data for a given topic. We discuss how we employ SRL for fact extraction and representation and give details on our method for aligning eight types of natural language questions to these facts. Finally, we discuss the visualization and results of the created QA system.

2 Method

In this section, we describe our method for gathering relevant text using a wiki seed and extracting facts using SRL. As a running example, we use the "Star Trek"-universe as the topic of interest.

2.1 Constructing Topic-Specific Corpora

As a first step, we select the appropriate wiki for the given topic and retrieve all its text as well as the names of the page titles. For the "Star Trek" example, the WIKIA project offers two wikis, namely *Memory Alpha* and *Memory Beta*[1], both of which we select as relevant. Using these wikis, we download over 95.000 pages or 250 MB of text content for the domain of interest.

We then determine combinations of search keywords using the page titles and use these as queries in search engines like BING[2] or FAROO[3]. Examples of such queries are "Kirk Spock Star Trek" or "Picard Data Star Trek". While FAROO (unlike BING) does not limit the number of allowed queries per month, its index is much smaller. We therefore developed the following strategy to use the FAROO index in our text gathering effort: For each combination of search keywords, we retrieve all matching pages and then follow their outgoing links to find more possibly related Web pages. We check each Web page to contain at least one mention of the domain keyword ("Star Trek") as a simple sanity check to ensure that the crawler has not left the domain of interest. We download all pages we reach with this method.

Using this method, we find over 500 MB of text for the "Star Trek"-domain. As this is an ongoing effort, the corpus size is expected to expand further. The generated corpus is then passed to the fact extraction step of the pipeline.

2.2 Fact Extraction

We detect English language sentences in the gathered corpus and apply SRL to detect predicate-argument structures for each verb. We use the ClearNLP toolkit (Choi and Adviser-Palmer, 2012) for this task; it links each predicate to a PROPBANK (Martha and Palmer, 2002) verb sense and its arguments to PROPBANK semantic roles. We choose PROPBANK over FRAMENET (Baker et al., 1998) as it models semantics more broadly and has a more complete coverage of verb frames. For our purpose, we are especially interested in the argument roles: PROPBANK gives us verb-specific argument roles as well as universal roles such as temporals (TMP), locatives (LOC), causal adverbials (CAU) and adverbials

[1]Available at http://en.memory-alpha.org/ and http://memory-beta.wikia.com/ respectively.

[2]http://www.bing.com

[3]http://www.faroo.com/

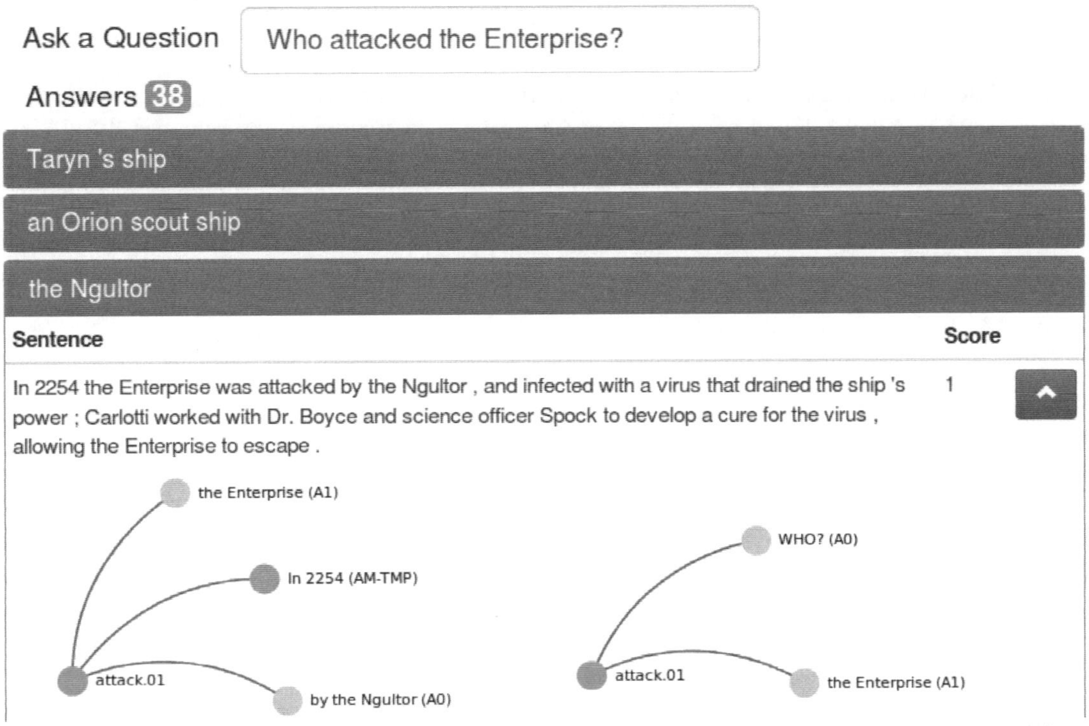

Figure 1: The QA-view of the Web demonstrator. The user types in a question and receives a list of arguments as answers below. For the question "*Who attacked the Enterprise?*" the user receives a total of 38 answers, three of which are shown here, namely "*Taryn's ship*", "*an Orion scout ship*" and "*the Ngultor*". By clicking on one of the answers, the user inspects the predicate-argument structures of both question (lower right graph) and the answer (lower left graph), as well as the sentence in which the answer is found.

of manner (MNR) and purpose (PRP). In this work, we treat the predicate-argument structures as N-ary facts and store these in a graph database.

To illustrate the fact extraction process, consider the sentence "*In 2254, the Enterprise was attacked by the Ngultor*". Using SRL, we determine a predicate-argument structure in which "attack" is the predicate and there are three arguments: Two arguments with verb-specific roles, namely "*by the Ngultor*" (attacker) and "*the Enterprise*" (that which is attacked), as well as the argument "*in 2254*", which is recognized to be of type *AM-TMP*, meaning that it confers additional temporal information to the ternary fact. This predicate-argument structure is illustrated in Figure 1.

2.3 Question Parsing

The question parsing process is similar to fact extraction; we apply SRL to a question to determine its predicate-argument structure. We then try to find matching predicate-argument structures in the fact base by searching for facts that share the same predicate and as many arguments as possible. The greater the number of matching arguments, the higher the score of the matching fact. In addition, we require matching facts to also contain an *answer argument* labeled with a specific semantic role which is determined through the question type.

We allow seven basic types of questions and one type of composite question. The basic question types we support are factual questions beginning with the question words "who", "where", "when", "whom", "what", "how" and "why". Depending on the question type, we require answer arguments to be labeled with a different semantic role. For "where"-questions, for example, we require answer arguments to be labeled as an *AM-LOC* argument. For "when"-questions, the answer argument must be labeled as an *AM-TMP* argument. For "who"-questions, we require an argument that shares the semantic role of the question word, which typically will be either *A0* or *A1*. These answer arguments are returned answers to the question.

We illustrate this in Figure 1. The question "*Who attacked the Enterprise?*" is parsed into a predicate-argument structure. It is aligned with the predicate-argument structure of the sentence "*In 2254 the Enterprise was attacked by the Ngultor*" because they share the same predicate as well as the argument "*the Enterprise*" with the role *A1*. Of the two remaining arguments, namely "*in 2254*" and "*the Ngultor*" the latter is selected as the answer argument because it carries the same semantic role as was assigned to the token "who" in the question, namely *A0*. In case of a "when"-question, "*in 2254*" would instead be selected as answer argument, as it is labeled with the required *AM-TMP* role.

In addition, we support one type of composite question, namely questions beginning with "which", as in "*Which captain was born on Earth?*". Such questions are decomposed into two separate "who"-questions, namely "*Who is a captain?*" and "*Who was born on Earth?*". We then determine answer arguments that match both questions and return these.

3 Demonstration

We present a Web demonstrator [4] in which users can query the fact base in one of two views:

QA view. In this view, users pose natural language questions and are presented with matching answers if they exist. For each answer, both the source sentences as well as the URLs to the original Web pages are displayed. Answers are ranked by a score which is determined through the number of matching arguments between the predicate-argument structures of the question and the answer. As illustrated in Figure 1, users inspect a visualization of these predicate-argument structures. This view is primarily designed to aid with understanding issues with *precision*, i.e. to understand how answers to questions come to be and how fact extraction and question parsing function.

Graph exploration view. In this view, users can browse the graph database directly for facts. Together with the QA view, this view is designed to examine issues of *recall*, i.e. to help understand the scope of the extracted information and why some questions are not answered.

4 Discussion

With our method, we find a total of 7 million facts for "Star Trek", 6.5 million for "Star Wars" and, due to its smaller wiki size, 3.5 million for "The Simpsons". Next to the availability of large amounts of Web text, our focus on topics of popular culture has the advantage that there are a large number of resources available online that can be used to analyze the QA capabilities of our system. In our analysis, we make use of ABSURDTRIVIA[5], a community powered Web site where users write and rate trivia quizzes on items of popular culture. The trivia quizzes consist of a set of multiple-choice questions. We crawl 50 of these questions on the NERDLE topics that conform to our question types and pose them to NERDLE. We find that NERDLE chooses the correct answer for 16 questions, a wrong answer for 5 questions and no answer at all for 29 questions.

Our demonstrator allows us to inspect wrong and unanswered questions. We find that the system often either lacks the correct facts in the fact base or cannot align questions to answers due to problems of synonymy, entailment and coreferences. An example of this is the question "*Who played Phlox?*" to which no answer is found, while the correct answer is found for "*Who portrayed Phlox?*". This suggests that the coverage of the system might be improved by adding knowledge on synonymous arguments as well as synonymous or entailing verbs. Future work will accordingly examine how synonyms and entailment could be added to improve the coverage of the system. One idea is to leverage wiki page links to identify synonymous entities similar to the work presented in (Spitkovsky and Chang, 2012). In addition, we will expand our crawling efforts to gather larger text corpora and add more question types to the question parser.

Future work will continue to emphasize the visualization of question parsing and answer alignment in order to aid discussion with the research community about the strengths and limitations of SRL for QA.

[4]The demonstrator is available online at http://www.textmining.tu-berlin.de/nerdle/

[5]http://www.absurdtrivia.com

Acknowledgements

We would like to thank the anonymous reviewers for their helpful comments. Umar Maqsud, Sebastian Arnold, Michael Hülfenhaus and Alan Akbik received funding from the European Union's Seventh Framework Programme (FP7/2007-2013) under grant agreement no ICT-2009-4-1 270137 'Scalable Preservation Environments' (SCAPE).

References

Collin F Baker, Charles J Fillmore, and John B Lowe. 1998. The berkeley framenet project. In *Proceedings of the 36th Annual Meeting of the Association for Computational Linguistics and 17th International Conference on Computational Linguistics-Volume 1*, pages 86–90. Association for Computational Linguistics.

Jinho D Choi and Martha Adviser-Palmer. 2012. Optimization of natural language processing components for robustness and scalability.

Anthony Fader, Luke S Zettlemoyer, and Oren Etzioni. 2013. Paraphrase-driven learning for open question answering. In *ACL (1)*, pages 1608–1618.

Paul Kingsbury Martha and Martha Palmer. 2002. From treebank to propbank.

Deepak Ravichandran and Eduard Hovy. 2002. Learning surface text patterns for a question answering system. In *Proceedings of the 40th Annual Meeting on Association for Computational Linguistics*, pages 41–47. Association for Computational Linguistics.

Dan Shen and Mirella Lapata. 2007. Using semantic roles to improve question answering. In *EMNLP-CoNLL*, pages 12–21. Citeseer.

Valentin I Spitkovsky and Angel X Chang. 2012. A cross-lingual dictionary for english wikipedia concepts. In *LREC*, pages 3168–3175.

NTU-MC Toolkit: Annotating a Linguistically Diverse Corpus

Liling Tan
Universität des Saarland
Campus, 66123 Saarbrücken, Germany
alvations@gmail.com

Francis Bond
Nanyang Technological University
14 Nanyang Drive, Singapore 637332
bond@ieee.org

Abstract

The NTU-MC Toolkit is a compilation of tools to annotate the Nanyang Technological University - Multilingual Corpus (NTU-MC). The NTU-MC is a parallel corpora of linguistically diverse languages (Arabic, English, Indonesian, Japanese, Korean, Mandarin Chinese, Thai and Vietnamese). The NTU-MC thrives on the mantra of "*more data is better data and more annotation is better information*". Other than increasing parallel data from diverse language pairs, annotating the corpus with various layers of information allows corpora linguists to discover linguistic phenomena and provides computational linguists with pre-annotated features for various NLP tasks. In addition to the agglomeration existing tools into a single python wrapper library, we have implemented three tools (`Mini-segmenter`, `GaChalign` and `Indotag`) that (i) provides users with varying analysis of the corpus, (ii) improves the state-of-art performance and (iii) reimplements a previously unavailable annotation tool as a free and open tool. This paper briefly describes the wrapper classes available in the toolkit and introduces and demonstrates the usage of the `Mini-segmenter`, `GaChalign` and `Indotag`.

1 Introduction

The NTU-MC Toolkit was developed in conjunction with the compilation of the Nanyang Technological University - Multilingual Corpus (NTU-MC) (Tan and Bond, 2012). It is an agglomeration of existing state-of-art tools into a single python wrapper library. The NTU-MC Toolkit provides python wrapper classes for tokenizers and Part-of-Speech (POS) taggers for the respectively languages:

- Stanford Segmenter and POS taggers (Arabic and Chinese)
- POSTECH `POSTAG/K` tagger (Korean)
- `tinysegmenter` and `MeCab` (Japanese)
- `JVnTextPro` (Vietnamese)

Additionally, we implemented three tools to provide complementary or better annotations, viz.:

- `Mini-segmenter` (Chinese): Dictionary based Chinese segmenter
- `GaChalign` (Crosslingual): Gale-Church Sentence-level Aligner with variable parameters
- `Indotag` (Indonesian): Conditional Random Field (CRF) POS tagger.

The following sections of the paper will briefly describe the wrapper classes available in the toolkit (Section 2) and introduce and demonstrate the usage of the `Mini-segmenter` (Section 3), `GaChalign` (Section 4) and `Indotag` (Section 5).

2 Tokenization and POS Tagger Wrappers

Python wrapper classes were written for (i) Stanford Segmenter and POS tagger (Chang et al., 2008; Toutanova et al., 2003), (ii) POSTECH `POSTAG/K` tagger (Lee et al., 2002), (iii) `tinysegmenter` and `MeCab` (Kudo et al., 2004) and (iv) `JVnTextPro` (Nguyen et al., 2010). Although scientifically uninteresting, it simplifies usage of annotation tools especially for beginner who are new to Natural Language Processing or python programming. The wrapper classes are also compatible with corpora readers of the Natural Language Toolkit (NLTK).

Usage Users can either invoke the wrapper classes programmatically[1]:

```
$ python
»> from ntumc.tk import postech
»> sentence = u"싱가포르에서가장유명한하이난식치킨라이스음식점중하나인Tian
Tian Hainanese Chicken Rice는맥스웰푸드센터(Maxwell Food Centre)에위치해
있으며, 음식점앞에는손님들이매일길게줄지어서있습니다."
»> postech.postagk(sentence)
[(u'싱가포르', 'NNP'), (u'에서', 'JKB'), (u'가장', 'MAG'), (u'유명',
'XR'), (u'하', 'XSA'), (u'ㄴ', 'ETM'), (u'하이난식', 'NNG'), ...]
```

or via command line:

```
$ echo "싱가포르에서가장유명한하이난식치킨라이스음식점중하나인Tian Tian
Hainanese Chicken Rice는맥스웰푸드센터(Maxwell Food Centre)에위치해있으며,
음식점앞에는손님들이매일길게줄지어서있습니다." > input.txt
$ python ntumc/tk/postech.py input.txt > output.txt
```

3 Mini-segmenter

The `mini-segmenter` is dictionary based Chinese segmenter that capitalizes on token length as heuristics for Chinese text tokenization. The tool includes a dictionary of Singaporean Chinese NEs crawled from Wikipedia titles and articles on Singapore.

Motivation The mini-segmenter was created to resolve the problem of segmenting localized Chinese words from the Singaporean variety of Mandarin Chinese in the NTU-MC. After manual inspection, the Stanford Chinese segmenter[2] was segmenting the Chinese tokens with the wrong word boundary. For example, the Stanford Chinese word segmenter wrongly tokenized 乌节路 *wujielu* "Orchard road" as 乌_节路 wu jielu "black joint-road". Originally, these topological terms were re-segmented with a manually crafted dictionary built using Wikipedia's Chinese translations of English names of Singapore places and streets. Then we found more localized Named Entities (NEs) for person names, organizations and food terms. Short of building a manually segmented corpus and retraining the Stanford segmenter models, a simple dictionary approach to segmentation could resolve out-of-domain issue.

Innovation A lightweight lexicon/dictionary based Chinese text segmenter. The advantage of using a lexicon/dictionary for text segmentation is the ability to localize and scale according to the Chinese variety or domain. The `mini-segmenter` ranks the token boundaries based on sum of the square of the tokens' character length, $\sum_i^n len(token_i)^2$, where *n* is the number of tokens and *len(token)* is the character length of each token. This novel scoring is based on the preference for larger chunks than smaller chunks in a sentence.

Usage The full documentation of the `mini-segmenter` can be found on `https://code.google.com/p/mini-segmenter/`

[1]The example sentence in English, *"One of the most famous Hainanese chicken rice stalls in Singapore, Tian Tian Hainanaese Chiken Rice is located in the Maxwell Food Centre, with long queues forming in front of the stall every day."*

[2]both Penn Chinese Treebank (ctb) and Peking University (pku) models

Results We evaluate the `mini-segmenter` output against the Stanford segmenter output with the `fish-head-curry.txt` from the NTU-MC which was was previously selected at random as a text sample for human annotators to verify the tagger accuracy. The Stanford segmenter with Stanford POS tagger, it achieved 85.94% POS accuracy with 19% mis-segments. Using the `mini-segmenter` with the Stanford POS tagger, it achieved 91.27% POS accuracy with 11.43% mis-segments.

4 GaChalign

The `GaChalign` tool is sentence alignment tool to align sentences given a bitext. The tool is a modification of the original Gale-Church algorithm that capitalized on ratio of characters/tokens of two languages in the bitext to align the sentences (Gale and Church, 1993).

Motivation The Gale-Church algorithm had parameters tuned to suit Indo-European languages more specifically German-English language pairs. When using state-of-art sentence alignment tool based on Gale-Church algorithm to align Chinese, Japanese or Korean texts to their respective English texts, the NTU-MC reported a poor performance in F-measure metrics adheres to standards set by the ARCADE II project (Chiao et al. 2006). We want to see whether it is possible to improve the algorithm by tune algorithm using language-pair specific parameters.

Innovation We replaced the mean, variance and penalty parameters from the Gale-Church algorithm with language-pair specific parameters automatically calculated from a non-aligned corpus.

Results Our experiment with English-Japanese corpus has shown that (i) simply using the calculated character mean from the unaligned text improves precision and recall of the algorithm; from 61.0% (default parameters) to 62.0% (language specific) F-scores and (ii) using language specific penalties further increased the F-scores to 62.9%. However, aligning syllabic/logographic language (Japanese) to alphabetic language (English) remains a challenge for Gale-Church algorithm[3].

5 Indotag

The `Indotag` is a probabilistic Conditional Random Field (CRF) Bahasa Indonesian Part of Speech (POS) tagger with the specifications recommended by (Pisceldo et al., 2009). The pre-trained model is based on the unigram CRF with 2-left and 2-right context features using the Universitas Indonesia's 1 million word corpus compiled under the Pan Asia Networking Localization (PANL10N) project.

Motivation To reimplement the Indonesian POS tagger described in Pisceldo et al. (2010) using free and open data and licensing it as open source tool.

Innovation None or not much. An open source reimplementation of a Bahasa Indonesian POS tagger.

Result The IndoTag achieved 78% accuracy when annotating the the `fish-head-curry.txt` text sample from the NTU-MC.

6 Discussion

While English POS tagging reports >97% accuracy (Manning, 2011) and sentence alignments for Indo-European languages performs well at >96% (Gale and Church, 1993; Varga et al., 2007), there is much room for improvement with regards to POS tagger accuracy for Asian languages and automatic sentence alignments from syllabic/logographic languages to alphabetic ones. Even though the languages in the NTU-MC are not considered low-resource languages, the tools to annotate them have limited performance. While the maintainers of the NTU-MC continues to push the performance of the individual tools for these languages, we urge researchers to work on improving NLP tools/application for Asian languages.

[3]Detailed evaluation on the `GaChalign` experiments can be found on `https://code.google.com/p/gachalign/`

7 Conclusion

We have introduced the NTU-MC Toolkit that was compiled to annotated the linguistically diverse NTU-MC. The toolkit agglomerate existing tools into a single python wrapper library. The toolkit also implemented the novel dictionary-based segmenter (`Mini-segmenter`) to improve state-of-art performance for Chinese segmentation, an modified Gale-Church algorithm (`GaChalign`) to improve sentence alignments for syllabic-alphabetic language pairs and reimplemented an open source `Indotag` Bahasa Indonesian POS tagger.

Acknowledgements

This research was partially funded by a joint JSPS/NTU grant on Revealing Meaning through Multiple Languages and the Erasmus Mundus Action 2 program MULTI of the European Union, grant agreement number 2009-5259-5.

The research leading to these results has received funding from the People Programme (Marie Curie Actions) of the European Union's Seventh Framework Programme FP7/2007-2013/ under REA grant agreement n ° 317471.

References

Pi-Chuan Chang, Michel Galley, and Christopher D Manning. 2008. Optimizing chinese word segmentation for machine translation performance. In *Proceedings of the Third Workshop on Statistical Machine Translation*, pages 224–232. Association for Computational Linguistics.

William A. Gale and Kenneth Ward Church. 1993. A program for aligning sentences in bilingual corpora. *Computational Linguistics*, 19(1):75–102.

Taku Kudo, Kaoru Yamamoto, and Yuji Matsumoto. 2004. Applying conditional random fields to japanese morphological analysis. In *EMNLP*, pages 230–237.

Gary Geunbae Lee, Jeongwon Cha, and Jong-Hyeok Lee. 2002. Syllable-pattern-based unknown-morpheme segmentation and estimation for hybrid part-of-speech tagging of korean. *Computational Linguistics*, 28(1):53–70.

Christopher D Manning. 2011. Part-of-speech tagging from 97% to 100%: is it time for some linguistics? In *Computational Linguistics and Intelligent Text Processing*, pages 171–189. Springer.

Cam-Tu Nguyen, Xuan-Hieu Phan, and Thu-Trang Nguyen. 2010. Jvntextpro: A java-based vietnamese text processing tool. `http://jvntextpro.sourceforge.net/`.

Femphy Pisceldo, Ruli Manurung, and Mirna Adriani. 2009. Probabilistic part-of-speech tagging for bahasa indonesia.

Liling Tan and Francis Bond. 2012. Building and annotating the linguistically diverse ntu-mc (ntu-multilingual corpus). In *International Journal of Asian Language Processing, 22(4)*, page 161–174.

Kristina Toutanova, Dan Klein, Christopher D Manning, and Yoram Singer. 2003. Feature-rich part-of-speech tagging with a cyclic dependency network. In *Proceedings of the 2003 Conference of the North American Chapter of the Association for Computational Linguistics on Human Language Technology-Volume 1*, pages 173–180. Association for Computational Linguistics.

Daniel Varga, Peter Halacsy, AndraS Kornai, Viktor Nagy, Laszlo Nemeth, and Viktor TrOn. 2007. Parallel corpora for medium density languages. *Recent Advances in Natural Language Processing IV: Selected Papers from RANLP 2005*, 292:247.

RDF Triple Stores and a Custom SPARQL Front-End for Indexing and Searching (Very) Large Semantic Networks

Milen Kouylekov[♣] **and Stephan Oepen**[♣♡]
[♣] University of Oslo, Department of Informatics
[♡] Potsdam University, Department of Linguistics
{milen|oe}@ifi.uio.no

Abstract

With growing interest in the creation and search of linguistic annotations that form general graphs (in contrast to formally simpler, rooted trees), there also is an increased need for infrastructures that support the exploration of such representations, for example logical-form meaning representations or semantic dependency graphs. In this work, we lean heavily on semantic technologies and in particular the data model of the Resource Description Framework (RDF) to represent, store, and efficiently query very large collections of text annotated with graph-structured representations of sentence meaning. Our full infrastructure is available under open-source licensing, and through this system demonstration we hope to receive feedback on the general approach, explore its application to additional types of meaning representation, and attract new users and possibly co-developers.

1 Motivation: The Problem

Much work in the creation and use of language resources has focused on *tree*-shaped data structures,[1] as are commonly used for the encoding of, for example, syntactic or discourse annotations. Conversely, there has been less focus on supporting general *graphs* until recently, but there is growing interest in graph-structured representations, for example to annotate and process natural language semantics. In this work, we demonstrate how *semantic technologies*, and in particular the data model of the Resource Description Framework (RDF) can be put to use for efficient indexing and search in (very) large-scale collections of semantic graphs.

We develop a mapping to RDF graphs for a variety of semantic representations, ranging from underspecified logical-form meaning representations to 'pure' bi-lexical semantic dependency graphs, as exemplified in Figures 1 and 2 below, respectively. Against this uniform data model, we populate off-the-shelf RDF triple stores with semantic networks comprising between tens of thousands and tens of millions of analyzed sentences. To lower the technological barrier to exploration of our triple stores, we implement a compact 'designer' query language for semantic graphs through on-the-fly expansion into SPARQL. In sum, the combination of standard RDF technologies and specialized query and visualization interfaces yields a versatile and highly scalable infrastructure for search (and in principle limited forms of reasoning) over diverse types of graph-structured representations of sentence meaning.

In our view, there is little scientific innovation in this work, but our approach rather demonstrates substantial design and engineering creativity. Our semantic search infrastructure is built from the combination of industrial-grade standard technologies (Apache Jena, Lucene, and Tomcat) with an open-source application for, among others, format conversion, query processing, and visualization implemented in Java. Thus, the complete tool chain is available freely and across platforms. Its application to additional types of meaning representation (and possibly other graph-structured layers of linguistic analysis) should be relatively straightforward, and we thus believe that our infrastructure can be of immediate value to both providers and consumers of large-scale linguistic annotations that transcend tree structures.

[1] Formally, trees are a restricted form of graphs, where every node is reachable from a distinguished root node by exactly one directed path.

$$\langle\, h_1,$$
$$h_4\text{:\_a\_q}(x_6, h_7, h_5), h_8\text{:\_similar\_a\_to}(e_9, x_6), h_8\text{:comp}(e_{11}, e_9, \_), h_8\text{:\_technique\_n\_1}(x_6),$$
$$h_2\text{:\_almost\_a\_1}(e_{12}, h_{13}), h_{14}\text{:\_impossible\_a\_for}(e_3, h_{15}, i_{16}),$$
$$h_{17}\text{:\_apply\_v\_to}(e_{18}, i_{19}, x_6, x_{20}), h_{21}\text{:udef\_q}(x_{20}, h_{22}, h_{23}), h_{24}\text{:\_other\_a\_1}(e_{25}, x_{20}), h_{24}\text{:\_crop\_n\_1}(x_{20}),$$
$$h_{24}\text{:\_such+as\_p}(e_{26}, x_{20}, x_{27}), h_{40}\text{:implicit\_conj}(x_{27}, x_{33}, x_{38}),$$
$$h_{31}\text{:udef\_q}(x_{33}, h_{32}, h_{34}), h_{35}\text{:\_cotton\_n\_1}(x_{33}), h_{46}\text{:\_and\_c}(x_{38}, x_{43}, x_{47}),$$
$$h_{41}\text{:udef\_q}(x_{43}, h_{42}, h_{44}), h_{45}\text{:\_soybean\_u\_unknown}(x_{43}), h_{48}\text{:udef\_q}(x_{47}, h_{49}, h_{50}), h_{51}\text{:\_rice\_n\_1}(x_{47})$$
$$\{\, h_{49} =_q h_{51}, h_{42} =_q h_{45}, h_{32} =_q h_{35}, h_{22} =_q h_{24}, h_{15} =_q h_{17}, h_{13} =_q h_{14}, h_7 =_q h_8, h_1 =_q h_2 \,\}\,\rangle$$

Figure 1: Example logical form meaning representation (MRS; taken from DeepBank).

2 Technology: Core Components

Our system architecture comprises two core components, viz. (a) the RDF repository, a database storing semantic networks in RDF triple form, and (b) the Web application, an interface for interactive search and visualization over the RDF repository.

Representing Semantic Graphs in RDF The RDF data model is based on statements about resources in the form of *subject–predicate–object* triples. The subject denotes the resource, and the predicate denotes traits or aspects of the resource, thus expressing a relationship between the subject and the object. A database that can store such expression and evaluate queries to them is called a triple store.

In Kouylekov and Oepen (2014), we describe the conversion of different types of semantic structures into RDF graphs. To date, we have addressed three types of meaning representations, viz. (in decreasing complexity) (a) scope-underspecified logical formulas in *Minimal Recursion Semantics* (MRS; Copestake et al., 2005); (b) variable-free *Elementary Dependency Structures* (EDS; Oepen and Lønning, 2006); and (c) bi-lexical dependency graphs as used in Task 8 at SemEval 2014 on *Broad-Coverage Semantic Dependency Parsing* (SDP; Oepen et al., 2014; Ivanova et al., 2012). For all three formats, we draw on (a) gold-standard annotations from DeepBank (Flickinger et al., 2012), a re-annotation of the venerable Penn Treebank WSJ Corpus (Marcus et al., 1993); and on (b) much larger collections of automatically generated analyses over the full English Wikipedia from the WikiWoods Treecache (Flickinger et al., 2010).

To store MRS, EDS, and SDP structures, we created small ontologies for each type of representation, building on a common core of shared ontology elements. In a nutshell, the EDS and SDP ontologies provide a generic representation of directed graphs with (potentially complex) node and edge labels; the dependencies proper, i.e. labeled arcs of the graph, are encoded as RDF object properties. The MRS ontology, on the other hand, distinguishes different types of nodes, corresponding to full predications vs. individual logical variables vs. hierarchically organized sub-properties of variables. Mapping the (medium-complexity) EDS graphs from DeepBank and WikiWoods onto RDF, for example, yields around 12 million and 4.3 billion triples, respectively (for the semantic dependencies of about 37 thousand and 48 million sentences in the two resources).

Web Application The core of our Web application is a search engine that executes SPARQL queries against the RDF repository. SPARQL is an RDF query language to search triple stores, allowing one to retrieve and manipulate RDF data. It is fully standardized and considered one of the key technologies of the Semantic Web. A SPARQL query can consist of triple patterns, conjunctions, disjunctions, and optional filters and functions. The query processor searches for sets of triples that match the patterns expressed in the query, binding variables in the query to the corresponding parts of each triple.

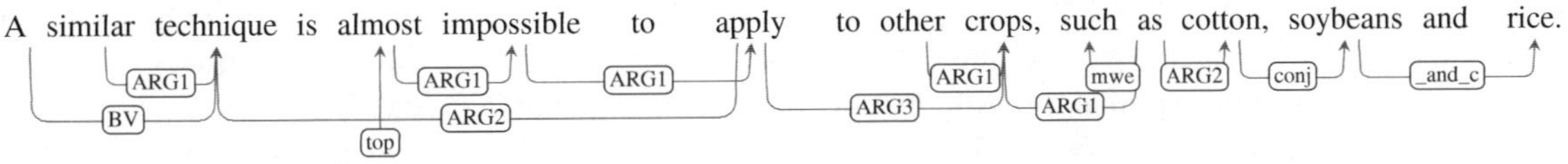

Figure 2: Example bi-lexical semantic dependencies (SDP; taken from DeepBank).

```
PREFIX sdp:<http://wesearch.delph-in.net/rdf/sdp#>
PREFIX dm:<http://wesearch.delph-in.net/rdf/sdp/dm#>
select ?graph
where {
 GRAPH ?graph {
  ?101 sdp:form "quarterly"^^xsd:string .
  ?x dm:lemma "result"^^xsd:string .
  {
   ?100 dm:pos "vbp"^^xsd:string
   UNION ?100 dm:pos "vbg"^^xsd:string
   UNION ...
  }
  ?101 dm:arg1 ?x .
  {
   ?100 dm:arg1 ?x UNION ?100 dm:arg2 ?x
   UNION ?100 dm:arg3 ?x UNION ?100 dm:arg4
  }
  FILTER
  ((!bound(?101) || !bound(?100) || ?101 != ?100)
   && (!bound(?101) || !bound(?x) || ?101 != ?x)
   && (!bound(?100) || !bound(?x) || ?100 != ?x))
 }
}
GROUP BY ?graph
ORDER BY ?graph
```

Figure 3: Core of the auto-generated SPARQL query corresponding to our running example.

Our infrastructure supports the definition of families of 'meta' query languages, to address semantic structures in a form that is more compact and much better adapted to the specific target format than SPARQL. An example of such a 'designer' language is the WeSearch Query Language (WQL), which was used in the context of the SemEval 2014 SDP task.[2] By way of informal introduction, consider the following example query:

(1)
```
/v*[ARG* x]
quarterly[ARG1 x]
x:+result
```

This example is comprised of three *predications*, one per line. The following characters have *operator* status: '/' (slash), '*' (asterisk), '[' and ']' (left and right square bracket), ':' (colon), and '+' (plus sign). This is a near-complete list of operator characters in WQL. Each predication can be composed of (i) an *identifier*, followed by a colon if present; (ii) a *form* pattern; (iii) a *lemma* pattern, prefixed by a plus sign, if present; (iv) a *part-of-speech* (PoS) pattern, prefixed by a slash, if present; and (v) a list of *arguments*, enclosed in square brackets, if present. Patterns can make use of Lucene-style wildcards, with the asterisk matching any number of characters, and a question mark ('?') to match a single character.

Thus, our example query searches for a verbal predicate (any PoS tag starting with 'v'), that takes any form of the lemma 'result' as its argument (in the range $\text{ARG}_1 \dots \text{ARG}_n$), where this argument is further required to be the ARG_1 of a node labeled 'quaterly'.

The auto-generated SPARQL expression that corresponds to this example query is shown in Figure 3. The query generator replaces the wildcarded PoS pattern by the union of all matching tags (that start with 'v', e.g. '?100 dm:pos "vbp" UNION ...' Likewise, the underspecified argument relation of this predication is replaced by the union of all possible argument types. Finally, the query processor ensures a one-to-one correspondence between query elements and matching graph elements, i.e. multiple distinct query components cannot match against the same target (graph component), or vice versa. This is accomplished in SPARQL through the filter expressions towards the end of the generated query.

[2]See http://wesearch.delph-in.net/sdp/ for an on-line demonstration and additional documentation.

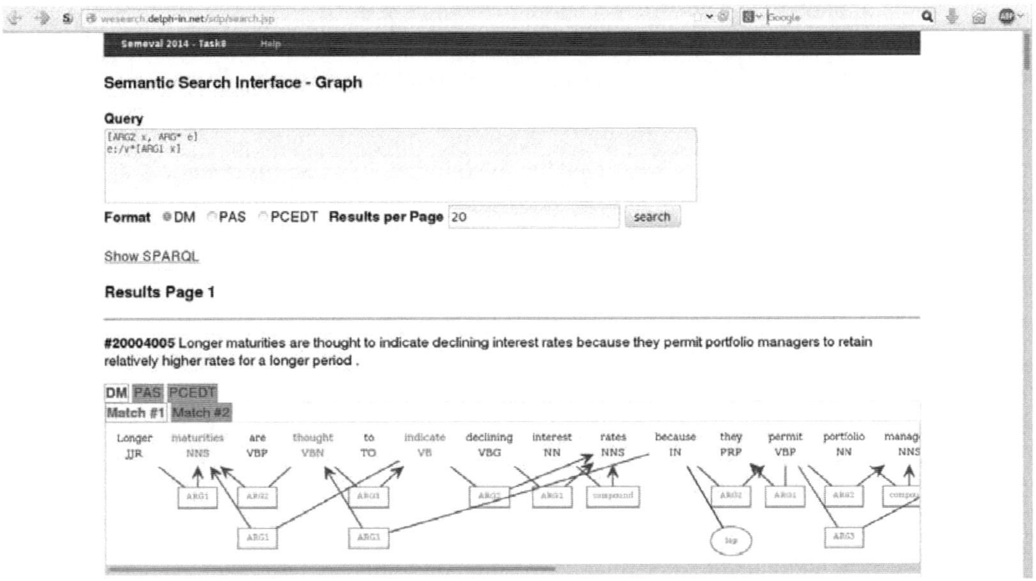

Figure 4: Screenshot of the interactive search interface, querying (semantic) object control structures.

Figure 4 shows a screenshot from the SemEval SDP user interface, demonstrating how WQL facilitates concise (and reasonably transparent) search for semantic 'object' control, i.e. a configuration involving two predicates sharing an argument in a specific assignment of roles.

Within the capabilities of the SPARQL back-end, different dialects of the meta query language can be implemented in a modular fashion, for example distinguishing different types of nodes and introducing additional node properties, as in the more complex MRS universe. Our query front-end transforms 'meta' queries into equivalent SPARQL expressions, and the search interface allows users to inspect the result of this transformation (and matching results), to possibly refine the search incrementally either at the 'meta' query layer or directly in SPARQL.

3 Demonstration: Indexing and Search

Our proposed interactive demonstration will seek to highlight (a) the flexibility of our infrastructure, i.e. walk through a series of queries of increasing complexity against different target formats; (b) its scalability, by comparing response times for different types of queries and different target formats over the large DeepBank and the vast WikiWoods indexes; and (c) the ease of 'behind the scenes' functionality, showing how additional semantic annotations in various formats can be ingested into the index. As part of this latter aspect of the demonstration, we will optionally discuss how we apply string-level indexing (in Apache Lucene) and basic frequency statistics in query interpretation and optimization, which jointly with parallelization over 'striped' RDF triple stores can yield greatly reduced response times for common types of queries to the WikiWoods index. We envision that parts of the demonstration can be organized in an audience-driven manner, for example taking as input the (possibly informal) characterization of a semantic configuration, collectively transforming it into a query against our DeepBank or WikiWoods stores, observing linguistic or technical properties of matching results, and refining the search incrementally.

Our software infrastructure is entirely open-source and (increasingly) modularized and parameterized to facilitate adaptation to additional types of annotation. Please see the project web page for licensing and access information, as well as for pointers to a variety of existing on-line demonstrations:

```
http://wesearch.delph-in.net/
```

References

Copestake, A., Flickinger, D., Pollard, C., and Sag, I. A. (2005). Minimal Recursion Semantics. An introduction. *Research on Language and Computation, 3*(4), 281 – 332.

Flickinger, D., Oepen, S., and Ytrestøl, G. (2010). WikiWoods. Syntacto-semantic annotation for English Wikipedia. In *Proceedings of the 7th International Conference on Language Resources and Evaluation.* Valletta, Malta.

Flickinger, D., Zhang, Y., and Kordoni, V. (2012). DeepBank. A dynamically annotated treebank of the Wall Street Journal. In *Proceedings of the 11th International Workshop on Treebanks and Linguistic Theories* (p. 85 – 96). Lisbon, Portugal: Edições Colibri.

Ivanova, A., Oepen, S., Øvrelid, L., and Flickinger, D. (2012). Who did what to whom? A contrastive study of syntacto-semantic dependencies. In *Proceedings of the Sixth Linguistic Annotation Workshop* (p. 2 – 11). Jeju, Republic of Korea.

Kouylekov, M., and Oepen, S. (2014). Semantic technologies for querying linguistic annotations. An experiment focusing on graph-structured data. In *Proceedings of the 9th International Conference on Language Resources and Evaluation.* Reykjavik, Iceland.

Marcus, M., Santorini, B., and Marcinkiewicz, M. A. (1993). Building a large annotated corpora of English: The Penn Treebank. *Computational Linguistics, 19*, 313 – 330.

Oepen, S., Kuhlmann, M., Miyao, Y., Zeman, D., Flickinger, D., Hajič, J., . . . Zhang, Y. (2014). SemEval 2014 Task 8. Broad-coverage semantic dependency parsing. In *Proceedings of the 8th International Workshop on Semantic Evaluation.* Dublin, Ireland.

Oepen, S., and Lønning, J. T. (2006). Discriminant-based MRS banking. In *Proceedings of the 5th International Conference on Language Resources and Evaluation* (p. 1250 – 1255). Genoa, Italy.

What or Who is Multilingual Watson?

Keith Cortis
IBM Ireland
keithcor@ie.ibm.com

Urvesh Bhowan
IBM Ireland
URVESHBH@ie.ibm.com

Ronan Mac an tSaoir
IBM Ireland
ronan.mcateer@ie.ibm.com

D.J. McCloskey
IBM Ireland
dj_mccloskey@ie.ibm.com

Mikhail Sogrin
IBM Ireland
SOGRIMIK@ie.ibm.com

Ross Cadogan
IBM Ireland
ROSSCADO@ie.ibm.com

Abstract

IBM Watson is an intelligent open-domain question answering system capable of answering questions posed in natural language. However, the system originally developed to compete against human players on Jeopardy! is heavily reliant on English language components, such as the English Slot Grammar parser, which impacts multilingual extensibility and scalability. This paper presents a working prototype for a multilingual Watson, introducing the major challenges encountered and their proposed solutions.

1 Introduction

IBM Watson is an intelligent open-domain question answering (QA) system capable of answering questions posed in natural language (Ferrucci, 2012). The open-domain QA problem is one of the most challenging in computer science and artificial intelligence, as it touches on aspects of information retrieval, Natural Language Processing (NLP), knowledge representation, machine learning and reasoning. Since Jeopardy! in 2011 (Ferrucci et al., 2010), Watson has been applied successfully to other domains, such as healthcare, finance and customer engagement. However, like Jeopardy!, these application areas deal exclusively with English data. The system is therefore heavily reliant on English NLP components, in particular, the rule-based English Slot Grammar (ESG) parser used throughout. While the ESG parser performs well and has limited multilingual capabilities, the required grammar or slot rules are language-specific, impacting scalability and deployment speed. This paper presents some of the major challenges and proposed solutions to extend Watson to support any natural languag. We introduce a robust cross-lingual method for identifying crucial characteristics in a question (such as the Lexical Answer Type), which shows similar expressiveness to the hand-crafted English-based implementation. We outline a system for detecting the same named entities across text in multiple languages, and our current effort to train a multilingual Watson system using Wikipedia data for demonstration at Coling 2014. The demo setup and a brief discussion of results is also presented.

2 Overview of Watson Architecture

This section presents an overview of the DeepQA architecture for multilingual Watson. In **Question Analysis** a detailed syntactic and semantic analysis is performed on the input question. Unstructured text is converted to structured information for use in later components. This process uses a series of NLP technologies, such as a statistically trained natural language parser, and components for named entity recognition, anaphora resolution and relation extraction. The Lexical Answer Type and Focus are important examples, described later. The **Hypothesis Generation** phase produces all possible candidate answers for a given question. Watson searches its corpora for relevant content. Example sources include unstructured knowledge, such as Wikipedia and structured resources including DBpedia and PRISMATIC. Potential answers to the question are generated from the retrieved content as unscored hypotheses. In **Supporting Evidence Retrieval**, the system gathers additional supporting evidence for each hypothesis by searching for occurrences of the candidate answer in the context of analysed question data.

Hypothesis and Evidence Scoring uses many scoring algorithms to determine the relevance of retrieved candidate answers. Each scorer, whether context dependent or independent, produces a measure of how well the evidence supports a candidate answer for a question. The **Final Merging and Ranking** phase merges equivalent candidate answers and uses a machine learning model to rank the final merged set of answers accordingly.

3 NLP and Parsing in Multilingual Watson

Syntactic parsing plays an important role throughout the major stages in Watson architecture, from question analysis, to primary search and answer scoring. We aim to investigate the impact of deep syntactic parsing compared to shallow methods for named entities, temporal and geographic references, etc. It is thought that accurate determination of the roles these aspects play requires a deeper analysis of sentence structure. For example, in the original system, the rules which detect the question focus and LAT are heavily dependent on the deep syntactical parse. Our experiments have show comparable results in this task with shallow methods. However, in corpus ingestion aspects such as building syntactic frames in order to learn axioms, such as "is _a(liquid, fluid)" and vice-versa, the subject-verb-object directionality of a statement is paramount.

Watson uses the rule-based ESG parser (McCord et al., 2012), which performs exceptionally well in terms of parse quality and throughput, and defines our parsing benchmark. The XSG formalism underpinning ESG supports new languages through the generation of language-specific grammar or slot rules. This activity requires significant effort from highly skilled linguists for each new language. As the system further evolves for new domains and use-cases, such rules must be revised and extended, resulting in a long term requirement for this specialised skillset. To address this skill requirement and enable a more scalable approach, a move towards statistical parsing methods is being investigated. We identified the following attributes of our ideal parsing technology. It should be multilingually capable, fast (compared to XSG, currently 2 orders of magnitude faster than current statistical parsers); highly accurate (comparable with XSG); easily extensible to new languages with low effort (relative to XSG); easy (and fast) to train on a new language or domain; memory efficient; robust to noisy/ungrammatical input; support a rich set of annotation features (ESG has 70+); facilitate overriding of biases in training data.

Our investigations indicate that meeting all of these requirements will be a challenge in any single parsing formalism. Statistical dependency parsing allowing for non-projective trees appears to be a good fit for the variation in language structure that we will need to support (McDonald et al., 2013). Experiments with MSTParser and the Eisner algorithm in Italian have shown promise from a quality point of view. We have also identified a language-independent formal representation of a parse. McDonald et al. (2013) present a harmonized set of dependency labels for multilingual parsing which has been adapted for other typologically diverse languages, such as Chinese and Finnish and encourages convergence for reuse. Our initial investigations using this set for English, Spanish, French, Brazilian Portugese and German text, suggest minimal modification is required to adapt for use in question answering. Modification of existing pipeline components to a more streamlined dependency structure than the XSG formalism, will form part of ongoing research.

Treebanks of parse data with part-of-speech and dependency labels will be required in order to train the chosen parser. There are several examples of existing Treebanks for the chosen languages, such as the IULA Spanish LSP Treebank[1]. However, the context of the data included is very rarely representative of question-answering scenarios. For example, in the IULA corpus, there are less than 10 questions. We will therefore be supplementing this training data with our own hand-annotated corpora, in order to increase the validity of the trained parser for use in question answering. As mentioned previously, we will also be adapting these resources to use the UniPos and UniDep part-of-speech and dependency label sets. In parallel to the

[1] http://www.iula.upf.edu/recurs01_tbk_uk.htm

investigations for multilingual parsing, we have also considered the requirements of a parser-independent system which can leverage shallow parse data in order to perform reasonably well at the same task. The multilingual LAT detection component which builds on part-of-speech data to identify noun phrases and associated head words and modifiers, may be additionally used to generate a simple linked parse structure without dependency labels. As the number of supported languages in the system grows, it is important to have a meaningful baseline upon which to build, even while a parser or appropriate training data for the new language is still being prepared. The parser-independent capability will be particularly useful in this context.

4 Other Challenges Faced in Multilingual Watson

4.1 Multilingual Lexical Answer Type (LAT)

For the Jeopardy! challenge, one of the most critical elements in the system design was the recognition of what is termed the LAT (Ferrucci et al., 2010). This is typically a noun or noun-phrase in the question which identifies the type of answer required, without any attempt to evaluate its semantics. Similarly influential, the Focus is the part of the sentence that, if replaced with the answer, makes the question a standalone statement. For example, in the question "What countries share a border with China?", the LAT is "countries", and the Focus is "What countries". Replacing this piece of text with the answer becomes a valid standalone statement, such as "Russia, Mongolia, India, ..., share a border with China". Ferrucci et al. (2010) found that identifying a candidate answer as an instance of a LAT is an important part of the answer scoring mechanism, and a common source of critical errors.

In the original system, a Prolog component was used to match specific English language patterns for various purposes including LAT detection. In a multilingual context, we require a more robust method that retains the same potential expressiveness and performance of a good Prolog implementation, while facilitating cross-lingual pattern recognition. Our multilingual prototype uses lexical features, such as part-of-speech and lemma. Pattern matching rules over these features were developed using the IBM LanguageWare[2] rules engine which provides a comparable level of expression with standard Prolog implementations. While maintaining pipeline accuracy for English, this prototype was also 4 times faster than the original Prolog modules. A statistical method that was originally used in the Jeopardy! pipeline is also being adapted for use in a multilingual context. This approach will reduce the dependency on hard-coded language-specific parsing rules. The use of harmonized Stanford dependencies (McDonald et al., 2013) will further enhance these efforts.

4.2 Detecting Concepts across Multiple Languages

One of the most challenging aspects of multilingual NLP is the recognition of identical concepts across text in multiple languages. Wikipedia and Wiktionary provide translations of words from one language to another, however they do not establish language-independent identifiers for concepts. Open Multilingual Wordnet (OMW) project[3] links WordNet style structured resources, in up to 150 languages, to the Princeton Wordnet of English[4]. While Princeton Wordnet is made specifically for English, its numeric ID system is in fact a set of language-independent identifiers, and may be used to relate concepts and words. The OMW project provides links to the same IDs from words in other languages. The Extended version of the OMW dataset additionally links Wiktionary data with these WordNet structured resources, thus greatly improving coverage of vocabulary.

In the multilingual Watson system, we can perform semantic analysis using domain knowledge irrespective of the language of the question, or the domain. This is enabled by a process of concept identification that maps instances of concepts in natural language text to a set of

[2] http://www-01.ibm.com/software/globalization/topics/languageware/
[3] http://compling.hss.ntu.edu.sg/omw/
[4] http://wordnet.princeton.edu/

language-independent identifiers. Our implementation takes inspiration from efforts, such as the OMW and the Unstructured Medical Language System[5] in the biomedical domain, which use alphanumeric labels to identify individual semantic concepts, irrespective of the forms these concepts take in any language. In addition to these unique identifiers, our design incorporates fully qualified URI namespaces for these instances, as proposed by the W3C Semantic Web Standard, in order to distinguish between instances of a concept in various contexts.

In parallel with this concept ID system, we have developed a lexicon expansion framework that incorporates pluggable transformation modules to generate alternative forms for lexicon entries. This facilitates the increased coverage of semantic concepts in the chosen domain text, which remain linked to their respective namespace-qualified unique identifiers.

4.3 Machine Learning Challenges

The original Watson system uses a cascade of multiple trained machine-learning models to decide if a candidate answer is correct. In each cascade, questions are categorised and routed to models trained for different types of English Jeopardy! questions. Training these models requires questions with known answers for the different question types. However, the same Jeopardy! style question characteristics may not apply or be evident in different languages. To address this, we simplified the hand-crafted model routing in the multilingual system to make no *a priori* assumptions about the question type. While this requires good model generalisation over a potentially broad range of questions, this is offset by the smaller but highly-focused feature set used in this multilingual system. Initial features were chosen by ranking scorers whose output showed the highest correlation to the correct class on experiments with English questions.

5 Multilingual Watson on Wikipedia-based Questions

5.1 Searching over Wikipedia

Ingestion is the process of transforming documents for use by Watson. Raw Wikipedia XML documents[6] are transformed into the TREC standard[7]. These TREC files must conform to the UTF-8 character encoding scheme. The TREC-formatted documents are then transformed into Lucene[8] search indices. During the TREC transformation process, text normalisation and character replacement was being conducted for English text. All corpora text in Unicode was normalised to ASCII, e.g., for the term *Japón*, the accent was stripped from the *ó* character, thus normalising to *Japon*. In addition, characters with particular ISO8859 codes, were replaced, such as π with the character *n*. Since the Jeopardy! pipeline handles only ASCII character encoding, this prevents the system from generating correct answers which contain non-ASCII characters, dramatically lowering recall on multilingual questions. These issues are resolved in the multilingual Watson system, which uses Unicode in the Normalisation Form Compatibility Composition.

5.2 Wikipedia-based Questions and Answers

We used 3732 English questions with known answers (originally gathered by the Watson team) as our question base (split into 3359 training and 373 test questions). These questions were machine translated to Spanish, French and Brazilian Portugese using IBM's n.Fluent Translation service[9] . The test set was manually reviewed to correct any translation errors, and questions deemed unanswerable (where Watson had no means of retrieving the correct answer from the source Wikipedia corpus) were removed. To assist in identifying which questions are unanswerable, the MediaWiki API[10] (an open web API service providing access to Wikipedia meta-data) was

[5]http://www.nlm.nih.gov/research/umls/

[6]Obtained from: http://dumps.wikimedia.org/

[7]For the Text REtrieval Conference (TREC) standard see: http://trec.nist.gov/

[8]http://lucene.apache.org/

[9]http://www-03.ibm.com/press/us/en/pressrelease/28887.wss

[10]http://www.mediawiki.org/wiki/API

used to filter questions whose answers could not be mapped to an article title in the Wikipedia source corpus.The MediaWiki API also has a cross-language aspect which provides useful redirect information between Wikipedia article titles, which we used to supplement our answers, e.g., "JFK" in English redirects to "John F. Kennedy" in Spanish. The manual curation of the translated English questions for English, Spanish, French and Brazilian Portuguese ensure that the same question set is used across the different languages, and that these common questions are all answerable with respect to their respective Wikipedia corpus.

6 Demo Setup and Discussion of Results

The setup of the demo will include a multilingual QA system (for several languages, such as English, Spanish, French, Brazilian Portuguese, etc.). The participants attending the Coling conference will be able to ask the multilingual Watson QA system a question via its web user interface. The system will then attempt to answer the question in real-time, and will return a list of the five top-ranked candidate answers and their confidence scores. The confidence score for each candidate answer represents the likeliness that it is correct, based on the analysis of all supporting evidence gathered by the system. Any supporting evidence can also be examined for a given answer, such as the passage or document hits from the search process.

For disclosure purposes we are unable to provide details on our multilingual experimental results. Therefore, we will briefly discuss our initial baseline results and the improvements made in our current system. Our initial baseline is based on the results using the English test questions, which achieved very high (near perfect) recall and high accuracy rates. In terms of multilingual Watson, our initial recall results were very low compared to English. As a result, recall became the primary focus of our multilingual investigation. Recall was improved by around 6% with the full Unicode text normalisation support and parser-independent changes (discussed in Sections 3 and 5.1 respectively). In addition, the answer curation discussed in Section 5.2 improved recall by 9%. Other language specific improvements and customisation to the primary search components in multilingual Watson, in particular, the Lucene analyser and search query, resulted in a further 29% increase in recall. These combined efforts produced comparable recall rates for Spanish, French and Brazilian Portuguese test questions to the English questions. The next area of our investigation will be focused on accuracy improvements.

References

David A. Ferrucci, Eric W. Brown, Jennifer Chu-Carroll, James Fan, David Gondek, Aditya Kalyanpur, Adam Lally, J. William Murdock, Eric Nyberg, John M. Prager, Nico Schlaefer, and Christopher A. Welty. 2010. Building Watson: An Overview of the DeepQA Project. *AI Magazine*, 31(3):59–79.

David A. Ferrucci. 2012. Introduction to "this is watson". *IBM Journal of Research and Development*, 56(3):235–249.

Michael C. McCord, J. William Murdock, and Branimir Boguraev. 2012. Deep parsing in watson. *IBM Journal of Research and Development*, 56(3):3.

Ryan T. McDonald, Joakim Nivre, Yvonne Quirmbach-Brundage, Yoav Goldberg, Dipanjan Das, Kuzman Ganchev, Keith B. Hall, Slav Petrov, Hao Zhang, Oscar Täckström, Claudia Bedini, Núria Bertomeu Castelló, and Jungmee Lee. 2013. Universal dependency annotation for multilingual parsing. In *ACL (2)*, pages 92–97. The Association for Computer Linguistics.

A Marketplace for Web Scale Analytics and Text Annotation Services

Johannes Kirschnick[1], Torsten Kilias[1], Holmer Hemsen[1]
Alexander Löser[2], Peter Adolphs[3], Heiko Ehrig[3], Holger Düwiger[3]
(1) Technische Universität Berlin, Einsteinufer 17, 10587 Berlin, Germany
{firstname.lastname}@tu-berlin.de
(2) Beuth Hochschule für Technik Berlin, Luxemburger Straße 10, 13353 Berlin, Germany
aloeser@beuth-hochschule.de
(3) Neofonie GmbH, Robert-Koch-Platz 4, 10115 Berlin, Germany
{firstname.lastname}@neofonie.de

Abstract

We present MIA, a data marketplace which enables massive parallel processing of data from the Web. End users can combine both text mining and database operators in a structured query language called MIAQL. MIA offers many cost savings through sharing text data, annotations, built-in analytical functions and third party text mining applications. Our demonstration showcases MIAQL and its execution on the platform for the example of analyzing political campaigns.

1 Introduction

Data-driven services and data marketplaces are young phenomena (Schomm et al., 2013). Commonly known commercial examples are *Factual.com* for location-related data, *Amazon* as a marketplace for infrastructure and data, and Microsoft's *datamarket.azure.com*. These marketplaces offer common data flow and service characteristics (Muschalle et al., 2012). MIA is such a marketplace, it offers data driven services in the area of natural language processing in combination with business intelligence services for analyzing more than 600 million pages of the German language Web (from 2013-2014). The user can combine linguistic components with standard SQL operators in data execution pipes to create new data sets. The marketplace permits the user to keep the insightful data exclusive or to grant access permissions to other users for data, annotation services or pipelines. MIA enables to turn the Web, a particular rich source of information using extraction, processing and enrichment tasks (e.g., parsing or semantically annotating) into a valuable knowledge resources to support various business intelligence (BI) tasks. Such tasks are exemplified by the following questions from the area of political campaign analysis:

- What is the polarity (sentiment) associated with events found in online news media?
- Which newspapers are biased in the last years towards certain political parties?

The MIA project started in 2011, since then we observed many similar queries and demands from sales departments (monitor and identify leads that soon will buy a car), human resources (identify professionals with capabilities in text mining), market research (monitor the effectiveness of a campaign) as well as product development (incorporate feedback from customers into the development process).

1.1 Background

Transforming huge volumes of text into structured information that is suitable and useful for empowering applications in heterogeneous and previously unknown application areas is a challenge. MIA addresses this using own and third party research in the areas of text mining and distributed databases.

Single system for analytical and NLP tasks. The parse tree database (PTDB) by Tari (2012) stores dependency tagged sentences and retrieves subtrees with a key value index based on *Lucene*. MIA goes drastically beyond this functionality. It enables GATE (gate.ac.uk) and UIMA (uima.apache.org) developers to integrate their components. This greatly expands the available processing modules on the platform as existing pipelines can be easily incorporated into the marketplace. Furthermore, it gives users the ability to store and retrieve lexical, syntactic and semantic annotations. The MIA platform executes these components as user-defined functions in a massively parallel database, enables the aggregation of resulting annotations with other data sources, such as in-house relational databases, and conducts these operations, all in a single system. AnnoMarket (Tablan et al., 2013) is a marketplace for executing GATE pipelines and permits to upload third party extractors, but lacks the functionality to aggregate and join results. Rather, it requires the user to ship preliminary results to a database where the user conducts advanced analytical tasks. However, companies may eschew the high investment risk and the technical difficulties to ship and analyze hundreds of millions of documents.

Declarative languages for text mining. System-T (Chiticariu et al., 2010) includes AQL, a declarative language for defining extractors through rules. MIAQL extends this idea with SQL predicates for sub-queries, views, joins and for data crawling that operate on datasets represented as collections of nested tuples. MIA's data model incorporates a span-algebra and operators for processing sequences or trees (Kilias et al., 2013). MIA also leverages our research for extracting relations (Akbik et al., 2012) and for restricting attribute types (Kirschnick et al., 2013) which builds on the provided abstractions.

1.2 Our Contribution

MIAQL: Text mining and analytical tasks with a single structured query language. We demonstrate how our declarative language MIAQL empowers end users to describe text mining tasks. MIAQL also supports common SQL-92 operations, such as joins, views, sub-queries, aggregations and group by. We showcase how our parallel execution framework compiles a MIAQL query into a dataflow representation and finally into a set of map/reduce tasks (Dean and Ghemawat, 2008).

Data marketplace for annotation services. We showcase how data providers can integrate data sets, developers can share modules for text mining or data analytics, application vendors can offer specialized applications and analysts can use the raw or annotated data for ad-hoc queries.

Optimizations for Web-scale corpora. We showcase on 600 million pages from the German language Web how our parallel execution framework optimizes queries for distributed multi-core environments and for file-, key-value- and column-based datastores, such as HBase[1] or the Parquet.io[2] file format.

2 Demonstration

Scenario: How biased are newspapers? Consider an analyst with the hypothesis that certain newspapers bias their reports towards certain political parties. Listing 1 shows a set of queries for determining such a bias. For solving this task the analyst must first obtain a news corpus, either by crawling or by buying and downloading the documents. Next, the analyst formulates a query for spotting sentences that mention a politician and computes the subjectivity. Finally, the analyst counts these tuples over all documents, groups them by the newspaper/party, aggregates the subjectivity and sorts the results.

2.1 Execution Environment for the Obtain-Annotate-Join-Aggregate-Process

This and many other monitoring processes follow the same schema: Obtaining already exclusive data, such as fresh data, and make data even more exclusive by complementing (joining), aggregating and sorting it. Nearly every company uses similar processes in the data warehouse on relational data but not on text data from the Web. MIA supports this process now also on hundreds of millions of Web pages with the following technologies:

Simple SQL interface for analysts. MIAQL provides standard SQL-92 statements for data aggregation, such as COUNTS, MIN, MAX, AVG, GROUP BY, including sub-queries and views. As a result, MIAQL presents a familiar environment for data analysts and reduces the necessity to learn a new query language. For example, listing 1 shows aggregations for counting and averaging the subjectivity for each

[1]https://hbase.apache.org (Last visited: 16/5/2014)

[2]http://parquet.io (Last visited: 16/5/2014)

```
CREATE VIEW sentences AS
SELECT srcName,text,unnest(splitSentences(text)) AS sentence
FROM news2013;

CREATE VIEW sentencesWithPOSTags AS
SELECT *,annotatePOSTags(sentence) AS posTags
FROM sentences;

CREATE VIEW sentencesWithSubjectivity AS
SELECT *,isSentenceSubjective(text,sentence,posTags) AS
     sentenceSubjective
FROM sentencesWithPOSTags;

CREATE VIEW sentencesWithEntities AS
SELECT *,unnest(annotateEntites(sentence, posTags)) AS entity
FROM sentencesWithSubjectivity;

CREATE VIEW filterSentencesWithPoliticians AS
SELECT
     srcName,party,politician,booleanToInt(sentenceSubjective)
     AS subjectivity
FROM sentencesWithEntities AS s
     JOIN politicians AS p ON s.uri=p.uri;

SELECT srcName,party,politician,COUNT(*), AVG(subjectivity)
FROM filterSentencesWithPoliticians
GROUP BY srcName, party, politician;
```

Listing 1: The listing shows a set of views in MIAQL for correlating mentions of politicians in newspapers and detecting whether the reporting is subjective. The MIAQL optimizer compiles this into an execution plan, see Figure 1 for an example.

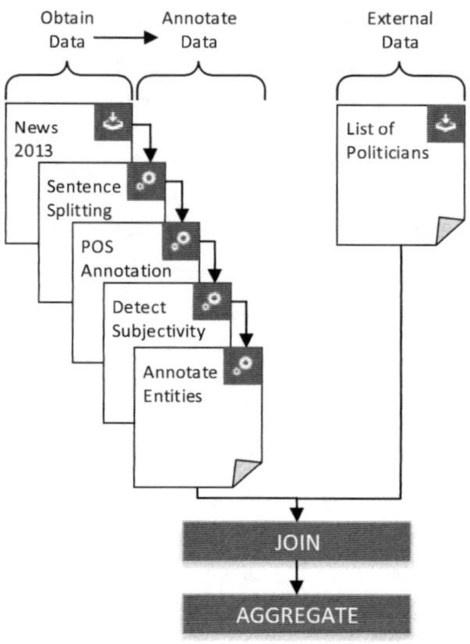

Figure 1: MIA supports user defined functions, optimizes equi, theta and cross joins into local, broadcast and repartitioning joins and supports common aggregate functions of SQL-92.

newspaper and politician/party pair. The query is transparently compiled into the data flow description language Pig Latin (Olston et al., 2008). This allows programs defined in MIAQL to be processed in a massively parallel way on a Hadoop system (Dean and Ghemawat, 2008). Figure 1 highlights the execution plan for the sample MIAQL query, which uses different data sources, processes them by executing a chain of annotators, joins the results and aggregates them to produce the final answer.

Reuse base annotators and user defined annotators. We observed from our users the need to enrich raw data with linguistic annotations at various levels. Users of the platform might be interested in named entities and their referents, topic labels or sentiment judgements for which they need to run specialized annotators. These annotators in turn might also depend on other levels of linguistic analysis. To prevent multiple processing of the same data with the same tools, the MIA platform crawls raw data and annotates it on ingestion at the most common linguistic levels. Multiple users can access these annotations across their projects and can thus save costs. For example, MIA performs **sentence splitting**, **tokenization**, **lemmatization**, **part-of-speech tagging**, **named-entity recognition** and a document-specific **topic detection** for each document. Other processing steps such as dependency parsing or entity linking (Kemmerer et al., 2014) can be applied on the fly at query time. Analysts may reuse this data in domain specific annotation functions. In the above listing the subjectivity analysis function reuses for example sentence boundaries and part-of-speech tags. The system executes such transformations as user-defined functions. Multiple functions are grouped into logical modules and registered on the platform for reuse, each with an associated description and a schema mapping from input to output tuples.

Complement Web data with in-house data. MIA permits users to upload in-house data to the distributed file system with restricted visibility. Our users join this data with the goal of complementing with existing data. For example, in the listing above a list of German politicians is joined with the list of extracted sentences to filter out all sentences that are not mentioning one of the defined politicians.

3 Lessons Learned

Data freshness, completeness and veracity. MIA's strongest asset is the ability to complement existing (possibly exclusive) in-house data with 'signals' from the Web, avoiding huge data set shipments.

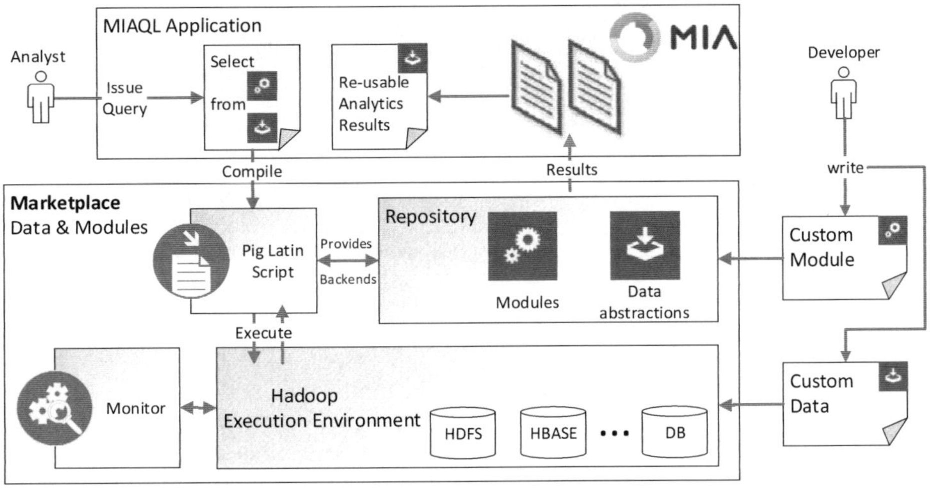

Figure 2: This figure shows the architecture of the marketplace. It contains the repository for data sets and text mining code modules. Developers can upload text mining modules, content providers can upload data sets and grant selected analysts reuse permissions. The application provides analysts with a Web interface for browsing the repository, authoring new MIAQL queries and downloading analytic results. Queries are transparently compiled into Pig Latin and executed on the distributed platform.

The Pig-Latin-based query processing engine provides users with answers within minutes. Currently, our users tolerate these answering times, for example for monitoring applications. However, users also often request fresh (minutes- hours) data, for tighter feedback loop integrations. Realizing short updates and low latency response times are research topics of the project, as well as delivering higher level insights beyond tabular reports, such as automated visualization and result clustering.

Cloud-based one-stop-shop marketplace vs. on-premise solution. Users can protect their data, functionality and processing results. However, some require running the MIA platform 'behind their firewalls'. Currently, they need to 'download' the processed results and execute the join in-house with their 'secret' data. For these users, we investigate operations for selecting the likely minimal and fresh but still highly complete data sets, such as Löser et al. (2013).

4 Current Status

The marketplace is currently available in private beta mode and accessible via a Web UI, which is displayed in Figure 3. Users can author, execute and monitor new jobs as well as inspect and download the results, while developers can create and upload new processing modules. New modules can be created by adhering to a simple tuple based processing interface defined by the platform, which greatly reduces the friction of writing new modules and leveraging existing text pipelines. The available public datasets are constantly expanded by continuously crawling the German Web, uploading new news articles and incorporating new social media posts.

While the project is targeted at providing large scale processing for German language texts, the core software platform is not tied to a particular language. All language specific contributions are packaged into separate data and processing modules. Supporting a new language sums up to creating and uploading new data and algorithm packages. More information as well as a demonstration video for MIA can be found at the project website `www.neofonie.de/forschung/mia`. We furthermore encourage requesting a demo login to the system.

Acknowledgments

We would like to thank the anonymous reviewers for their helpful comments. The work to build the demonstrator and the underlying technologies received funding from the German Federal Ministry of

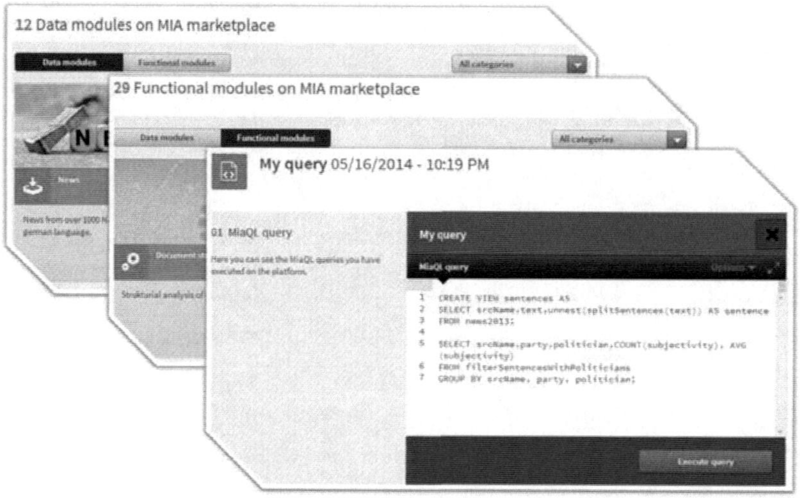

Figure 3: This figure shows the sophisticated execution environment presented by the MIA platform. The Web-driven UI supports the analysts with query authoring, data and function modules browsing as well as job monitoring and results download.

Economics and Energy (BMWi) under grant agreement 01MD11014A, "A cloud-based Marketplace for Information and Analytics on the German Web" (MIA).

References

Alan Akbik, Larysa Visengeriyeva, Priska Herger, Holmer Hemsen, and Alexander Löser. 2012. Unsupervised Discovery of Relations and Discriminative Extraction Patterns. In *COLING*, pages 17–32.

Laura Chiticariu, Rajasekar Krishnamurthy, Yunyao Li, Sriram Raghavan, Frederick Reiss, and Shivakumar Vaithyanathan. 2010. SystemT: An Algebraic Approach to Declarative Information Extraction. In *ACL*, pages 128–137.

Jeffrey Dean and Sanjay Ghemawat. 2008. MapReduce: Simplified Data Processing on Large Clusters. *Commun. ACM*, 51(1):107–113, January.

Steffen Kemmerer, Benjamin Großmann, Christina Müller, Peter Adolphs, and Heiko Ehrig. 2014. The neofonie nerd system at the erd challenge 2014. *SIGIR Forum*. To appear.

Torsten Kilias, Alexander Löser, and Periklis Andritsos. 2013. INDREX: in-database distributional relation extraction. In *DOLAP*, pages 93–100.

Johannes Kirschnick, Alan Akbik, Larysa Visengeriyeva, and Alexander Löser. 2013. Effective Selectional Restrictions for Unsupervised Relation Extraction. In *IJCNLP*. The Association for Computer Linguistics.

Alexander Löser, Christoph Nagel, Stephan Pieper, and Christoph Boden. 2013. Beyond search: Retrieving complete tuples from a text-database. *Information Systems Frontiers*, 15(3):311–329.

Alexander Muschalle, Florian Stahl, Alexander Löser, and Gottfried Vossen. 2012. Pricing Approaches for Data Markets. In *BIRTE*, pages 129–144.

Christopher Olston, Benjamin Reed, Utkarsh Srivastava, Ravi Kumar, and Andrew Tomkins. 2008. Pig latin: a not-so-foreign language for data processing. In Jason Tsong-Li Wang, editor, *SIGMOD Conference*, pages 1099–1110. ACM.

Fabian Schomm, Florian Stahl, and Gottfried Vossen. 2013. Marketplaces for data: an initial survey. *SIGMOD Record*, 42(1):15–26.

Valentin Tablan, Kalina Bontcheva, Ian Roberts, Hamish Cunningham, and Marin Dimitrov. 2013. AnnoMarket: An Open Cloud Platform for NLP. In *ACL (Conference System Demonstrations)*, pages 19–24.

Luis Tari, Phan Huy Tu, Jörg Hakenberg, Yi Chen, Tran Cao Son, Graciela Gonzalez, and Chitta Baral. 2012. Incremental information extraction using relational databases. *IEEE Trans. Knowl. Data Eng.*, 24(1):86–99.

DKPro Agreement: An Open-Source Java Library for Measuring Inter-Rater Agreement

Christian M. Meyer,[†] **Margot Mieskes,**[§†] **Christian Stab,**[†] **and Iryna Gurevych**[†‡]
[†] Ubiquitous Knowledge Processing Lab (UKP-TUDA)
Computer Science Department, Technische Universität Darmstadt
[‡] Ubiquitous Knowledge Processing Lab (UKP-DIPF)
German Institute for Educational Research
[§] Information Center for Education
German Institute for Educational Research (DIPF)
http://www.ukp.tu-darmstadt.de

Abstract

In this paper, we introduce a novel Java implementation of multiple inter-rater agreement measures, which we make available as open-source software. Besides assessing the reliability of coding tasks using S, π, κ, α, etc., we particularly support unitizing tasks by measuring α_U as the agreement of the boundaries of the identified annotation units. We provide a unified interface and data model for both tasks as well as multiple diagnostic devices for analyzing the results.

1 Introduction

Reliability is a necessary precondition for obtaining high-quality datasets and thus for drawing valid conclusions from an annotation study. Assessing the reliability by means of inter-rater agreement measures has been an established scientific practice in psychology (e.g., Cohen, 1960), medicine (Cicchetti et al., 1978), and content analysis (Krippendorff, 1980) for decades. In the computational linguistics and natural language processing community, reliability discussions have long been limited or completely ignored. It was not until Carletta's (1996) appeal that researchers started measuring the inter-rater agreement at a larger scale. However, there are still numerous papers published every year that lack a proper discussion of data quality. The reliability of the utilized datasets is, for example, not discussed at all in six out of the thirteen task description papers of SemEval-2013, and it remains shallow in another four papers, which do not provide a suitable inter-rater agreement figure.[1] A major reason for this is the limited availability of software components, which support the standard measures and are well-integrated with existing systems. In fact, many researchers currently rely on manual calculations, hasty implementations of single coefficients, or free online calculators that often lack documentation of the implementation details.

In this work, we present the novel Java-based software library *DKPro Agreement* for computing multiple inter-rater agreement measures using a shared interface and data model. For the first time, we provide a unified model for analyzing *coding* (i.e., assigning categories to fixed items) and *unitizing studies* (i.e., segmenting the data into codable units). By supporting these two fundamental annotation setups, our software can be used for analyzing many different annotation tasks including syntactic (e.g., part-of-speech tagging), semantic (e.g., word sense assignment, keyphrase identification), and discourse annotation tasks (e.g., dialogue act tagging). We particularly provide diagnostic devices for analyzing systematic disagreement, which is often overlooked in reliability discussions. DKPro Agreement is available as open-source software, thoroughly tested on a wide range of examples, and well-documented for getting started quickly.[2] Our implementation is targeted at scientists and software developers working in Java, including the large communities around the major Java-based toolkits *OpenNLP*, *DKPro*, and *GATE*.[3] The software integrates more easily with existing Java applications than statistics software such as *Octave*, *R*, or *SPSS*, and its usage requires a less pronounced statistics background.

[1] All SemEval task descriptions (http://www.cs.york.ac.uk/semeval-2013) have been discussed among the authors.

[2] DKPro Agreement is part of the DKPro Statistics library. The project is available from https://code.google.com/p/dkpro-statistics/ and licensed under the Apache License 2.0.

[3] http://opennlp.apache.org, http://code.google.com/p/dkpro-core-asl, http://gate.ac.uk

2 Related Work

Reliability is the subject of an extensive body of literature. Artstein and Poesio (2008) and Krippendorff (1980) give a general introduction to this topic. Implementations of inter-rater agreement measures exist both as stand-alone and as online tools (e.g., `http://uni-leipzig.de/~jenderek/tool/tool.htm`, `http://terpconnect.umd.edu/~dchoy/thesis/Kappa`). Most of them focus on one type of agreement measure (e.g., `http://vassarstats.net/kappa.html` and Randolph (2005) for κ as well as `http://ron.artstein.org/software.html` for α). Others are limited to a few different measures (e.g., `https://mlnl.net/jg/software/ira` and `http://dfreelon.org/utils/recalfront/recal3`). Frameworks offering a wider range of measures are either commercial with a high price tag (e.g., `http://www.medcalc.org/manual/kappa.php`) or limited to specific platforms (e.g., `http://www.agreestat.com/agreestat.html`). The situation is even worse for unitizing studies, for which we are only aware of Perry and Krippendorff's (2013) implementation available at `http://www.gabriela.trindade.nom.br/2013/02/calculating-alpha-d-and-alpha-u/`. To the best of our knowledge, there is no software library providing a large variety of agreement measures and diagnostic devices, which covers both coding and unitizing studies and which integrates well with existing systems.

3 Implementation

The standard workflow for using DKPro Agreement is (1) representing the annotated data using our unified data model, (2) measuring the agreement among the individual raters, and (3) analyzing the results using diagnostic devices and visualizations.

Data model. We provide the Java interface `IAnnotationStudy` as the basic representation of the annotated data. An annotation study consists of a set of *raters*, a set of codable *units*, and a set of *categories*, which may be used by the raters to code a unit. The categories do not have a specific type, such that any Java object (including integers and enums) may be used without any extensions.

Following Krippendorff's (1980) terminology, we distinguish two basic annotation setups: In *coding studies*, the raters receive a set of *annotation items* with fixed boundaries (e.g., full articles from a newspaper), which each of them should code ("annotate") with one of the categories (e.g., politics, economics). We consider each rater's annotation of an item a single *annotation unit*. In *unitizing studies*, the raters are asked to identify the annotation units themselves by marking their boundaries (e.g., highlighting key phrases). Depending on the task definition, the identified units may be coded with one of multiple categories or just distinguish identified segments from so-called *gaps* between these segments.

Figure 1 illustrates this data model for both setups. The framed boxes show the annotation units and the categories assigned to them. In coding studies, the units with identical index (i.e., the columns) yield the annotation items. In unitizing studies, the units may be positioned arbitrarily within the continuum. We represent missing annotations as empty boxes (coding studies) and as horizontal lines between the identified units (unitizing studies).

Software developers can either instantiate our default implementation (e.g., by reading data from flat files or databases) or implement the provided Java interfaces in order to reuse their own data model. For coding studies, there is an `addItem` method with a *varargs* parameter (i.e., a method taking an arbitrary number of parameters) for specifying the annotation of each rater for a certain item. The line `study.addItem("B", "C", null, "B")` indicates that four raters coded an item with the categories B, C, *null*, and B. We use *null* to represent missing annotations. Similarly, unitizing studies provide an `addUnit` method, which takes the boundaries and the category assigned to the unit by a certain rater. The line `study.addUnit(10, 4, 2, "A")` indicates, for instance, a unit of length 4, which starts at position 10 and which has been annotated as category A by rater 2.

Coding measures. Table 1 shows an overview of the inter-rater agreement measures currently available in DKPro Agreement. Artstein and Poesio (2008) give an overview of these measures. While the *percentage agreement* simply divides the number of agreements by the item count, all other measures perform a *chance correction*. A major difference is the assumed probability distribution for the expected agreement, which is considered different for each study and rater (i.e., *rater-specific*), the same for all

Measure	Type	Raters	Chance correction	Weighted
Percentage agreement	coding	≥ 2	–	–
Bennett et al.'s S (1954)	coding	2	uniform	–
Scott's π (1955)	coding	2	study-specific	–
Cohen's κ (1960)	coding	2	rater-specific	–
Randolph's κ (2005) [multi-S]	coding	≥ 2	uniform	–
Fleiss's κ (1971) [multi-π]	coding	≥ 2	study-specific	–
Hubert's κ (1977) [multi-κ]	coding	≥ 2	rater-specific	–
Krippendorff's α (1980)	coding	≥ 2	study-specific	✓
Cohen's weighted κ_{w} (1968)	coding	≥ 2	rater-specific	✓
Krippendorff's α_{u} (1995)	unitizing	≥ 2	study-specific	–

Table 1: Implemented inter-rater agreement measures

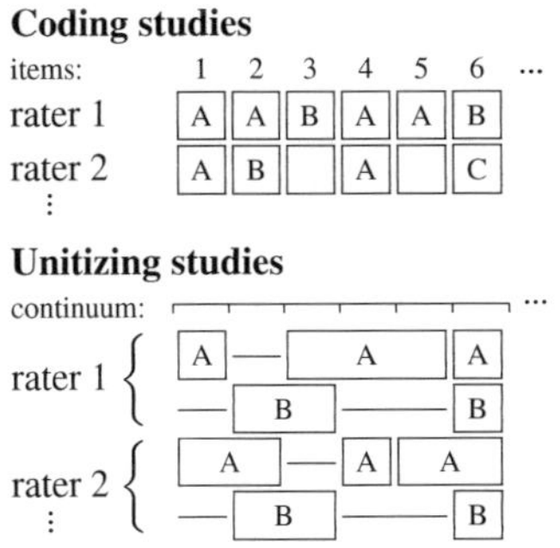

Figure 1: Data model

raters (*study-specific*), or the same for all studies and raters (*uniform*). As all of these measures are used in the literature, we need implementations for each of them to be able to compare different results. This is particularly important for κ measures, because many different definitions exist. Cohen's κ (1960) is, for instance, often compared to Fleiss's κ (1971), although both measures assume a different probability distribution. Since all measures implement a standardized interface, different results can be easily compared using our software. The line `new PercentageAgreement(study).calculateAgreement()` returns, for instance, the percentage agreement of the given study, while the line `new FleissKappaAgreement(study).calculateAgreement()` returns Fleiss's κ (1971) for the very same study.

Most early measures consider an agreement if, and only if, the categories assigned to an item are identical. *Weighted measures* allow for defining a *distance function* that expresses the similarity of two categories. We provide distance functions for nominal, ordinal, interval, and ratio scales (Krippendorff, 1980), as well as the MASI distance function for set-valued data (Passonneau, 2006). Set annotations are an example for a more complex type of category, as they facilitate assigning multiple categories to a given unit. Additionally, researchers can easily define new study-specific distance functions.

Unitizing measures. Although unitizing has long been identified as a major issue of reliability analysis (cf. Auld and Whitea, 1956), there are so far only few formalizations. The most elaborate measure is Krippendorff's α_{U} (1995), which is based on a distance function for comparing units with identical, overlapping, or disjoint boundaries. As a model for expected disagreement, α_{U} considers all possible unitizations for the given continuum and raters. Thereby, α_{U} becomes fully compatible with Krippendorff's α (1980) for coding tasks. Due to the lack of implementations and the complex statistics, α_{U} is almost never reported in the literature. While our implementation follows the original definition, it does not require to explicitly encode the gaps, because we generate them automatically. This simplifies the usage of this measure substantially, since, for example, UIMA[4] annotations can be directly used to represent the annotation units. While the original definition focuses on only one category, we additionally support Krippendorff's later definition of an aggregating α_{U} over all categories (Krippendorff, 2004).

Analysis. The raw inter-rater agreement scores are useful for comparing multiple annotation studies with each other, but they are of limited help for diagnosing disagreement and potential systematic issues with certain categories, items, or raters. This is why we provide interfaces for measuring the agreement of a specific category, item, or rater. Fleiss (1971) defines, for instance, a category-specific κ_c that we realize in our software. The same holds for the unitizing measure α_{U}, which also provides a category-specific agreement score. Besides measuring a rater-specific agreement score, DKPro Agreement facilitates the computation of pairwise inter-rater agreement in order to identify the pair of raters with the highest and lowest agreement. Finally, each measure can return some of its intermediate results, for example, the expected agreement P_{e} of Scott's π (1955).

Another means of analysis is to display the annotation units and the disagreement among the raters. Coding studies can be displayed as a *coincidence table* or as a *reliability matrix* (Krippendorff, 1980). For studies with two raters, our software also allows printing a *contingency table*. In addition to that,

[4]Unstructured Information Management Architecture, http://uima.apache.org

we provide a formatter for the *weighing matrix* of a distance function and a basic visualization of the continuum of annotation units in unitizing studies – similar to the representation in Figure 1.

Code example. Consider the coding study described by Krippendorff (1980, p. 139) consisting of nine annotation items that have been categorized as category 1, 2, 3, or 4 by three raters. We can (re-)analyze this study with DKPro Agreement using the following Java code:

```
CodingAnnotationStudy study = new CodingAnnotationStudy(3); ❶
study.addItem(1, 1, 1); study.addItem(1, 2, 2); study.addItem(2, 2, 2); ❷
study.addItem(4, 4, 4); study.addItem(1, 4, 4); study.addItem(2, 2, 2);
study.addItem(1, 2, 3); study.addItem(3, 3, 3); study.addItem(2, 2, 2);
PercentageAgreement pa = new PercentageAgreement(study); ❸
System.out.println(pa.calculateAgreement());
KrippendorffAlphaAgreement alpha = new KrippendorffAlphaAgreement(
    study, new NominalDistanceFunction());
System.out.println(alpha.calculateObservedDisagreement());
System.out.println(alpha.calculateExpectedDisagreement());
System.out.println(alpha.calculateAgreement());
System.out.println(alpha.calculateCategoryAgreement(1)); ❹
System.out.println(alpha.calculateCategoryAgreement(2));
new CoincidenceMatrixPrinter().print(System.out, study); ❺
```

The first step is ❶ the instanciation of an `IAnnotationStudy` for the three human raters. Then, ❷ we add all $3 \cdot 9 = 27$ annotation units to the study by providing the category chosen by each rater to code the nine annotation items. Note that most reliability analyses would read the raters's decisions from a file, database, or other data structure rather than typing them in manually like in this example. Once the data model is complete, ❸ we calculate the inter-rater agreement. Following the original publication, we calculate the raw agreement and Krippendorff's α (1980) and thus print 0.740 (percentage agreement), 0.259 (observed disagreement D_{O}), 0.724 (expected disagreement D_{E}), and 0.642 (α coefficient). Finally, ❹ we analyze the agreement by calculating the category-specific α for the categories 1 and 2 yielding a system output of 0.381 and 0.711, and ❺ we print a coincidence matrix on the system console.

4 Evaluation and Publication

Automatic tests. Even though the agreement measures are clearly defined in the literature, their implementation is error-prone due to the varying notations and the required changes to take efficiency and numerical stability into account. A single confused index (e.g., p_{ij} instead of p_{ji}) could easily yield invalid conclusions for many studies. This is why we provide 61 unit tests to evaluate the correctness of our implementation. Besides manually devised examples, we use 46 examples from the literature (e.g., from Krippendorff, 1980). All examples contain references to their original documentation.

Numerical stability. We especially test the analysis of larger annotation studies, which raise issues of numerical stability. When scaling the example by Artstein and Poesio (2008, p. 558) with factor 500, an implementation potentially returns a Cohen's κ of 0.82, although it is only 0.35. This phenomenon is due to arithmetic overflows, instable division operations, and rounding errors. Krippendorff's α_{U} depends, for instance, on the cubic factor $2l_{hj}^3$, which can raise such issues even for rather small studies. Where necessary, we use logarithms or Java's `BigDecimal` type to ensure accurate results.

Open-source software. We publish our implementation as open-source software under the Apache License. By providing access to our source code, researchers can learn how the measures work and how the software is used. Moreover, they can easily contribute in order to extend the library and evaluate its correctness in a peer review, which is an essential step to establish the credibility of the software. Finally, our choice of a free license should ease (re-)using the software in many projects and thus facilitate the reproduction and comparison of annotation results, which often falls short in our community.

Documentation. DKPro Agreement is fully documented using Javadoc comments. In addition to that, we provide a general introduction and a getting-started tutorial on the project page, which also points the users to our numerous usage examples in the form of test cases.

5 Conclusion and Future Work

We have presented an open-source Java software for measuring inter-rater agreement of coding and unitizing studies. In future work, we plan to provide additional diagnostic devices and elaborated visualizations (such as Hinton diagrams) and to integrate our measures with existing annotation workbenches. An early software version has, for example, already been used in the *CSniper* (Eckart de Castilho et al., 2012) and *WebAnno* (Yimam et al., 2013) systems. We plan to extent this to other systems and also make use of the newly introduced unitizing setup.

Acknowledgments

This work has been supported by the Volkswagen Foundation as part of the Lichtenberg-Professorship Program under grant No. I/82806.

References

Ron Artstein and Massimo Poesio. 2008. Inter-Coder Agreement for Computational Linguistics. *Computational Linguistics*, 34(4):555–596.

Frank Auld, Jr and Alice M. Whitea. 1956. Rules for Dividing Interviews Into Sentences. *The Journal of Psychology: Interdisciplinary and Applied*, 42(2):273–281.

Edward M. Bennett, R. Alpert, and A. C. Goldstein. 1954. Communications Through Limited Response Questioning. *Public Opinion Quarterly*, 18(3):303–308.

Jean Carletta. 1996. Assessing Agreement on Classification Tasks: The Kappa Statistic. *Computational Linguistics*, 22(2):249–254.

Domenic V. Cicchetti, Chinyu Lee, Alan F. Fontana, and Barbara Noel Dowds. 1978. A Computer Program for Assessing Specific Category Rater Agreement for Qualitative Data. *Educational and Psychological Measurement*, 38(3):805–813.

Jacob Cohen. 1960. A Coefficient of Agreement for Nominal Scales. *Educational and Psychological Measurement*, 20(1):37–46.

Jacob Cohen. 1968. Weighted kappa: Nominal scale agreement with provision for scaled disagreement or partial credit. *Psychological Bulletin*, 70(4):213–220.

Richard Eckart de Castilho, Sabine Bartsch, and Iryna Gurevych. 2012. CSniper – Annotation-by-query for non-canonical constructions in large corpora. In *Proceedings of the 50th Meeting of the Association for Computational Linguistics: System Demonstrations*, pages 85–90, Jeju Island, Korea.

Joseph L. Fleiss. 1971. Measuring Nominal Scale Agreement among many Raters. *Psychological Bulletin*, 76(5):378–382.

Lawrence Hubert. 1977. Kappa revisited. *Psychological Bulletin*, 84(2):289–297.

Klaus Krippendorff. 1980. *Content Analysis: An Introduction to Its Methodology*. Beverly Hills, CA: Sage Publications.

Klaus Krippendorff. 1995. On the reliability of unitizing contiguous data. *Sociological Methodology*, 25:47–76. Published for American Sociological Association.

Klaus Krippendorff. 2004. *Content Analysis: An Introduction to Its Methodology*. Thousand Oaks, CA: Sage Publications, 2nd edition.

Rebecca J. Passonneau. 2006. Measuring agreement on set-valued items (MASI) for semantic and pragmatic annotation. In *Proceedings of the Fifth International Conference on Language Resources and Evaluation*, pages 831–836, Genoa, Italy.

Gabriela Trindade Perry and Klaus Krippendorff. 2013. On the reliability of identifying design moves in protocol analysis. *Design Studies*, 34(5):612–635.

Justus J. Randolph. 2005. Free-marginal multirater kappa (multirater κ_{free}): An alternative to Fleiss' fixed-marginal multirater kappa. In *Proceedings of the 5th Joensuu University Learning and Instruction Symposium*, Joensuu, Finland.

William A. Scott. 1955. Reliability of Content Analysis: The Case of Nominal Scale Coding. *Public Opinion Quaterly*, 19(3):321–325.

Seid Muhie Yimam, Iryna Gurevych, Richard Eckart de Castilho, and Chris Biemann. 2013. WebAnno: A Flexible, Web-based and Visually Supported System for Distributed Annotations. In *Proceedings of the 51st Annual Meeting of the Association for Computational Linguistics: System Demonstrations*, pages 1–6, Sofia, Bulgaria.

Distributional Semantics in R with the `wordspace` Package

Stefan Evert
Professur für Korpuslinguistik
Friedrich-Alexander-Universität Erlangen-Nürnberg
Bismarckstr. 6, 91054 Erlangen, Germany
stefan.evert@fau.de

Abstract

This paper introduces the `wordspace` package, which turns Gnu R into an interactive laboratory for research in distributional semantics. The package includes highly efficient implementations of a carefully chosen set of key functions, allowing it to scale up to real-life data sets.

1 Introduction

Distributional semantic models (DSMs) represent the meaning of a target term (which can be a word form, lemma, morpheme, word pair, etc.) in the form of a feature vector that records either co-occurrence frequencies of the target term with a set of feature terms (*term-term model*) or its distribution across text units (*term-context model*). Such DSMs have become an indispensable ingredient in many NLP applications that require flexible broad-coverage lexical semantics (Turney and Pantel, 2010).

Distributional modelling is an empirical science. DSM representations are determined by a wide range of parameters such as size and type of the co-occurrence context, feature selection, weighting of co-occurrence frequencies (often with statistical association measures), distance metric, dimensionality reduction method and the number of latent dimensions used. Despite recent efforts to carry out systematic evaluation studies (Bullinaria and Levy, 2007; Bullinaria and Levy, 2012), the precise effects of these parameters and their relevance for different application settings are still poorly understood.

The `wordspace` package for Gnu R (R Development Core Team, 2010) aims to provide a flexible, powerful and easy to use "interactive laboratory" that enables its users to build DSMs and experiment with them, but that also scales up to the large models required by real-life applications.

2 Related work

One reason for the popularity of distributional approaches is that even large-scale models can be implemented with relative ease. In the geometric interpretation, most operations involved in building and using a DSM can be expressed concisely in terms of matrix and vector algebra: matrix multiplication, inner and outer products, matrix decomposition, and vector norms and metrics.

In order to make DSMs accessible to a large group of users, several dedicated software packages have been developed. Most of these packages either implement a particular model, limiting their flexibility, or impose a complex framework of classes, making it hard for users to carry out operations not envisioned by the package developers. Examples of the first category are HiDeX (Shaoul and Westbury, 2010), a modern reimplementation of the HAL model, and Semantic Vectors (Widdows and Cohen, 2010), which enforces a random indexing representation in order to improve scalability.

A typical example of the second category is the S-Space package (Jurgens and Stevens, 2010), which defines a complete pipeline for building and evaluating a DSM; researchers wishing e.g. to evaluate the model on a different task need to implement the evaluation procedure in the form of a suitable Java class. Two Python-based software packages in this category are Gensim (Řehůřek and Sojka, 2010) and DISSECT (Dinu et al., 2013), which has a particular focus on learning compositional models.

In order to avoid locking its users into a particular framework or class of distributional model, the `wordspace` package takes a different approach. It builds on the statistical software environment Gnu R, which provides efficient dense and sparse matrix algebra, sophisticated statistical analysis and visualization, as well as numerous machine learning methods as part of its core library and through a wealth of add-on packages. R itself is already an excellent environment for the interactive exploration of DSMs.

Like many other R packages, `wordspace` does not define its own complex framework. It extends functionality that is already available (and easy to use) with a small set of carefully designed functions that (i) encapsulate non-trivial R operations in a convenient and user-friendly way and (ii) provide highly efficient and memory-friendly C implementations of key operations in order to improve scalability. Of the other DSM software packages available, DISSECT seems closest in spirit to `wordspace`. Therefore, it is used as a point of reference for the performance comparison in Sec. 5.

3 The `wordspace` package

The `wordspace` package is an open-source project distributed under the GNU General Public License. Since the pacakge is linked to the R interpreter and its functions are always invoked from interpreted code, this does not preclude commercial applications involving closed-source components. The package source code is hosted on R-Forge.[1] It can easily be installed from the Comprehensive R Archive Network (CRAN), which provides pre-compiled binaries for Windows and Mac OS X.

3.1 Input formats

The most general representation of a distributional model takes the form of a sparse matrix, with entries specified as a triplet of row label (target term), column label (feature term) and co-occurrence frequency (cf. left panel of Fig. 1). The `wordspace` package creates DSM objects from such triplet representations, which can easily be imported into R from a wide range of file and database formats. Ready-made import functions are provided for TAB-delimited text files (as used by DISSECT), which may be compressed to save disk space, and for term-document models from the text-mining framework `tm` for R.

The native input format is a pre-compiled sparse matrix representation generated by the UCS toolkit.[2] In this way, UCS serves as a hub for the preparation of co-occurrence data, which can be collected from dependency pairs, extracted from a corpus indexed with the IMS Corpus Workbench,[3] or imported from various other formats such as the Ngram Statistics Package (NSP).[4]

3.2 Features

The `wordspace` package offers flexible convenience functions to filter DSMs by properties of their rows (targets) and columns (features), combine multiple co-occurrence matrices by rows or by columns, and merge data obtained from different corpora. Co-occurrence frequencies can be weighted by a tf.idf scheme or one of various statistical association measures, rescaled e.g. by a logarithmic transformation, standardized and row-normalized.

Efficient implementations are provided for dimensionality reduction by randomized SVD (Halko et al., 2009) or random indexing, for computing a distance matrix between a set of row vectors, and for the identification of the nearest neighbours of a given target term. Additional functions compute centroid representations for sentence contexts and support the evaluation of DSMs in standard classification, clustering and regression tasks. Several freely available gold standard data sets are included in the package.

Due to its philosophy, `wordspace` only provides essential functionality that cannot easily be achieved with basic R functions or does not scale well in the standard implementation. Many further analyses and operations (e.g. partial least-squares regression for learning compositional DSMs) can be performed with standard R functions or one of more than 5000 add-on packages available from CRAN.

[1] `http://wordspace.r-forge.r-project.org/`
[2] `http://www.collocations.de/software.html`
[3] `http://cwb.sourceforge.net/`
[4] `http://ngram.sourceforge.net/`

dog-n	walk-v	6343
dog-n	walk-n	2461
dog-n	bite-v	1732
cat-n	tail-n	1285
cat-n	jump-v	541
...	...	...

noun	rel	verb	f	mode
dog	subj	bite	3	spoken
dog	subj	bite	12	written
dog	obj	bite	4	written
dog	obj	stroke	3	written
...	...	...	...	...

Figure 1: Typical input data: triplet representation of a sparse co-occurrence matrix (left panel) and verb-noun cooccurrences from the BNC used as example data in Sec. 4 (right panel).

4 Example session

Fig. 3 shows the full set of R commands required to compile and use a DSM with the `wordspace` package, based on a built-in table containing co-occurrence counts of verbs and their subject/object nouns in the British National Corpus (BNC), an excerpt of which is shown in the right panel of Fig. 1.

After loading the package (line 1), we use a standard R function to extract data for the written part of the BNC (line 3). The `dsm()` function constructs a basic DSM object from co-occurrence data in various sparse matrix representations (line 4). Note that multiple entries for the same noun-verb combination are automatically aggregated, resulting in a 19831×4854 noun-verb co-occurrence matrix. Highly sparse vectors are unreliable as indicators of word meaning, so we filter out rows and columns with less than 3 nonzero entries using the `subset()` method for DSM objects. The required nonzero counts have automatically been added by the `dsm()` constructor. Since deleting rows and columns changes the nonzero counts, we apply the process recursively until both constraints are satisfied (line 9).

Co-occurrence counts are then weighted by the log-likelihood association measure, log-transformed to deskew their distribution, and row vectors are normalized to Euclidean unit length. This is achieved with a single function call and minimal memory overhead (line 13). For dimensionality reduction, the efficient randomized SVD algorithm is used (line 15), resulting in a plain R matrix `VObj300`.

Typical applications of a DSM are to compute distances or cosine similarities between pairs of target terms (line 17) and to find the nearest neighbours of a given term (line 20). The final DSM can be evaluated e.g. by comparison with the RG65 data set of semantic similarity ratings (Rubenstein and Goodenough, 1965). Here, we obtain a Pearson correlation of $r = 0.521$ (with 95% confidence interval $0.317 \dots 0.679$) and a Spearman rank correlation of $\rho = 0.511$ (line 26). The correlation can also be visualized with a built-in plot method (line 29), shown in the left panel of Fig. 2.

The commands in lines 31–37 illustrate the use of standard R functions for further analysis and visualization. Here, an implementation of non-metric multidimensional scaling in the R package `MASS` produces a semantic map of the nearest neighbours of *book*. A slightly more polished version of this plot is shown in the right panel of Fig. 2. The only step that takes a non-negligible amount of time is dimensionality reduction with randomized SVD (approx. 14 seconds on the reference system, see Sec. 5).

5 Performance comparison

In order to determine the usefulness of the `wordspace` package for realistically sized data sets, a benchmark was carried out using the $W \times W$ projection of the Distributional Memory tensor (Baroni and Lenci, 2010), resulting in a sparse 30686×30686 matrix with 60 million nonzero entries (6.4% fill rate). Execution times of key operations and file sizes of the native serialization format are shown in Table 1 and compared against DISSECT v0.1.0 as the closest "competitor". Tests were carried out on a 2012 MacBook Pro with a 2.6 GHz 4-core Intel Core i7 CPU, 16 GiB RAM and a 768 GB SSD.

Runtimes for nearest neighbours (NN) are averaged over 198 nouns, and those for cosine similarity are averaged over 351 noun pairs. Both sample sets were taken from the WordSim-353 data set. DISSECT requires about 2.5 GiB RAM to carry out the complete process, while R requires slightly above 4 GiB. Most of the RAM is needed to load the non-native input format (which happens to be the native format of DISSECT). For the remaining steps, memory usage remains well below 3 GiB.

	wordspace	DISSECT	size (.rda / .pkl)
build model from triples file	186.0 s	503.3 s	
save model	57.6 s	1.5 s	228.9 MB / 725.7 MB
normalize row vectors	0.5 s	1.3 s	
SVD projection to 300 latent dimensions	353.6 s	296.6 s	
save latent vectors	10.4 s	0.4 s	71.5 MB / 185.0 MB
20 nearest neighbours (full matrix)	119 ms	1269 ms	
20 nearest neighbours (300 dims)	10 ms	92 ms	
cosine similarity (full matrix)	4 ms	< 1 ms	
cosine similarity (300 dims)	< 1 ms	< 1 ms	

Table 1: Performance comparison: wordspace vs. DISSECT on Distributional Memory.

6 Further development

The wordspace package is under very active development. Main objectives for the near future are (i) sparse SVD using SVDLIBC (which is more efficient than randomized SVD in certain cases), (ii) sparse non-negative matrix factorization (NMF), and (iii) built-in support for a wider range of file and database formats. In addition, new weighting functions and distance metrics are continuously being added.

References

Marco Baroni and Alessandro Lenci. 2010. Distributional Memory: A general framework for corpus-based semantics. *Computational Linguistics*, 36(4):673–712.

John A. Bullinaria and Joseph P. Levy. 2007. Extracting semantic representations from word co-occurrence statistics: A computational study. *Behavior Research Methods*, 39(3):510–526.

John A. Bullinaria and Joseph P. Levy. 2012. Extracting semantic representations from word co-occurrence statistics: Stop-lists, stemming and SVD. *Behavior Research Methods*, 44(3):890–907.

Georgiana Dinu, Nghia The Pham, and Marco Baroni. 2013. DISSECT – distributional semantics composition toolkit. In *Proceedings of the 51st Annual Meeting of the Association for Computational Linguistics: System Demonstrations*, pages 31–36, Sofia, Bulgaria, August.

N. Halko, P. G. Martinsson, and J[oel] A. Tropp. 2009. Finding structure with randomness: Stochastic algorithms for constructing approximate matrix decompositions. Technical Report 2009-05, ACM, California Institute of Technology, September.

David Jurgens and Keith Stevens. 2010. The S-Space package: An open source package for word space models. In *Proceedings of the ACL 2010 System Demonstrations*, pages 30–35, Uppsala, Sweden, July.

R Development Core Team, 2010. *R: A Language and Environment for Statistical Computing*. R Foundation for Statistical Computing, Vienna, Austria. ISBN 3-900051-07-0. See also http://www.r-project.org/.

Radim Řehůřek and Petr Sojka. 2010. Software framework for topic modelling with large corpora. In *Proceedings of the LREC 2010 Workshop on New Challenges for NLP Frameworks*, pages 45–50, Valletta, Malta, May. ELRA.

Herbert Rubenstein and John B. Goodenough. 1965. Contextual correlates of synonymy. *Communications of the ACM*, 8(10):627–633.

Cyrus Shaoul and Chris Westbury. 2010. Exploring lexical co-occurrence space using HiDEx. *Behavior Research Methods*, 42(2):393–413.

Peter D. Turney and Patrick Pantel. 2010. From frequency to meaning: Vector space models of semantics. *Journal of Artificial Intelligence Research*, 37:141–188.

Dominic Widdows and Trevor Cohen. 2010. The Semantic Vectors package: New algorithms and public tools for distributional semantics. In *IEEE Fourth International Conference on Semantic Computing (ICSC 2010)*, pages 9–15.

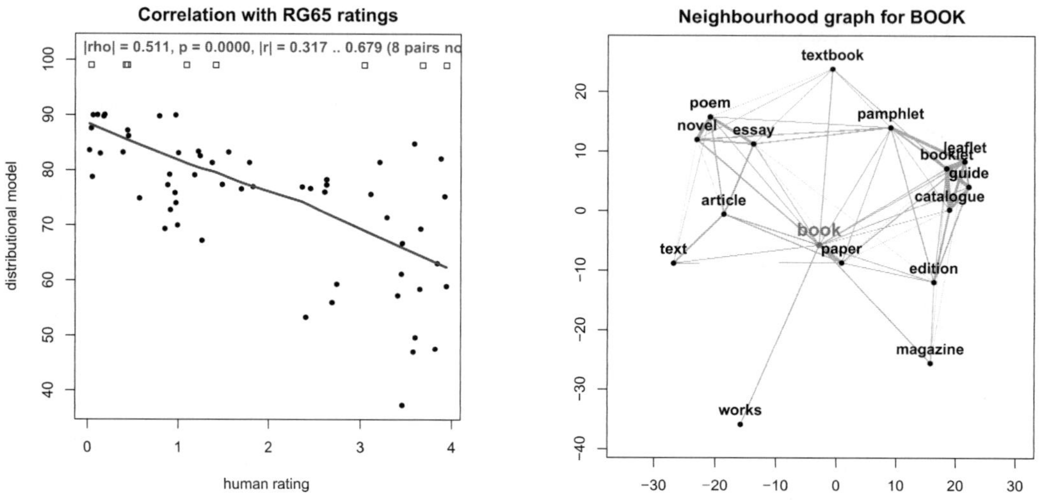

Figure 2: Two visualizations created by the sample code in Fig. 2.

```
library(wordspace)

Triples <- subset(DSM_VerbNounTriples_BNC, mode == "written")
VObj <- dsm(target=Triples$noun, feature=Triples$verb, score=Triples$f,
            raw.freq=TRUE, sort=TRUE)
dim(VObj)
  [1] 19831  4854

VObj <- subset(VObj, nnzero >= 3, nnzero >= 3, recursive=TRUE)
dim(VObj)
  [1] 12428  3735

VObj <- dsm.score(VObj, score="simple-ll", transform="log", normalize=TRUE)

VObj300 <- dsm.projection(VObj, method="rsvd", n=300, oversampling=4)

pair.distances("book", "paper", VObj300, method="cosine", convert=FALSE)
  book/paper
   0.7322982
nearest.neighbours(VObj300, "book", n=15) # defaults to angular distance
     paper     novel  magazine     works   article  textbook     guide      poem
  42.92059  48.03492  49.10742  49.33028  49.54836  49.82660  50.29588  50.37111
     essay   leaflet   edition      text  pamphlet   booklet catalogue
  50.45991  50.53009  50.78630  50.95731  51.12786  51.21351  52.43824

eval.similarity.correlation(RG65, VObj300, format="HW")
               rho      p.value missing        r   r.lower   r.upper
  RG65 0.5113531 1.342741e-05       8 0.520874 0.3172827 0.6785674
plot(eval.similarity.correlation(RG65, VObj300, format="HW", details=TRUE))

nn <- nearest.neighbours(VObj300, "book", n=15)
nn.terms <- c("book", names(nn)) # nn = distances labelled with the neighbour terms
nn.dist <- dist.matrix(VObj300, terms=nn.terms, method="cosine")
library(MASS) # a standard R package that includes two MDS implementations
mds <- isoMDS(nn.dist, p=2)
plot(mds$points, pch=20, col="red")
text(mds$points, labels=nn.terms, pos=3)
```

Figure 3: Complete example code for building, using and evaluating a DSM with `wordspace`.

Method51 for Mining Insight from Social Media Datasets

Simon Wibberley
University of Sussex
simon.wibberley
@sussex.ac.uk

Jeremy Reffin
University of Sussex
j.p.reffin
@sussex.ac.uk

David Weir
University of Sussex
d.j.weir
@sussex.ac.uk

Abstract

We present Method51, a social media analysis software platform with a set of accompanying methodologies. We discuss a series of case studies illustrating the platform's application, and motivating our methodological proposals.

1 Introduction

Social scientists wish to apply language processing technology on social media datasets to answer sociological questions. To that end, the technology should support methodologies that allow analysts to gain valuable insight from the datasets under examination. In previous work we have argued for the importance of agility when dealing with social media datasets (Wibberley et al., 2013). In this paper we present a series of case studies, carried out on Twitter, that illustrate the importance of that agile paradigm, and how they have motivated the development of several additional methodologies, including 'Twitcident', 'Patterns of Use', and 'Russian Doll' analysis. First, we present Method51[1], the technological counterpart to our methodological paradigm.

2 Method51

Method51 uses active learning, coupled with a Naïve Bayes model, to allow social scientists to construct chains of linked, bespoke classifiers. The framework, initially an extension of DUALIST (Settles, 2011), utilises an EM step to harness information from large amounts of unlabelled data, and allows the analyst to expedite learning by specifying features that are highly indicative of a class. Using this approach, a classifier can be trained within minutes (Settles, 2011). This enables analysts to evolve the way that the data is being analysed without significant loss of effort. Method51 provides significant additional functionality including collaborative gold standard and classifier construction, processing pipeline construction, data collection and storage, data visualisation, various filtering and processing modules, and time-based data selection. Figure 1a show the pipeline construction interface, which allows analysts to knit together chains of bespoke classifiers.

Figure 1b shows the 'Coding' interface which is the primary point of contact between the analyst and the data, where documents and features are labelled. Classifier evaluation statistics are also displayed, so analysts can rapidly assess whether the data and technology are amenable to their analytical approach. Method51 aims to put social science researchers at the centre of the data exploration process. Insight is generated through the iterative interaction of the subject matter expert and the data itself.

Method51 combines two strands of existing work. The first body of work employs tailored automatic data analysis, using supervised machine-learning approaches (Carvalho et al., 2011; Papacharissi and de Fatima Oliveira, 2012; Meraz and Papacharissi, 2013; Hopkins and King, 2010; Burnap et al., 2013b). A second body of work focusses on providing user interfaces that enable researchers to customise their processing pipeline, based on the requirements of their investigation (Blessing et al., 2013; Black et al., 2012; Burnap et al., 2013a).

[1] Method51 has been released under an open source license, and is available at https://github.com/simonwibberley/method51

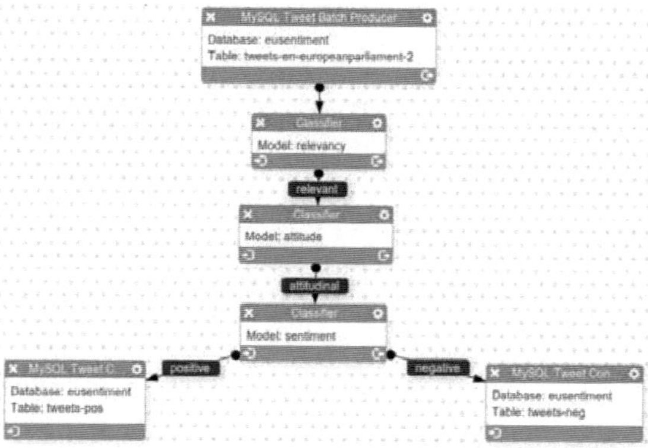

(a) Pipeline Construction Interface

(b) Coding interface

3 Case Studies

Over the past 18 months we have conducted a wide range of studies using Method51. Three illustrative case studies are presented here in chronological order; each investigation highlighted new analytical challenges and therefore motivated methodological and technological development.

3.1 EU Sentiment

In the first study, we examined the attitudes of EU citizens towards the Eurozone crisis of 2013 (Bartlett et al., textitforthcoming). We set out with a preconceived structure and methodology. We tracked 6 topics, referencing EU institutions or prominent people, and collected Tweets in 3 languages (English, French, and German) to create 18 distinct streams of messages. For each stream, we constructed a bespoke classification pipeline with a common analytical architecture of three successive layers: a classifier for relevancy, a classifier to determine whether Tweets were attitudinal, and a classifier to determine the polarity of the sentiment being expressed.

We found that, broadly, the data did not fit the pre-conceived analytical architecture neatly and that classifier performance was a poor fit with human judgements, particularly for the attitudinal and sentiment layers. Table 1 illustrates the range of performance of classifiers measured against human-annotated gold standard. Although relevancy classifiers performed adequately, the reliability of attitudinal and sentiment classifiers varies widely across streams.

Investigation revealed a number of underlying issues and prompted a series of methodological responses:

Need for flexible architecture We observed that each stream presented different challenges that could only be appropriately addressed by a bespoke architecture tailored to the anatomy of the stream. For example, relevancy classification was only sometimes required. The 'Euro' stream was targeted towards conversation about the Euro currency, but required relevancy filtering as the query '#euro' matched conversations regarding a wide variety of other topics such as sport competitions. Conversely, the 'Barroso' stream, tracking messages regarding the president of the European Commission, José Manuel Barroso, was of sufficiently high precision not to warrant relevancy filtering.

'Twitcident' analysis We observed that attitudes were typically only exposed when some event in the world "provoked" a burst of reactions that was related to the topic of interest. These response bursts, which usually occur over a matter of hours to days, have been labelled 'Twitcidents'. We found that the nature of the response — and how this should be mapped onto the broader topic — was unique to the event itself. The 'Twitcident' analysis principle states that each event needs to be studied separately in order to be correctly interpreted. Using a common classification architecture, or otherwise aggregating results across Twitcidents, is likely to create a misleading picture of how opinions are being shaped by events over time. As an example, a speech by the UK Prime Minister expressing a sceptical view of the EU prompted many enthusiastic responses. Messages that commented positively on his speech were contributing evidence of negative sentiment towards the EU. Clearly the reaction to that speech had to be analysed separately in order to allow for this reversal of sentiment polarity.

Exploratory 'Patterns of Use' analysis The poor fit between the data and the imposed classification architecture prompted us to adopt a new approach to constructing pipelines. The framework enables analysts to 'fail fast': engage actively with the data and explore how it is structured, before committing to the pipeline framework. This is feasible because Method51 enables classifiers to be built quickly.

This 'Patterns of Use' analysis is inspired by Grounded Theory (Glaser et al., 1968), and mandates that classification categories should arise from an unbiased examination of the available data. Categories arise naturally from the analyst's engagement with the data.

3.2 Father's Day

Our initial ideas about 'Patterns of Use' analysis were explored further in the Father's Day study. Our aim here was to identify users likely to respond positively to a targeted advertisement for Father's Day gift ideas, that assessment being driven by the content of a Tweet sent by the user. We collected and analysed Tweets mentioning Father's Day in the days leading up to the event, and our first attempts at analysing underlying patterns prompted a revision to our methodology.

'Russian Doll' approach We observed that at any stage the data tends to be dominated by one pattern of usage, obscuring other underlying patterns. We developed a 'Russian Doll' approach, which mandates that at each layer a classifier is built to unpack from the data Tweets that match this most prominent pattern of usage. With this usage pattern stripped out, new structure is typically revealed in the remaining data, which can in turn be unpacked using simple bespoke classifiers. Chained together, this pipeline of classifiers removes successive different patterns of usage to expose underlying structure.

In this case, our a-priori expectation was that the stream would contain marketing Tweets, general conversation about Father's Day, and our target subset: people expressing uncertainty about what gift to get. Our analysis revealed, however, a significant critical class of Tweets (and Tweeters) the presence of which was unexpected — a category for which targeted marketing Tweets would be wholly inappropriate. The content of the Tweets matching this category (dubbed 'Sad/Distressed') was negative, with Tweeters venting sad or angry feelings towards absent fathers, generally though family breakdown or bereavement. It was only through this careful patterns of use analysis that we identified this critical subgroup.

The final architecture consisted of two layers that dealt with existing marketing Tweets, a layer that assessed the suitability of the Tweet as a potential target for a marketing campaign, and a final layer that identified explicit requests for gift ideas. This pipeline showed good performance as measured by F-scores against gold-standard annotated data (see Table 2). The unexpected 'Sad/Distressed' category constituted a high proportion (10%) of all Tweets in the data set. Of the remaining tweets, 50% were classified 'Marketing', 36% were classified 'Miscellaneous' comments about Father's Day, and 4% as 'Gift Idea Request', our target group.

3.3 Mark Duggan

Our final case study illustrates an analysis conducted using the 'Twitcident' and 'Patterns of Use' techniques. The aim was to dissect the online reaction to developments in the Mark Duggan inquest, an enquiry into the shooting by police in London of a young black man. Over the course of about a month, Tweets regarding Mark Duggan were collected with a view to analysing reactions as the case progressed. The response showed the familiar 'Twitcident' pattern (see Figure 2). Twitcidents were examined individually, culminating in an analysis of the large response on Twitter to the final verdict. Four specific categories of response were identified and analysed. These were: (i) 'No Justice' — where a Tweet included accusations of institutional racism and/or claims that Duggan was unarmed; (ii) 'Justice' — that Duggan "had it coming", and/or that Duggan was armed; (iii) 'Riot' — warning of possible rioting,

	Range	Split
Relevance	0.5 - 0.9	2-way
Attitudinal	0.3 - 0.9	2-way
Sentiment	0.1 - 0.8	3-way

Table 1: Range of F1-scores of EU Sentiment

	Individual	Marketing
F1	0.873	0.844

(a) Marketing level 1

	Individual	Marketing
F1	0.834	0.490

(b) Marketing level 2

	Suitable	Sad	Marketing
F1	0.785	0.564	0.227

(c) Suitability

	Request	Other
F1	0.583	0.959

(d) Gift request

Table 2: F-scores of Russion Dolls Analysis

	Justice	No Justice	Riot	Watching
F1	0.636	0.842	0.737	0.451
Split	58%	17%	7%	18%

Table 3: Verdict classifier performance

making calls for calm; and (iv) 'Watching' — people neutrally expressing interest in a case. Pipeline performance was good as measured by F-scores against gold-standard (see Table 3)

This case further illustrates how patterns of response are specific to a particular situation, greatly limiting the usefulness of pre-defined classifiers (e.g. for sentiment) in real-world investigations.

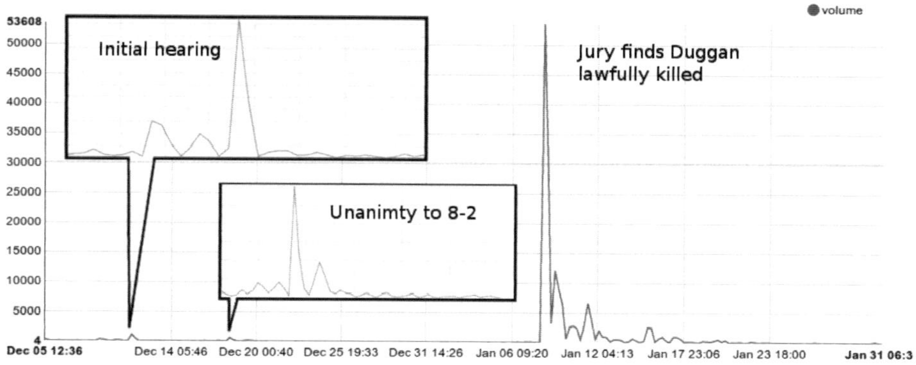

Figure 2: Mark Duggan 'Twitcidents'

4 Discussion

We will end with a discussion of how we have interpreted the developments in methodology described above, and how that interpretation leads to an intuitive framework for further work.

We have presented the application of three distinct methodologies for mining insight from social media data. The insights gained from each case study are the result of three interdependent factors; (i) the question that is being posed, (ii) the extend to which the answers to the question reside in the data, and (iii) the extent to which the technology is capable of addressing the question given the data. We encapsulate this line of interpretation as 'Question, Data, and Technology'. By considering these factors analysts can remain plastic about how the 'Data' and 'Technology' can mutually constrain and inform the 'Question'. For example, if answers to the question are not represented in the data in a form the technology can recognise, then the question should be revised. Conversely, the technology may reveal unexpected characteristics in the data that contribute towards the analysts understanding of what the question should be. Careful alignment between all three tend to result in valuable insights being discovered.

Crucial to this alignment is assessing the performance of the technology on the data, given the question being posed. Method51 provides some functionality towards supporting this, such as accuracy and F-scores. However, these measures indirectly indicate whether the classifier is behaving sensibly by virtue of the gold standard evaluation data being an i.i.d sample of the unlabelled data.

The behaviour of classifiers on unlabelled data forms a crucial role in how the technology supports the analyst in their investigation. Directly exposing that behaviour and developing an informed understanding of the relationship between 'Question, Data, and Technology' would only expedite and contribute towards reliable insights being discovered. Incorporating technology into Method51 that exposes how unlabelled data are effected by analytical processes is an area for further work.

In general, we have found that considering the interaction between 'Question, Data, and Technology' provides an intuitive framework for refining the focus of methodological and technological development towards demonstrably useful innovations.

Acknowledgments

This work was supported by the ESRC National Centre for Research Methods grant DU/512589110. We are grateful to our collaborators at the Centre for the Analysis of social media, Jamie Bartlett and Carl Miller for valuable contributions to this work. We thank the anonymous reviewers for their helpful comments. This work was partially supported by the Open Society Foundation.

References

J. Bartlett, Miller C, J. Reffin, D. Weir, and Wibberley S. *forthcoming*. Vox digitas. *http://www.demos.co.uk/publications*.

W. Black, R. Procter, S. Gray, and S. Ananiadou. 2012. A data and analysis resource for an experiment in text mining a collection of micro-blogs on a political topic. In *LREC*. ELRA.

A. Blessing, J. Sonntag, F. Kliche, U. Heid, J. Kuhn, and M. Stede. 2013. Towards a tool for interactive concept building for large scale analysis in the humanities. In *LaTeCH, Social Sciences, and Humanities*. ACL.

P. Burnap, N. Avis, and O. Rana. 2013a. Making sense of self-reported socially significant data using computational methods. *International Journal of Social Research Methodology*.

P. Burnap, O. Rana, N. Avis, M. Williams, W. Housley, A. Edwards, J. Morgan, and L. Sloan. 2013b. Detecting tension in online communities with computational twitter analysis. *Technological Forecasting and Social Change*.

P. Carvalho, L. Sarmento, J. Teixeira, and M. Silva. 2011. Liars and saviors in a sentiment annotated corpus of comments to political debates. In *ACL: Human Language Technologies*.

Barney G Glaser, Anselm L Strauss, and Elizabeth Strutzel. 1968. The discovery of grounded theory; strategies for qualitative research. *Nursing Research*.

D. J. Hopkins and G. King. 2010. A method of automated nonparametric content analysis for social science. *American Journal of Political Science*.

Sharon Meraz and Zizi Papacharissi. 2013. Networked gatekeeping and networked framing on #egypt. *The International Journal of Press/Politics*, 18(2):138–166.

Zizi Papacharissi and Maria de Fatima Oliveira. 2012. Affective news and networked publics: the rhythms of news storytelling on #egypt. *Journal of Communication*, 62(2):266–282.

B. Settles. 2011. Closing the loop: Fast, interactive semi-supervised annotation with queries on features and instances. In *Empirical Methods in Natural Language Processing*.

Simon Wibberley, David Weir, and Jeremy Reffin. 2013. Language technology for agile social media science. In *Proceedings of the 7th Workshop on Language Technology for Cultural Heritage, Social Sciences, and Humanities*, pages 36–42, Sofia, Bulgaria, August. Association for Computational Linguistics.

MT-EQuAl: a Toolkit for Human Assessment of Machine Translation Output

Christian Girardi[(1)] **Luisa Bentivogli**[(1)]
Mohammad Amin Farajian[(1,2)] **Marcello Federico**[(1)]
[(1)] FBK - Fondazione Bruno Kessler, Trento, Italy
[(2)] University of Trento, Italy
{cgirardi,bentivo,farajian,federico}@fbk.eu

Abstract

MT-EQuAl (Machine Translation Errors, Quality, Alignment) is a toolkit for human assessment of Machine Translation (MT) output. MT-EQuAl implements three different tasks in an integrated environment: annotation of translation errors, translation quality rating (*e.g.* adequacy and fluency, relative ranking of alternative translations), and word alignment. The toolkit is web-based and multi-user, allowing large scale and remotely managed manual annotation projects. It incorporates a number of project management functions and sophisticated progress monitoring capabilities. The implemented evaluation tasks are configurable and can be adapted to several specific annotation needs. The toolkit is open source and released under Apache 2.0 license.

1 Introduction

It is widely recognized within the MT field that human evaluation can play a crucial role in improving MT technology. Despite the well-known difficulties in collecting human annotations (the process is time-consuming, costly and often subjective), state of the art MT research is now moving towards integrating as much as possible human quality assessment into the MT workflow. The most commonly used human evaluation methodologies are based on absolute adequacy and fluency scores, relative ranking of alternative MT outputs, and, more recently, human post-editing. Although very useful, these methods do not provide information about the specific problems of MT systems. To address this limitation, new approaches based on human error analysis have emerged, where annotators identify and classify translation errors thus giving precise indications about specific deficiencies of the evaluated MT systems. Given the outlined trend, it is of the utmost importance to make available to the MT community tools (i) able to support large-scale annotation projects involving a great variety of languages, (ii) addressing the most required MT assessment tasks, and (iii) designed in a way to reduce as much as possible the problems related to manual annotation. MT-EQuAl is a toolkit for the manual assessment of MT output, created with the aim of addressing the above requirements. The main characteristics of MT-EQuAl are the following:

- Web-based and multi-user: allows large-scale and remotely managed annotation projects. It incorporates project management functions and sophisticated progress monitoring capabilities.
- Three different MT assessment tasks in an integrated environment: annotation of translation errors, translation quality rating (*e.g.* adequacy, fluency, relative ranking), and word alignment. An integrated environment offering different tasks can address the needs of a higher number of potential users within the MT field.
- Highly configurable tasks: possibility to evaluate a single MT output as well as two or more automatic translations in parallel, which is useful if the purpose of the annotation is to compare MT systems. Furthermore, all tasks can be adapted to specific annotation needs (see Section 2).
- Fast and well-designed annotation interfaces: particular attention was paid to the usability of the interfaces, especially for the error annotation task where a lot of annotations, often overlapping and

covering long sequences of words, have to be made. A fast and easy-to-use interface can reduce the problems related to manual evaluation and ensure annotation speed and data quality.

- Open source: released under Apache 2.0 license at `http://github.com/hltfbk/mt-equal`.

We think that these features give to MT-EQuAl an added value with respect to other existing annotation tools which only partially fulfill the requirements illustrated above.

Over the years, various annotation tools with different characteristics have been made available for the assessment tasks offered by our toolkit. However, none of them incorporates all the features of MT-EQuAl: either the integration in a multi-task platform, or a web-based interface, or the implementation of the error annotation task which is the most needed to support the upcoming research. The most comparable tools to MT-EQuAl are PET (Aziz et al., 2012), COSTA (Chatzitheodorou and Chatzistamatis, 2013), TAUS DQF framework,[1] translate5,[2] Blast (Stymne, 2011), and Appraise (Federmann, 2012), since they all implement translation error annotation. These tools were created for different purposes and differ in various ways among each other and with respect to MT-EQuAl. All of them except Appraise do not support multiple MT outputs, and PET, COSTA, and Blast are stand-alone tools. From the error analysis point of view, their interfaces show different levels of flexibility. PET and COSTA permit only sentence-level annotation, which is not the suitable granularity for that kind of information. Appraise offers word-level annotation but displays the MT output word by word, which does not facilitate the annotator in getting a global view of the sentence and of the errors. Finally, the translate5 and Blast interfaces show the whole MT output and allow the annotator to mark the specific portion(s) of text where an error occurs. This type of annotation is the same implemented in MT-EQuAl. However, with respect to these tools, MT-EQuAl represents a step further as one of our main design goals was usability. The MT-EQuAl error analysis interface is simple and very intuitive, and offers visualization functions aimed at reducing annotators' cognitive load, so to enable them to focus on the task itself (see Section 2.2).

2 System Overview

MT-EQuAl is a web-based application implemented using PHP and JavaScript. It takes as input several UTF-8 encoded *csv* files: the source text, the reference translation (optional), and one file for each of the MT outputs to be evaluated. This allows the evaluation of single systems as well as the comparison of multiple systems. Each row in the input *csv* files contains one evaluation item, typically one sentence. In order to annotate translation errors, the sentences must be tokenized. To this purpose, the tool accepts input files already tokenized by the user or - if needed - it applies a simple tokenization based on spaces, punctuation, and other language-dependent rules (*e.g.* a character-based tokenization is applied to Chinese texts). The source and target languages must be declared in the *csv*, so that the tool can apply the most suitable text tokenization and visualisation (*e.g.* the text can be displayed left to right and viceversa). The annotated data can be exported both in *csv* and XML format.

As regards data storage, all recorded information is permanently stored in a MySQL database. An interesting feature is that immediate persistence of data is achieved without an explicit action by the user to save the data, since every annotation is immediately sent to the server and stored in the database. Finally - being a web-based application - if the server encounters some problems, annotation is blocked and the user is notified with a warning message.

The MT-EQuAl front-end is composed of a project management interface and three annotation interfaces, one for each evaluation task.

2.1 Project Management Interface

The various project management functions implemented in the tool are accessible to the project manager through an interface which is composed of four tabs:

- **Task**. In this tab the project manager creates the task and sets its specific features. For the error analysis task, a default error typology - based on (Vilar et al., 2006) - is available, but any alternative

[1] `https://evaluation.taus.net/tools`
[2] `http://www.translate5.net`

tagset can be adopted. In the rating task it is possible to decide the number of points in the rating scale, while in the alignment task the number of alignment types (*e.g.* sure, possible) can be set.

- **Data**. In this tab the project manager can import the input files and apply the tokenization module if desired. Moreover, a table summarizing the data stored in the database for each task is displayed.
- **Users**. In this tab the project manager can create accounts for users and assign them to different tasks. Each user will see only the task(s) s/he has been assigned to. Users do not see other users' annotations unless they are working in "revision mode", where an existing annotation is presented for revision.
- **Annotation**. This tab contains the progress monitoring and export functions. As regards progress monitoring, a report containing real-time information about the progress of the annotation is displayed both at the task level and the user level. Moreover, the project manager can monitor user activity through the visualization of the remote client interface in read-only mode. This feature is particularly useful as it addresses the typical problems related to training and supervision of remote annotators. Regarding annotation export, data can be exported (i) for all the tasks, (ii) for each single task, and (iii) for each user. Furthermore, the annotations carried out by a user can be directly copied into another user account for revision.

2.2 Error Annotation Interface

The error annotation interface requires the annotator to identify the type of errors present in the MT output, according to the adopted error typology, and to mark their position in the text. As shown in Figure 1, the annotator is presented with the source sentence, a reference translation (optional) and the MT output(s) to be analyzed. Two buttons allow the annotator to mark the MT output as containing "*no errors*" or "*too many errors*". In order to annotate the errors, the annotator selects with the mouse the word(s) to be annotated. The selected word(s) are highlighted and, by right-clicking, the error typology menu is displayed and the suitable error type can be chosen. It is possible to annotate single words (including punctuation), spaces (*e.g.* to indicate the correct place for missing words in the candidate translation), and sequences of words (very useful especially for reordering problems which can involve entire portions of the sentence). The annotated errors are listed at the right of the corresponding sentences, subdivided by error type. If the mouse hovers over a given error instance, the corresponding word(s) appear underlined in the text. It is possible to delete single error instances (by clicking on the bin icon) or all the errors of a give type (by clicking on the "reset" button).

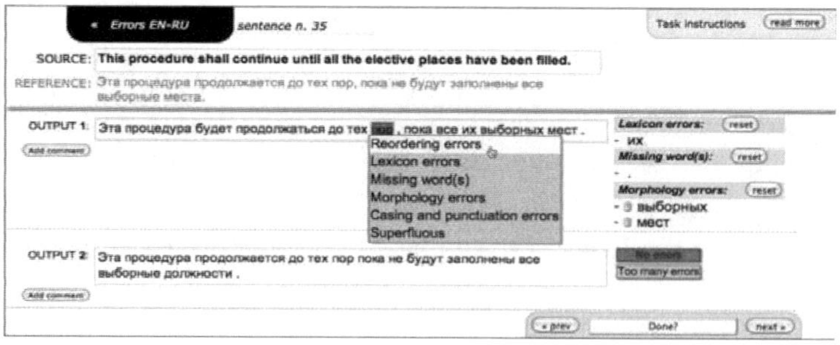

Figure 1: Error annotation interface configured for two MT outputs and with the default error typology.

2.3 Translation Quality Rating Interface

As shown in Figure 2(a), the quality rating interface displays the source sentence, a reference translation (optional) and the MT output(s) to be rated. When the assessor clicks on a point in the scale, the annotation is automatically saved and the point is highlighted in red. By clicking on the button "Done", the assessor confirms that the evaluation item has been completed. This layout is suitable for adequacy/fluency evaluation, ranking outputs relatively to each other, and in general all those assessment tasks that require rating MT outputs.

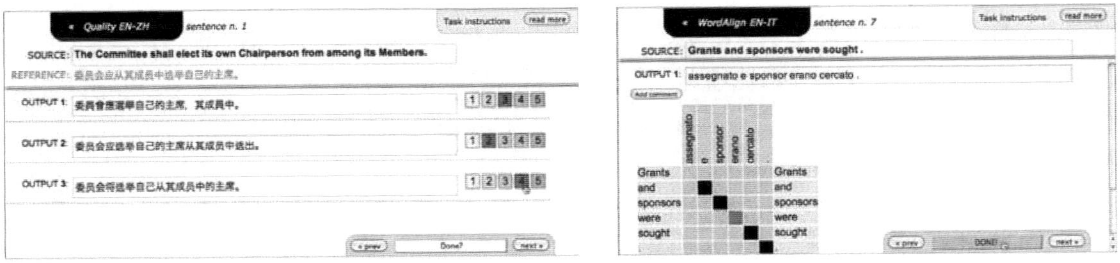

(a) Quality Rating

(b) Word Alignment

Figure 2: (a) Quality Rating interface with 3 systems and a 5-point scale (b) Word Alignment interface.

2.4 Word Alignment Annotation Interface

The word alignment interface displays a traditional alignment matrix, where the rows correspond to the words of the sentence in one language and the columns to the words of its translation. Word alignments can be edited by clicking the respective matrix cells to add or remove links between words. The interface is designed to allow the alignment of discontinuous text segments. Figure 2(b) shows an alignment example where light grey, dark grey, and black cells respectively represent unlinked words, possible and sure alignments.

3 Applications of MT-EQuAl and Forthcoming Extensions

MT-EQuAl is currently being used by professional translators on English to Italian data to assess the performance of the alignment models and annotate translation errors of the MT systems developed within the MateCat project.[3] MT-EQuAl was also extensively used within an industrial project for the evaluation of commercial MT systems. To this purpose, professional translators performed error annotation and quality rating on data for three different language pairs (English to Arabic/Chinese/Russian). MT-EQuAl is being actively developed on the basis of the feedback and requirements collected from its users. We are also currently implementing the automatic computation of Inter-Annotator Agreement scores, as an additional feature to further improve the toolkit.

Acknowledgments

This work has been partially supported by the EC-funded project MateCat (ICT-2011.4.2-287688).

References

Wilker Aziz, Sheila Castilho Monteiro de Sousa, and Lucia Specia. 2012. PET: a tool for post-editing and assessing machine translation. In *Proceedings of the Eight International Conference on Language Resources and Evaluation (LREC'12)*, Istanbul, Turkey, May. European Language Resources Association (ELRA).

Konstantinos Chatzitheodorou and Stamatis Chatzistamatis. 2013. COSTA MT Evaluation Tool: An Open Toolkit for Human Machine Translation Evaluation. *Prague Bulletin of Mathematical Linguistics*, pages 83–89.

Christian Federmann. 2012. Appraise: an open-source toolkit for manual evaluation of mt output. *Prague Bulletin of Mathematical Linguistics*, pages 25–35.

Sara Stymne. 2011. Blast: A tool for error analysis of machine translation output. In *Proceedings of the ACL-HLT 2011 System Demonstrations*, pages 56–61, Portland, Oregon, June. Association for Computational Linguistics.

David Vilar, Jia Xu, Luis Fernando D'Haro, and Hermann Ney. 2006. Error Analysis of Machine Translation Output. In *Proceedings of the Fifth International Conference on Language Resources and Evaluation (LREC'06)*, pages 697–702, Genoa, Italy, May. European Language Resources Association (ELRA).

[3] `www.matecat.com`

OpenSoNaR: user-driven development of the SoNaR corpus interfaces

Martin Reynaert
TiCC / Tilburg University
CLST / Radboud
Universiteit Nijmegen
reynaert@uvt.nl

Matje van de Camp
De Taalmonsters
matje@taalmonsters.nl

Menno van Zaanen
TiCC / Tilburg University
mvzaanen@uvt.nl

Abstract

OpenSoNaR is an online system that allows for analyzing and searching the large scale Dutch reference corpus SoNaR. Due to the size of the corpus, accessing the information contained in the dataset has proven to be difficult for less technically inclined researchers. The OpenSoNaR project aims to facilitate the use of the SoNaR corpus by providing a user-friendly online interface. To make sure that the resulting system is practically useful, several user groups have been identified, who drive the interface development process by providing practical use cases. The current system is already used in educational and research settings.

1 Introduction

Concerted efforts over the past years[1] in the Dutch language area in Europe, the Netherlands and the northern half of Belgium, Flanders, have yielded a corpus of over 500 million words of richly linguistically annotated contemporary written Dutch, called SoNaR (Oostdijk et al., 2013). After the SoNaR project finished, it became clear that the corpus is difficult to handle for most potential users because of its size and technical formats. The OpenSoNaR project[2] aims to resolve the practical problems of dealing with the SoNaR dataset. On the basis of an available corpus back-end system, BlackLab, that allows for searching through all the information contained in the SoNaR dataset, user interfaces, called WhiteLab, are developed that allow for user-desired types of corpus searches and investigations. We will first briefly describe the SoNaR dataset. Next, we discuss the OpenSoNaR project, treating the ideas behind the project as well as the description of the system, focusing mainly on WhiteLab.

2 SoNaR

The SoNaR project developed a large scale reference corpus for contemporary, written Dutch. This balanced corpus consists of about 540 million tokens of Dutch across a wide range of text types, such as books, magazine articles, reports, subtitles, but also data from the "new" media, such as chat texts, SMS and tweets. A unique aspect of this corpus is that for all texts, IPR regulations are explicitly known, in most cases settled by contract with the copyright holders. All texts are linguistically annotated on several layers. Documents, paragraphs, sentences and tokens are uniquely identified and lemmata, part-of-speech (POS), named entity information and morphological analyses have been automatically annotated in the data. All information, from tokenization, linguistic annotation to metadata, is marked in XML structures. The Folia XML format (van Gompel and Reynaert, 2013) is used to hold all the textual information and linguistic annotations. Metadata, which includes, for example, origin, author, text genre (as far as known), is stored in a separate document that is linked to the text document. Metadata is stored

[1]Funded in large part by the Dutch Language Union in the STEVIN programme described in the Open Access book 'Essential Speech and Language Technology for Dutch' http://www.springer.com/education+%26+language/linguistics/book/978-3-642-30909-0

[2]Homepage: http://opensonar.uvt.nl

in CMDI files (Broeder et al., 2011). The metadata files duplicate the number of documents in the corpus. SoNaR consists of approximately 2.4 million files.

3 OpenSoNaR

The aim of the OpenSoNaR project is to develop and implement a practically useful system that allows easy access to the SoNaR corpus. The project has been set up to make sure that the functionality of the system serves a wide range of users. As is implied by the name of the project, our wish is to make the system we build as open as possible to all users. We will provide a fully open online service to all, from schoolchildren onwards, based on the IPR-settlements negotiated during the SoNaR corpus building project. The SoNaR corpus has subsections which were obtained on the basis of Creative Common licenses, e.g. Wikipedia, which will be open. The system will further under CLARIN login be fully open and free to all non-commercial researchers. Restrictions on commercial research and/or use apply to some important subsections, e.g. the newspapers and periodicals incorporated in the corpus. For these, interested commercial parties need to negotiate access separately with the copyright owners.

3.1 Project

Technical issues stand in the way of most potential users actively conducting research on the SoNaR corpus. The OpenSoNaR project is to resolve these. The SoNaR-500 corpus[3] requires information retrieval tools for efficient searching, as trivial solutions are simply too slow or cumbersome to use. The XML format requires the search system to know about the XML structure that describes the linguistic information in somewhat more complex searches, for example, using a combination of token and linguistic information. Metadata selections are required just as well.

The aim of the OpenSoNaR system is to solve all these practical problems. Two components are developed: BlackLab that enables searching in the data, and WhiteLab providing the user-interface. In order to provide the most useful search interface, four main user groups have been identified. These consist of researchers in the areas of (corpus and cognitive) linguistics, communication and media studies, literary sciences, and cultural sciences. Each of these groups are asked to provide typical use cases, i.e. search operations that they would like to be able to ask the SoNaR corpus. To test practical usability, the system is also incorporated in education. Currently, OpenSoNaR has been successfully tested by students in courses on linguistics and research methodology. The results of these test provide feedback on what further developments the interfaces require to be practically of best possible use to all.

3.2 Related work

Throughout Europe, most national corpora available online are based on BlackLab's predecessor and source of inspiration, the notable Corpus Workbench system[4] (Christ, 1994). In the Netherlands, there is another concurrent project in which a corpus exploration and exploitation environment is being developed. This is the much larger and far more ambitious project Nederlab[5]. Nederlab aims to create a research portal to all digital corpora available for Dutch from its earliest days. There is cross-fertilization between both projects.

3.3 System

The OpenSoNaR system consists of two components that interact with each other. The *BlackLab* component is the back-end of the system and provides the actual search functionality. On top of BlackLab, the *WhiteLab* component provides the front-end, user interface.

[3]Available free for research from the Dutch HLT Agency TST-Centrale `http://tst-centrale.org/nl/producten/corpora/sonar-corpus/6-85`. The documentation link on the page offers access to the user manual.

[4]Homepage: `http://cwb.sourceforge.net/`

[5]`http://www.nederlab.nl/docs/Nederlab_NWO_Groot_English_aanvraagformulier.pdf`

3.3.1 BlackLab

As explained on its official GitHub site[6], BlackLab is a Java-based corpus retrieval engine built on top of Apache Lucene. It allows fast, complex searches with accurate hit highlighting on large, annotated, bodies of text, in our case text in FoLiA XML. This back-end system is further being developed at the Dutch Institute for Lexicology (INL) by Jan Niestadt. OpenSoNaR had a head start in its further interface development efforts in that BlackLab comes equipped with a fine basic user interface as is evidenced by the online INL corpora 'Letters as Loot'[7] and the corpus of Medieval Dutch 'Corpus Gysseling'[8].

3.3.2 WhiteLab

The Whitelab user interface[9] is currently available in two languages, Dutch and English. We hope to be able to extend the languages available. The Whitelab user by default lands on the **Search** page of OpenSoNaR when logging in. Next to this page we have the **Explore** page and the **Home** page.

Home The Home page provides information about the system. It provides a first-user manual which gives an overview of the main possibilities OpenSoNaR offers. It also provides the actual user manual of the SoNaR corpus which offers in-depth information on the composition of this corpus of contemporary written Dutch. Next, short films are available that provide tutorials of how to use the system.

Explore The Explore page gives statistical information about the corpus contents, providing insight into the distribution of the texts available per genre and according to their provenance, basically whether they were collected in the Netherlands or in Flanders. A third category contains texts with uncertain provenance, e.g. the texts from various European Union organizations or from Wikipedia. This page also affords access to n-gram (where n is 1 to 5) frequency lists derived from the whole corpus and its genre subsections for word forms, lemmata and the combination of lemmata with POS-tags.

Search The Search environment is the most elaborate. It provides four levels of access to the contents: Simple, Extended, Advanced and Expert.

The **Simple search** option provides Google-style, single query box access. Entering a search term here will instantiate a search over the full contents of the corpus. The search is for word forms, which may be phrases (n-grams), in which case exact matches are sought, i.e. respecting the actual sequence of words. This functionality is also provided by the next two search environments.

The **Extended search** environment allows one to impose selection filters on the search effected. These filters are of two kinds. First, there are filters on the metadata. Second, there are filters on the lexical level, allowing one to search for either word forms, lemmata or by POS-tags.

The metadata filters are at first hidden behind a bar visible above the actual lexical query fields. When the user wants to impose metadata filters the bar is expanded by a simple mouse click and the user is presented with a row consisting of three drop-down boxes. The middle box has just two options: 'is' or 'is not'. The left box gives access to all the metadata fields available in the corpus CMDI metadata files. The right box, upon selection of a particular metadata field in the left box, dynamically expands with the list of available metadata contents, where applicable. Metadata filters can be stacked. Through a 'plus' button to the right of the query row, one may obtain further rows in each of which further restrictions on the query may be imposed. The metadata selection interface further provides the option of grouping the query results obtained by a range of features. E.g, if one here selects the option of having the results presented by country of origin of the hit texts, one is not presented directly with the KWIC list of results, but rather with a bar representation of the number of hits per country. One may then click on one of these bars and be presented with the KWIC list. Alternatively, having made a selection of texts, one may opt to be presented with a word cloud of its most salient terms, for exploratory purposes.

The lexical filters allow one to perform optionally case-sensitive searches for either word forms, for lemmata and for POS-tags. When the search is for lemmata, all the word forms sharing the same lemma

[6] `https://github.com/INL/BlackLab`

[7] URL: http://brievenalsbuit.inl.nl/zeebrieven/page/search

[8] `http://gysseling.corpus.taalbanknederlands.inl.nl/gysseling/page/search`

[9] We provide screenshots of the interfaces at `http://opensonar.uvt.nl`

will be retrieved. For POS-tag searches the user is presented with a drop-down list which presents a layman's translation in plain language for the actual POS-tags involved. Combinations of, for instance, word forms and POS searches are possible to direct the search for the word 'drink' (ibidem in English) towards the first person singular of the present tense verb form, rather than its use as a noun.

For the **Advanced search** option we fully acknowledge to emulate the elegant interface to CQL-query building as provided by the Swedish Språkbanken[10]. Users are first presented with a single box containing three query fields. By horizontally or vertically adding further boxes as in Figure 1 they may build quite complex queries without the need to know the query language behind them. Users get to see the query they have built and have the option of further extending it, manually. Results are subsequently presented graphically, cf. Figure 2.

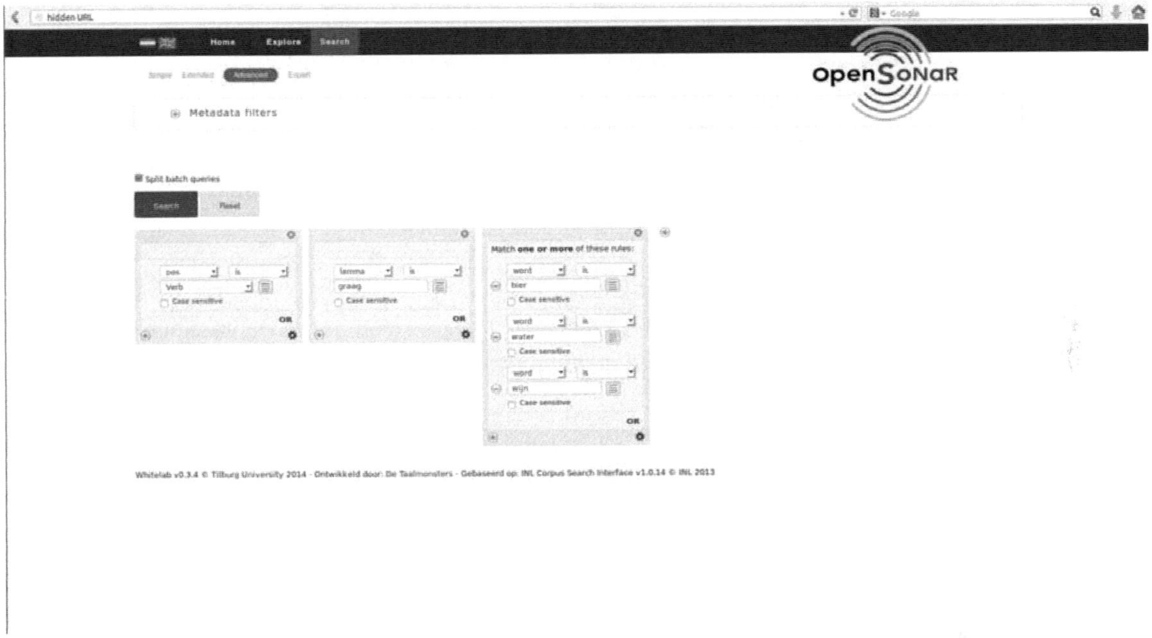

Figure 1: An advanced CQL-query having been built with Advanced Search query boxes

The **Expert search** requires knowledge of the query language incorporated in the system. It is CQL, the Corpus Query Language[11]. In its essence, this search option's limitations are defined mainly by the user's CQL proficiency.

Regardless of the search option one has chosen, by default, eventually a KWIC list of results is presented. One may then choose to 'Toggle titles' and by clicking on a title, move to full text view. There, moving the cursor over any of the words in the text, one gets to see a small window with the word form's unique ID, lemma and POS-tag.

A feature of the Extended and Advanced search options we have not seen in other corpus exploration environments is that multiple queries can be performed in one operation. This is facilitated by the fact that by clicking on the 'list' button to the right of the query boxes the user may effortlessly upload a pre-prepared list of query terms. After uploading, these query terms are converted by the system into actual, separate CQL queries which are accessible via a drop-down list above the query boxes. The user then has the option of having the output presented separately, per query, or mixed. As soon as the queries have run, the user has the further option of downloading the results. If in the Advanced search environment a user uploads more than one query list, the system makes a combination of all the query terms in the lists. Given x terms in list A and y terms in list B, this results in x times y queries. If this is not what the user intended, then he has the option of uploading a list of, for instance, word bigrams to be searched for in

[10] See 'Korp' at `http://spraakbanken.gu.se/eng/start`

[11] A nice tutorial is at: `http://cwb.sourceforge.net/files/CQP_Tutorial/`

Figure 2: Grouped results of the advanced CQL-query having been built with Advanced Search query boxes. After grouping, results are first presented graphically after which the user may further explore the text snippets retrieved.

the Extended search environment.

The query results are in a tab-separated format suitable for loading in a spreadsheet. The format should be easily convertible to the specific formats required by statistical packages such as R or SPSS.

4 Conclusion

In this OpenSoNaR system demonstration paper we have given an overview of ongoing work in the Netherlands to provide to all online access to the new richly annotated reference corpus for contemporary written Dutch called SoNaR.

Acknowledgements

The authors, TiCC senior scientific programmer Ko van der Sloot as Software Quality Control Officer, and Max Louwerse as Project Coordinator gratefully acknowledge support from CLARIN-NL in project OpenSoNaR (CLARIN-NL-12-013). The first author further acknowledges support from NWO in project Nederlab. We would like to specifically thank our colleagues at INL: Katrien Depuydt, Jesse de Does and Jan Niestadt.

References

Daan Broeder, Oliver Schonefeld, Thorsten Trippel, Dieter Van Uytvanck, and Andreas Witt. 2011. A pragmatic approach to XML interoperability – the Component Metadata Infrastructure (CMDI). In *Balisage: The Markup Conference 2011*, volume 7.

Oliver Christ. 1994. A Modular and Flexible Architecture for an Integrated Corpus Query System.

Nelleke Oostdijk, Martin Reynaert, Véronique Hoste, and Ineke Schuurman. 2013. The construction of a 500-million-word reference corpus of contemporary written Dutch. In *Essential Speech and Language Technology for Dutch: Results by the STEVIN-programme*, chapter 13. Springer Verlag.

Maarten van Gompel and Martin Reynaert. 2013. FoLiA: A practical XML Format for Linguistic Annotation - a descriptive and comparative study. *Computational Linguistics in the Netherlands Journal*, 3.

THE MATECAT TOOL

M. Federico and **N. Bertoldi** and **M. Cettolo** and **M. Negri** and **M. Turchi**
Fondazione Bruno Kessler, Trento (Italy)
M. Trombetti and **A. Cattelan** and **A. Farina** and
D. Lupinetti and **A. Martines** and **A. Massidda**
Translated Srl, Roma (Italy)
H. Schwenk and **L. Barrault** and **F. Blain**
Université du Maine, Le Mans (France)
P. Koehn and **C. Buck** and **U. Germann**
The University of Edinburgh (United Kingdom)

www.matecat.com

Abstract

We present a new web-based CAT tool providing translators with a professional work environment, integrating translation memories, terminology bases, concordancers, and machine translation. The tool is completely developed as open source software and has been already successfully deployed for business, research and education. The MateCat Tool represents today probably the best available open source platform for investigating, integrating, and evaluating under realistic conditions the impact of new machine translation technology on human post-editing.

1 Introduction

The objective of MateCat[1] is to improve the integration of machine translation (MT) and human translation within the so-called computer aided translation (CAT) framework. CAT tools represent nowadays the dominant technology in the translation industry. They provide translators with text editors that can manage several document formats and suitably arrange their content into text *segments* ready to be translated. Most importantly, CAT tools provide access to translation memories (TMs), terminology databases, concordance tools and, more recently, to machine translation (MT) engines. A TM is basically a repository of translated segments. During translation, the CAT tool queries the TM to search for exact or fuzzy matches of the current source segment. These matches are proposed to the user as translation suggestions. Once a segment is translated, its source and target texts are added to the TM for future queries. The integration of suggestions from an MT engine as a complement to TM matches is motivated by recent studies (Federico et al., 2012; Green et al., 2013; Läubli et al., 2013), which have shown that post-editing MT suggestions can substantially improve the productivity of professional translators. MateCat leverages the growing interest and expectations in statistical MT by advancing the state-of-the-art along three directions:

- *Self-tuning MT*, i.e. methods to train statistical MT for specific domains or translation projects;
- *User adaptive MT*, i.e. methods to quickly adapt statistical MT from user corrections and feedback;
- *Informative MT*, i.e. supply more information to enhance users' productivity and work experience.

Research along these three directions has converged into a new generation CAT software, which is both an enterprise level translation workbench (currently used by several hundreds of professional translators) as well as an advanced research platform for integrating new MT functions, running post-editing

[1]MateCat, acronym of Machine Translation Enhanced Computer Assisted Translation, is a 3-year research project (11/2011-10/2014) funded by the European Commission under FP7 (grant agreement no 287688). The project consortium is led by FBK (Trento, Italy) and includes the University of Edinburgh (United Kingdom), Université du Maine (Le Mans, France), and Translated Srl (Rome, Italy).

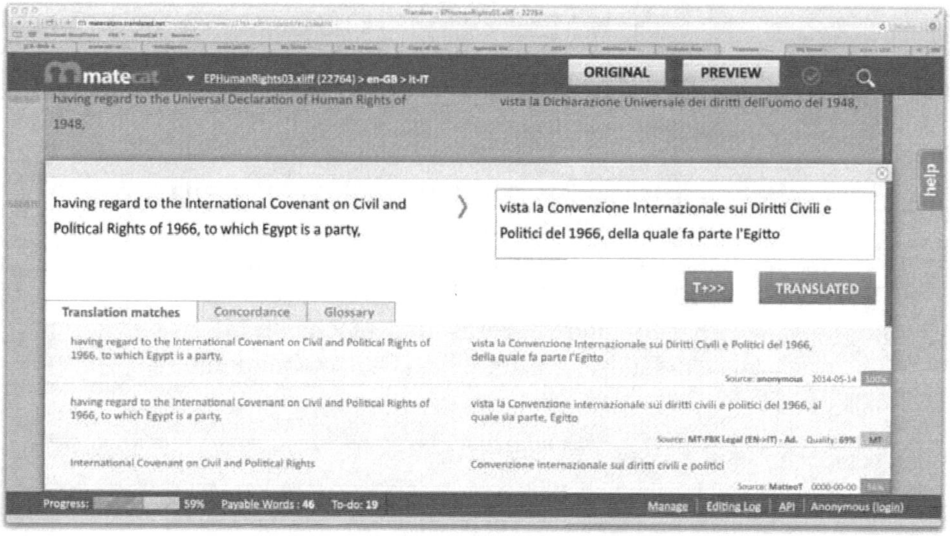

Figure 1: The MateCat Tool editing page.

experiments and measuring user productivity. The MateCat Tool, which is distributed under the LGPL open source license, combines features of the most advanced systems (either commercial, like the popular SDL Trados Workbench,[2] or free like OmegaT[3]) with new functionalities. These include: *i)* an advanced API for the Moses Toolkit,[4] customizable to languages and domains, *ii)* ease of use through a clean and intuitive web interface that enables the collaboration of multiple users on the same project, *iii)* concordancers, terminology databases and support for customizable quality estimation components and *iv)* advanced logging functionalities.

2 The MateCat Tool in a Nutshell

Overview. The MateCat Tool runs as a web-server accessible through Chrome, Firefox and Safari. The CAT web-server connects with other services via open APIs: the TM server MyMemory[5], the commercial Google Translate (GT) MT server, and a list of Moses-based servers specified in a configuration file. While MyMemory's and GT's servers are always running and available, customized Moses servers have to be first installed and set-up. Communication with the Moses servers extends the GT API in order to support self-tuning, user-adaptive and informative MT functions. The natively supported document format of MateCat Tool is XLIFF,[6] although its configuration file makes it possible to specify external file converters. The tool supports Unicode (UTF-8) encoding, including non latin alphabets and right-to-left languages, and handles texts embedding mark-up tags.

How it works. The tool is intended both for individual translators or managers of translation projects involving one or more translators. A translation project starts by uploading one or more documents and specifying the desired translation direction. Then the user can optionally select a MT engine from an available list and/or a new or existing private TM in MyMemory, by specifying its private key. Notice that the public MyMemory TM and the GT MT services are assumed by default. The following step is the *volume analysis* of the document, which reports statistics about the words to be actually translated based on the coverage provided by the TM. At this stage, long documents can be also split into smaller portions to be for instance assigned to different translators or translated at different times. The following step starts the actual translation process by opening the editing window. All source segments of the

[2] `http://www.translationzone.com/`
[3] `http://www.omegat.org/`
[4] `http://www.statmt.org/moses/`
[5] `http://mymemory.translated.net`
[6] `http://docs.oasis-open.org/xliff/v1.2/os/xliff-core.html`

document and their corresponding target segments are arranged side-by-side on the screen. By selecting one segment, an editing pane opens (Figure 1) including an editable field that is initialized with the best available suggestion or with the last post-edit. Translation hints are shown right below together with their origin (MT or TM). Their ranking is based on the TM match score or the MT confidence score. MT hints with no confidence score are assigned a default score. Tag consistency is automatically checked during translation and warnings are possibly shown in the editing window. An interesting feature of the MateCat Tool is that each translation project is uniquely identified by its URL page which also includes the currently edited segment. This permits for instance more users to simultaneously access and work on the same project. Moreover, to support simultaneous team work on the same project, translators can mark the status (*draft, translated, approved, rejected*) of each segment with a corresponding color (see Figure 1, right blue bar). The user interface is enriched with search and replace functions, a progress report at the bottom of the page, and several shortcut commands for the skilled users. Finally, the tool embeds a concordance tool to search for terms in the TM, and a glossary where each user can upload, query and update her terminology base. Users with a Google account can access a project management page which permits then to manage all their projects, including storage, deletion, and access to the editing page.

MT support. The tool supports Moses-based servers able to provide an enhanced CAT-MT communication. In particular, the GT API is augmented with feedback information provided to the MT engine every time a segment is post-edited as well as enriched MT output, including confidence scores, word lattices, etc. The developed MT server supports multi-threading to serve multiple translators, properly handles text segments including tags, and instantly adapts from the post-edits performed by each user (Bertoldi et al., 2013).

Edit Log. During post-editing the tool collects timing information for each segment, which is updated every time the segment is opened and closed. Moreover, for each segment, information is collected about the generated suggestions and the one that has actually been post-edited. This information is accessible at any time through a link in the Editing Page, named Editing Log. The Editing Log page (Figure 2) shows a summary of the overall editing performed so far on the project, such as the average translation speed and post-editing effort and the percentage of top suggestions coming from MT or the TM. Moreover, for each segment, sorted from the slowest to the fastest in terms of translation speed, detailed statistics about the performed edit operations are reported. This information, with even more details, can be also downloaded as a CSV file to perform a more detailed post-editing analysis. While the information shown in the Edit Log page is very useful to monitor progress of a translation project in real time, the CSV file is a fundamental source of information for detailed productivity analyses once the project is ended.

3 Applications.

The MateCat Tool has been exploited by the MateCat project to investigate new MT functions (Bertoldi et al., 2013; Cettolo et al., 2013; Turchi et al., 2013; Turchi et al., 2014) and to evaluate them in a real professional setting, in which translators have at disposal all the sources of information they are used to work with. Moreover, taking advantage of its flexibility and ease of use, the tool has been recently exploited for data collection and education purposes (a course on CAT technology for students in translation studies). An initial version of the tool has also been leveraged by the Casmacat project[7] to create a workbench (Alabau et al., 2013), particularly suitable for investigating advanced interaction modalities such as interactive MT, eye tracking, and handwritten input. Currently the tool is employed by Translated for their internal translation projects and is being tested by several international companies, both language service providers and IT companies. This has made possible to collect continuous feedback from hundreds of translators, which besides helping us to improve the robustness of the tool is also influencing the way new MT functions will be integrated to supply the best help to the final user.

[7] `http://www.casmacat.eu`

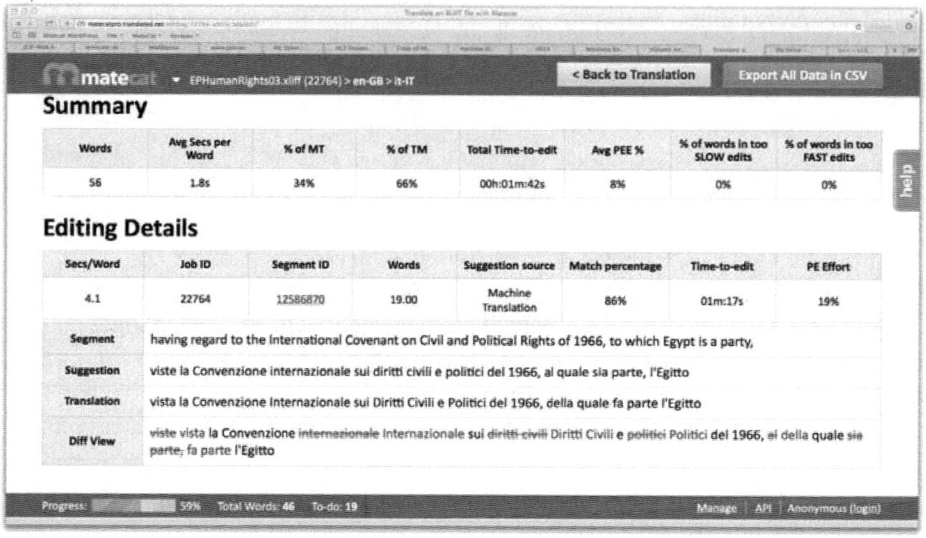

Figure 2: The MateCat Tool edit log page.

References

Vicent Alabau, Ragnar Bonk, Christian Buck, Michael Carl, Francisco Casacuberta, Mercedes Garca-Martínez, Jesús González, Philipp Koehn, Luis Leiva, Bartolomé Mesa-Lao, Daniel Oriz, Hervé Saint-Amand, Germán Sanchis, and Chara Tsiukala. 2013. Advanced computer aided translation with a web-based workbench. In *Proceedings of Workshop on Post-editing Technology and Practice*, pages 55–62.

Nicola Bertoldi, Mauro Cettolo, and Marcello Federico. 2013. Cache-based Online Adaptation for Machine Translation Enhanced Computer Assisted Translation. In *Proceedings of the MT Summit XIV*, pages 35–42, Nice, France, September.

Mauro Cettolo, Christophe Servan, Nicola Bertoldi, Marcello Federico, Loïc Barrault, and Holger Schwenk. 2013. Issues in Incremental Adaptation of Statistical MT from Human Post-edits. In *Proceedings of the MT Summit XIV Workshop on Post-editing Technology and Practice (WPTP-2)*, pages 111–118, Nice, France, September.

Marcello Federico, Alessandro Cattelan, and Marco Trombetti. 2012. Measuring user productivity in machine translation enhanced computer assisted translation. In *Proceedings of the Tenth Conference of the Association for Machine Translation in the Americas (AMTA)*.

Spence Green, Jeffrey Heer, and Christopher D Manning. 2013. The efficacy of human post-editing for language translation. In *Proceedings of the SIGCHI Conference on Human Factors in Computing Systems*, pages 439–448. ACM.

Samuel Läubli, Mark Fishel, Gary Massey, Maureen Ehrensberger-Dow, and Martin Volk. 2013. Assessing Post-Editing Efficiency in a Realistic Translation Environment. In Michel Simard Sharon O'Brien and Lucia Specia (eds.), editors, *Proceedings of MT Summit XIV Workshop on Post-editing Technology and Practice*, pages 83–91, Nice, France.

Marco Turchi, Matteo Negri, and Marcello Federico. 2013. Coping with the subjectivity of human judgements in MT quality estimation. In *Proceedings of the Eighth Workshop on Statistical Machine Translation*, pages 240–251, Sofia, Bulgaria, August. Association for Computational Linguistics.

Marco Turchi, Antonios Anastasopoulos, José G.C. de Souza, and Matteo Negri. 2014. Adaptive Quality Estimation for Machine Translation. In *Proceedings of the 52nd Annual Meeting of the Association for Computational Linguistics (ACL '14)*. Association for Computational Linguistics.

Author Index